Hizbu'llah

Critical Studies on Islam

Series editors: Azza Karam (Director of the Women's Programme at the World Conference on Religion and Peace, New York) and Ziauddin Sardar (Visiting Professor of Postcolonial Studies at City University, London)

The Iraqi Invasion of Kuwait
Religion, Identity and Otherness in the Analysis of War and Conflict
Hamdi A. Hassan

Hizbu'llah

Politics and Religion

Amal Saad-Ghorayeb

Pluto Press

LONDON • STERLING, VIRGINIA

First published 2002 by Pluto Press
345 Archway Road, London N6 5AA
and 22883 Quicksilver Drive,
Sterling, VA 20166–2012, USA

www.plutobooks.com

British Library Cataloguing in Publication Data
A catalogue record for this book is available from the British Library

Library of Congress Cataloging in Publication Data
  Hizbullah : politics and religion / Amal Saad-Ghorayeb.
    p. cm. — (Critical studies on Islam)
  ISBN 0–7453–1793–6 (hard) — ISBN 0–7453–1792–8 (pbk.)
  1. Hizballah (Lebanon) 2. Islam and politics—Lebanon. 3.
Shiites—Lebanon—Political activity. 4. Israel–Arab Border Conflicts,
1949—Lebanon. I. Title. II. Series.
  BP194.185 .S23 2001
  322.4'2'095692—dc21

                                                          2001002257

ISBN 0 7453 1793 6 hardback
ISBN 0 7453 1792 8 paperback

10   9   8   7   6   5   4   3   2

Designed and produced for Pluto Press by
Chase Publishing Services, Fortescue, Sidmouth EX10 9QG
Typeset from disk by Stanford DTP Services, Towcester
Printed in the United States of America by Phoenix Color

To my father

Contents

Critical Studies on Islam

Series Editors: Azza Karam and Ziauddin Sardar

Islam is a complex, ambiguous term. Conventionally it has been used to describe religion, history, culture, civilisation and worldview of Muslims. But it is also impregnated with stereotypes and post-modern notions of identity and boundaries. The diversity of Muslim peoples, cultures, and interpretations, with their baggage of colonial history and post-colonial present, has transformed Islam into a powerful global force.

This unique series presents a far-reaching, critical perspective on Islam. It analyses the diversity and complexity of Islam through the eyes of people who live by it. Provocative and thoughtful works by established as well as younger scholars will examine Islamic movements, the multilayered questions of Muslim identity, the transnational trends of political Islam, the spectre of ethnic conflict, the political economy of Muslim societies and the impact of Islam and Muslims on the West.

The series is built around two fundamental questions. How are Muslims living, thinking and breathing Islam? And how are they rethinking and reformulating it and shaping the global agendas and discourses?

As Critical Studies on Islam seeks to bridge the gap between academia and decision making environments, it will be of particular value to policy makers, politicians, journalists and activists, as well as academics.

Azza Karam is the Director of the Women's Programme at the World Conference on Religion and Peace, New York. She has published extensively on development, conflict, gender and democratisation issues. She is also author of *Islamism, State and Women* and co-author of *Islam in a Non-Polarized Society*.

Ziauddin Sardar is a well-known writer, broadcaster and cultural critic. A Visitng Professor of Postcolonial Studies at the City University, he is considered a pioneering writer on Islam. He is the author of several books for Pluto Press, most recently *Aliens R Us*.

ix

Acknowledgements

This book would not have been possible without the assistance of Professor Jorgen Nielsen, Director of the Centre for Islam and Christian-Muslim Relations at the University of Birmingham, whom I had the privilege of having as the supervisor for my PhD dissertation, upon which this book is based. The time and energy he exerted to offer me insightful comments and sound suggestions, in spite of his heavy workload, not to mention his prompt responses to my constant stream of e-mail queries, were of invaluable use to me.

I am also very much indebted to Professor Ghassan al-Zayn, who clarified various concepts to me and helped me organise the numerous ideas in my head into a comprehensive and meaningful whole.

Another person I owe great thanks to is my father, Abdo Saad. His extensive contacts with Hizbu'llah officials provided me with unparalleled access to many leading figures in the party, without whom this work would not have borne fruition. Yet over and above such concrete assistance, my father has indirectly helped me in completing this book by being my strongest source of intellectual inspiration.

Finally, but by no means last, I would like to thank my husband, Abdullah Ghorayeb, for his loving support. His patience (in enduring my fouler moods!), encouragement and motivation every step of the way were indispensable to the progression of my work.

Introduction

Background of the Study

The subject of this work is the largest and most prominent political party in Lebanon, and perhaps the most renowned Islamist movement in the world, the Hizbu'llah. The movement rose to notoriety because of its alleged involvement in the kidnapping of over 80 Westerners throughout the 1980s, including such prominent hostages as the Archbishop of Canterbury's special envoy, Terry Waite. Hizbu'llah's purported culpability for the attack on the US embassy in Beirut in April 1983, which killed 63 people, as well as the bombing of the US Marines' barracks in Beirut in October that same year, which resulted in the deaths of 241, also earned it world-wide infamy. The deaths of 29 people in the 1992 bombing of the Israeli embassy in Argentina, and another 100 in the 1994 attack on a Jewish cultural centre in London, did nothing to temper the opprobrium heaped upon Hizbu'llah, despite the absence of any concrete evidence connecting the organisation to either incident.

Public interest in the party was also sustained by its 18-year-long military struggle against Israeli occupation forces in South Lebanon. Hizbu'llah's unanticipated triumph over Israel, whose military forces prematurely withdrew from Lebanese territory in May 2000, further placed the movement under the international media's spotlight. The ability of a small and ill-equipped guerrilla group to thwart one of the most powerful armies in the world was met with astonishment by the international community and widespread acclaim in the Arab and Islamic world. Hizbu'llah's capture of three Israeli soldiers in the disputed territory of the Shiba' Farms[1] on 7 October 2000, and its seizure of a retired Israeli colonel who was supposedly lured into Lebanon, a few days later, also served to highlight the movement's continued importance as a strategic regional player, and hence its newsworthiness.

In Lebanon, Hizbu'llah's renown is not only attributable to such incidents, but also to its integration into the secular Lebanese political system as of 1990. The party's overall 'pragmatisation', or what many in Lebanon have called its 'Lebanonisation', after almost a decade of political radicalism, has rendered it a particularly

1

compelling case for observation and study by Lebanese journalists and academics.

Hizbu'llah's political evolution, together with its resistance activity, has earned it widespread kudos amongst many sectors of Lebanese society. The once common Lebanese perception of Hizbu'llah as a fanatical religious Iranian surrogate organisation that sought to impose its Islamic vision of the socio-political order, modelled on the Islamic Republic of Iran, onto Lebanese society, underwent a gradual change in the post-war period. This transformation was the product of the end of the civil war, which had effectively precluded the possibility of interreligious dialogue and reconciliation, as well as the change of the Hizbu'llah leadership.

The politically exclusive and intolerant tone adopted by Hizbu'llah's first secretary-general, Shaykh Subhi al-Tufayli, gave way to the politically inclusive and conciliatory discourse initiated by the party's second secretary-general, al-Sayyid 'Abbas al-Mussawi, who pursued the party's participation in the secular, democratic political system. After Mussawi's assassination by Israeli forces in February 1992, his successor, al-Sayyid Hassan Nasru'llah, continued this discourse and accentuated the themes of Christian-Muslim reconciliation and co-existence in a politically pluralist society, whilst overseeing the party's political integration.

The credibility of this discourse partly lay in the fact that Hizbu'llah's hands had not been stained with Christian blood at any point in the civil war, since the only local group it was in direct conflict with was its Shi'ite counterpart, the Amal militia. Although this did nothing to appease the Christian inhabitants of the former 'security zone' in South Lebanon, who remained fearful of Hizbu'llah's intentions in the event of an Israeli withdrawal from the area, these fears were laid to rest in the aftermath of Israel's withdrawal from the region. The non-materialisation of the anticipated hostilities between the Christian community in the liberated areas and Hizbu'llah's cadres, came as a welcome surprise to many Lebanese, notwithstanding the Christians' repeated call for the disarmament of the Islamic Resistance in the border areas and the deployment of the Lebanese army in its place.

Hizbu'llah's political performance in the resurrected Lebanese parliament, from 1992 until the present day, has added further credibility to its conciliatory discourse. Both the party's admirers and detractors agree that, of all the political forces in Lebanon, Hizbu'llah is the only political party which has not been tainted by charges of corruption or political opportunism and which has resolutely stuck to its principles. This perceived moral and ideological integrity was epitomised by the death of Nasru'llah's son in September 1997 whilst in combat with Israeli troops, which won the party leader the respect of all Lebanese sects.

More recently, this image of Hizbu'llah has been reinforced by its liberation achievement, which was attributed to the party's unswerving loyalty to its resistance priority. Thus, despite the fear of an Islamic or Muslim-dominated system, which continues to be harboured by Lebanon's increasingly marginalised Christians, Hizbu'llah has succeeded in preserving its core support base, winning over those who were formerly indifferent to it, and earning the respect of many of its opponents.

Objectives and Methodology

My acute interest in Hizbu'llah was very much the product of my mixed cultural upbringing. As a Briton, born in England to Lebanese parents, I was fascinated by this staunchly anti-Western, anti-Zionist, martyrdom-loving organisation. As a Lebanese, I was appalled by the apparent ease with which this movement was accused of sundry terrorist activities by Western journalists and policy-makers, and their insistence on referring to its guerrilla fighters, who were practising their legitimate right to resist a foreign occupation, as 'terrorists'.

A few years after my family and I emigrated to Lebanon, Hizbu'llah contested the 1992 parliamentary election and won twelve seats, four of which it allocated to non-Shi'ite allies. In the 1996 election again, the party won nine seats and the government's legitimisation of its Islamic Resistance. My initial interest in the party's antagonism towards the West, its abomination of Israel and its apotheosis of martyrdom, was now conjoined with a profound curiosity about the party's underlying political motives and strategy. This fascination impelled me to devote my PhD dissertation, which I began that same year and from which this book is adapted, to a study of Hizbu'llah.

I sought to shift the focus away from the party's alleged involvement in the Western hostage crises to an area which has not received the attention it deserves – the political mind of Hizbu'llah. In addition to studying the intellectual foundations of Hizbu'llah's political thought, I sought to examine the extent to which its political transformation clashed with those foundations and Islamic principles, and how the party rationalised the apparent contradiction between the two.

This book examines the central pillars of Hizbu'llah's intellectual structure[2] within the framework of Lebanese socio-political reality. The purpose of such an analysis is threefold. In the first place, it aims to examine each of the party's intellectual pillars in order to discern the degree to which they are compatible with the contemporary secular world and to appreciate the complexity of its political thought on a purely theoretical level. In the second place, it endeavours to assess how Hizbu'llah has responded to political developments which necessitate a reformulation of its intellectual structure. Third, it attempts to gauge the extent to which the party has been able to preserve its religious and moral principles and maintain its intellectual consistency whilst adapting to such developments.

With these objectives in mind, Chapter 1 examines the moral bases for political violence and accommodation in non-Islamic states, according to Hizbu'llah, both on a theoretical level and in relation to the Lebanese state. Chapter 2 analyses the party's Islamic state ideal and how this ideal squares with its relatively recent endorsement of democracy, while Chapter 3 explores Hizbu'llah's commitment to the concept of the *Wilayat al-Faqih*, both in the abstract and within the Lebanese situational context. The fourth chapter deliberates the party's Islamic universalism on the one hand, and its ability to reconcile this pan-Islamism with its Arab and Lebanese identity on the other. The perusal of the nature of Hizbu'llah's civilisational struggle with the West constitutes the fifth chapter in the study.

Chapter 6 deals with the most invariable of Hizbu'llah's intellectual pillars, its resistance to the Israeli occupation of South Lebanon, while Chapter 7 gauges the extent of Hizbu'llah's anti-Zionism and its abomination of Israel, both theoretically and in connection with various political developments. The final chapter analyses the anti-Judaic content and Qur'anic origins of Hizbu'llah's intellectual discourse on the Jews.

Each of Hizbu'llah's intellectual pillars will be explored both in the abstract and in relation to Lebanese reality through a close examination and analysis of the party's intellectual and political discourse between 1984 and 2000. Part of this discourse was gleaned from Hizbu'llah's media, such as its weekly newspaper *al-'Ahd*, its monthly English-language newsletter, *al-Maokif*, which is published by its Foreign Relations Unit, and several political and cultural television productions by its television station, al-Manar. Other aspects of the party's intellectual and political discourse were elicited from public speeches by party officials, especially those made by Hizbu'llah's secretary-general, al-Sayyid Hassan Nasru'llah, as well as interviews with Hizbu'llah leaders in the local, regional and international broadcast and print media.[3]

Additionally, the party's political and intellectual discourse was extracted from a series of interviews with Hizbu'llah officials, which I conducted between February 1997 and February 2000. While prospective interviewees were chosen in a manner which ensured the greatest possible representation of the party's leading suborganisations, accessibility was a central criterion in the selection of interviewees, in light of the Hizbu'llah leadership's semi-clandestine character. In fact, had it not been for my father's extensive political contacts which were cultivated as a result of his prominent role as an election researcher in Lebanon, I would not have had access to all nine of the officials that I interviewed.

The highest ranking of the nine officials interviewed is Shaykh Na'im Qasim, Hizbu'llah's deputy secretary-general, who was interviewed on 17 March 1998. In addition to his post as deputy secretary-general, Qasim also acts as one of the seven members of the party's supreme decision-making body, the *Majlis al-Shura al-Qarar* (the Decision-Making Council), and heads the party's strategic Planning Council, as well as the Parliamentary Works Council.

Also interviewed was Muhammad Ra'id, head of Hizbu'llah's Political Council, whom I met on 9 March 1998. Ra'id is also a member of Hizbu'llah's Decision-Making Council and serves as an MP for the party's parliamentary Loyalty to the Resistance Bloc, which *ipso facto* renders him a member of the party's Parliamentary Works Council.

I also held a lengthy interview with Muhammad Fnaysh, MP for the Loyalty to the Resistance Bloc and member of the Parliamentary Works Council, on 15 August 1997. Additionally, two lengthy interview sessions were held on 2 March 1997 and 18 February 2000 with 'Ali Fayyad, member of the Planning Council who also heads the Consultative Centre for Studies and Documentation (a research centre associated with Hizbu'llah).

The other interviewees were Muhammad Muhsin, media consultant to al-Manar Television, who was interviewed on 1 March 1997; Yussef Meri', head of Hizbu'llah's Foreign Relations Unit and member of the Political Council, interviewed on 10 April 1998; the alleged perpetrator of the 1983 bombing of the US Marines' barracks in Beirut, al-Sayyid Husayn al-Mussawi, head of Islamic Amal, an organisational affiliate of Hizbu'llah, and a member of the party's Planning Council, interviewed on 21 August 1997; one Hizbu'llah official interviewed on 13 February 2000, who for personal reasons preferred to remain anonymous; Rima Fakhri, head of the Beirut branch of Hizbu'llah's Women's Association, interviewed on 23 December 1997.

Although commonly associated with Hizbu'llah, al-Sayyid Muhammad Husayn Fadlu'llah is not used as a reference for the party's intellectual and political discourse. While some party observers, such as Magnus Ranstorp, Nizar Hamzeh and Judith Miller, maintain that Fadlu'llah is Hizbu'llah's political leader or spiritual guide, and others, including Mary-Jane Deeb and Gabriel Almond, Emmanuel Sivan and Scott Appleby, allege that the party was his 'brainchild',[4] I personally do not not believe that Fadlu'llah is affiliated to Hizbu'llah in the organisational sense.

Not only have Fadlu'llah and Hizbu'llah consistently denied any organisational association between the two, but both have also rejected the description of Fadlu'llah as the party's spiritual mentor. As contended by the party, its spiritual guide is 'Ali Khamini'i, the *Wali al-Faqih* (leader jurisprudent), and not Fadlu'llah.[5] Furthermore, although the party admits that it 'benefits greatly' from the 'opinions, positions and comments', of 'an eminent [religious] scholar' such as Fadlu'llah,[6] it does not view them as 'binding or obligatory'.[7] The relationship between the party and Fadlu'llah is not one of compulsory consultation but 'one of cooperation', which is rooted in the 'single social environment and culture', or '*al-hala al-Islamiyya al-Shi'iyya*' (the Islamic Shi'ite situation), to which both Fadlu'llah and the party belong.[8]

Such claims are not confined to the party, but are shared by Hala Jaber and Chibli Mallat who reason that Fadlu'llah's large following necessitates that he retain his institutional independence from Hizbu'llah.[9] Bearing these considerations in mind, Hala Jaber argues that Fadlu'llah would be better described as 'a strong source of inspiration rather than a spiritual mentor' for the party.[10] Jaber asserts that 'his views cannot always be deemed as typical of Hizbu'llah's perspectives'[11] – a conclusion which is echoed by Martin Kramer.[12] That is not to say, however, that Fadlu'llah's opinions digress significantly from the party's, only that they are not identical, and do not therefore merit more than an occasional reference insofar as they reflect the general tone of the party's views.

The Politicisation of the Lebanese Shi'ites and Subsequent Rise of Hizbu'llah

The emergence of Lebanon's Hizbu'llah was due not only to the Israeli invasion of 1982, Western intervention and the role of Iran and Syria in Lebanon, but also to the political mobilisation of the Lebanese Shi'ite community which began in earnest in the late 1960s. Thus, before turning to the circumstances surrounding the birth of Hizbu'llah, this section will first touch upon those factors which conduced to the Shi'ites' political awakening.

Socio-economic and Political Factors

Despite the mobilisational value of the Shi'ite cultural heritage of oppression and suffering, which accorded Shi'ite politicisation a distinctly communal character, the chief determinants of Shi'ite activism in Lebanon have been the same social, economic and political conditions which have spurred Third World radical and populist movements to action.

Of these conditions, the social mobilisation engendered by various aspects of the modernisation process is one which is closely correlated with political activism in modernising countries.[13] As one aspect of social mobilisation, the urbanisation of the Lebanese Shi'ites beginning in the late 1950s laid the foundation of their politicisation a decade later. Prompted by the extreme deprivation of the long neglected Shi'ite rural 'peripheries' of the South and Biqa', the Shi'ites' migration to the Beirut 'core', around which they settled in slums, fostered a communal consciousness among the socially, culturally and psychologically dislocated settlers.

As slum-dwellers in the 'belts of misery', the Shi'ites continued to constitute the most disadvantaged segment of Lebanese society. Although this 'community-class'[14] phenomenon was somewhat hidden in the communally segregated rural setting, the community's exposure to the affluent and Westernised lifestyles of their Christian and Sunni counterparts in the new urban milieu engendered a sense of relative deprivation and self-identification as 'the proletariat of Lebanon'.[15]

Although their general level of social mobilisation had risen by the late 1960s, in terms of media participation, literacy and education, it was still below par in comparison with other sects. Moreover, the gap between their social mobilisation and the economic and political opportunities afforded to them only widened, generating the potentially explosive phenomenon of 'rising expectations'.

The low level of political development characterising the Maronite-dominated Lebanese political system only exacerbated the Shi'ites' frustration and served to further radicalise them. The community's underrepresentation in parliament, the civil service and government, as enshrined in the *Mithaq al-Watani* (National Pact) of 1943, which distributed all parliamentary, government and public posts based on the population census of 1932, had the effect of delegitimising the state and alienating the great majority of Shi'ites.

Although these circumstances are usually conducive to the espousal of religion as 'a goal-replacement mechanism' in Islamic societies,[16] the political mobilisation of the Lebanese Shi'ites was initially channelled into non-Islamic avenues of political participation. The roots of Shi'ite political mobilisation, and hence the formation of Hizbu'llah, lie in the community's radicalisation by Arab nationalist, socialist and communist organisations. The loss of Palestine in 1948, signalled the inception of a Shi'ite political consciousness.[17]

Nevertheless, it was not until the rise of Jamal 'Abd al-Naser in the early 1950s, followed by the Ba'ath takeover in Syria in 1963 and the establishment of the Palestine Liberation Organisation (PLO) in 1964,[18] that the stage was set for Shi'ite political participation. The Shi'ites affiliated themselves with the Naserists, the Ba'ath Party, the Syrian Social Nationalist Party (SSNP) and other Arab nationalist parties.

The Shi'ites' affinity for Palestinian fida'i groups such as the Popular Front for the Liberation of Palestine (PFLP) was abetted by the Cairo Agreement of 1969 which confined the PLO's resistance activities to Lebanon.[19] While Shi'ite sympathy for the Palestinian resistance groups was sustained until the early 1970s, the ideological credibility of Arab nationalism was severely compromised by the 1967 war.[20] Dubbed the 'disaster', the Arab defeat by Israel greatly disheartened the community and paved the way for its identification with leftist organisations such as the Organisation of

Communist Action (OCA) and the Lebanese Communist Party (LCP), whose members were predominantly Shi'ite.

However, the Arab nationalist and leftist parties which won Shi'ite support did so not because of their secular nature, but in default of a viable communal or Islamic alternative at the time. Although Imam Musa as-Sadr presented the community with such an alternative when he founded the Movement of the Deprived in 1974, the organisation was sidelined by the beginning of the civil war a year later.

As a predominantly sectarian conflict, the war pitted Maronite militias and government forces against the Palestinians and their Lebanese progressive allies, the Lebanese National Movement (LNM). Comprising chiefly Muslim leftists and Arab nationalists, the movement drew most of its 'foot soldiers' from the Shi'ite community. This remained the case despite Sadr's creation of the Amal militia in 1975, which was subsumed under the LNM umbrella. Amal's defection from the LNM in 1976 at Sadr's behest greatly undermined its support base, thereby enabling the LNM's constituent groups to continue to monopolise the community's political allegiances.

Prior to the outbreak of the civil war in 1975, it was the Shi'ites' socio-economic and political deprivations which propelled them to political action, but once the war took its toll, it was the political mobilisation of the Maronites which instigated the Shi'ites' militant counter-mobilisation. Of all the Lebanese sectarian groups, the Shi'ites incurred the highest number of fatalities during the civil war, especially in its first year, at the hands of the Maronite militias amongst others.[21] In particular, it was the eviction of 100,000 Shi'ites from Nab'a in August 1976[22] and their resettlement in the overpopulated southern suburbs which radicalised the community.

It was not until the late 1970s that this radicalisation was rechannelled to Amal, which witnessed a considerable upsurge in popularity after Sadr's disappearance in 1978. Shi'ite support for the movement was further bolstered by the Israeli invasion of 1978 and the Islamic Revolution in Iran a year later.

The communal politicisation of the Shi'ites preceded their religious politicisation. They initially experienced a communal re-identification, not a Shi'ite Islamic retrospection. Accordingly, their political awakening had more in common with the politicisation of other Lebanese sects than with the universal Islamic revival. By the same token, the factors behind this communal re-identification only played an indirect role in the emergence of Hizbu'llah.

The Israeli Invasion

The pre-eminent factor directly responsible for the movement's birth, and hence the Islamicisation of the Lebanese Shi'ites, was the Israeli invasion of 1982. Although the process of Shi'ite radicalisation had already taken root over a decade earlier, and was reinforced in 1978 by Israel's first invasion of Lebanon, the scope of this radicalism was expanded and imbued with a distinctly Islamic character by the second invasion. The mass destruction wreaked by Israel's 1982 invasion, the brutality of its subsequent occupation of the South and the West's concomitant intervention in Lebanon spawned various Shi'ite Islamic resistance groups that coalesced to form Hizbu'llah.

Israel's aggression goes back to 1968 when the PLO began establishing bases in the South. Israel's actual occupation of a part of the South, its so-called 'security zone', began a decade later in the aftermath of Operation Litani, which resulted in the deaths of 2000 and the displacement of 250,000.[23] Interestingly though, the politicising impact of this invasion and the occupation which ensued did not translate itself operationally into an active resistance on the part of the Shi'ites. The Palestinian resistance's hegemony over the southern battlefield precluded the emergence of a Lebanese resistance force. It was Israel's success in eradicating the armed Palestinian presence in Lebanon in 1982 that permitted other resistance groups to come to the fore.

Another factor explaining the Shi'ites' non-resistance and the non-materialisation of the Islamic Resistance during the 1978 invasion was that the Islamic Revolution in Iran had not yet taken place. Thus, the Shi'ites reacted militantly to the 1982 invasion, after the Revolution's occurrence in 1979. It follows that the Shi'ites' Islamicisation – partly a product of the Revolution's 'demonstration effect' – was a necessary condition for their resistance to Israel and the advent of Hizbu'llah.

But in the final analysis, there is much doubt as to whether Hizbu'llah, the political movement-cum-party, would have emerged had it not originated as a conglomeration of armed Islamic groups resisting Israel. Although there had been a significant number of religious groups and associations prior to 1982, many of which arose as a direct result of the Iranian revolution, their merger was not inevitable in the absence of an Israeli invasion. In the words of Hizbu'llah parliamentarian Muhammad Fnaysh, 'the Israeli invasion helped these groups think more about coalescing', which may not otherwise have been the case.[24] Expressed more explicitly by Nasru'llah, 'had the enemy not taken this step [the invasion], I do not know whether something called Hizbu'llah would have been born. I doubt it'.[25]

Having established the Israeli invasion as Hizbu'llah's initial *raison d'être*, it is important to appreciate how the invasion effected such a high level of radicalisation amongst the community, and by association, how the Islamic Resistance perceived itself as a 'natural reaction' to it.[26] Aside from the religious foundations of the resistance to Israel, the enormity of the Israeli invasion and the brutality of its occupation generated a spontaneous resistance that would later form the backbone of Hizbu'llah. The damage caused to 80 per cent of southern villages, and the near destruction of seven of them,[27] did much to fuel the Shi'ites' wrath, as did the 19,000 deaths and 32,000 casualties inflicted by Israel.[28]

Another radicalising outcome of the invasion was the mass exodus from the South instigated by the destruction of southern produce, Israel's economic blockade of the region, and the flooding of Israeli goods into the Lebanese market. Consequently, a large influx of southerners further swelled the size of the Shi'ite 'belt of misery' which was transformed into a repository of militant Shi'ite groups. Even some Palestinian camps came to provide shelter for the most destitute of the southern refugees, one of which reportedly housed more Shi'ites than Palestinians.[29] Thus, the Sabra and Chatila massacres in 1982 not only victimised Palestinians, but Shi'ite refugees as well who constituted close to one-quarter of those slain.[30]

Yet as politicising as this harrowing episode was, it was the Israelis' desecration of an *'Ashura* ceremonial procession in Nabatiyyeh a year later which both expanded the resistance and inflamed the Shi'ites' fervour. As an intrinsic part of the Shi'ite cultural heritage, the annually held *'Ashura* ceremonies commemorate the 'martyrdom' of the third Shi'ite Imam, Husayn, who died on the tenth day of the Islamic month of Muharram 680 CE in the town of Karbala. On this date, Husayn and a number of his 72 companions who were en route to the town of Kufa, whose inhabitants had invited Husayn to assume leadership, were intercepted and slaughtered by forces loyal to the tyrannical Ummayad ruler Yazid.

While the event was construed throughout Shi'ite history as an act of redemptive suffering on Husayn's part, contemporary Shi'ite thinkers denuded the Karbala drama of its politically passive purport by reinterpreting Husayn's martyrdom as an exemplary act of heroism and sacrifice for all believers to emulate in their struggle against contemporary oppressors. It is against this backdrop that the politicising impact of the desecration of the *'Ashura* procession by Israeli troops must be viewed. Not only was the incident an act of profanity, it was one committed by a state whose oppressive practices in Lebanon were too easily analogised by Lebanese Shi'ites with the oppression typified by Yazid. As such, the Nabatiyyeh incident is considered a milestone in the Islamic resistance to Israel.[31]

Another seminal event in the movement's history was the 1984 assassination of Shaykh Raghib Harb, Imam of Jibshit village, which exalted the Imam's stature among Hizbu'llah adherents to *'Shaykh al-Shuhada'* (the master/leader of all martyrs), thereby adding further impetus to the resistance to Israel's occupation.

Israel's mass detention of Lebanese southerners was another driving force behind the resistance's zeal. By 1983, 10,000 Lebanese and Palestinians were held captive in Israeli-controlled jails.[32] The Ansar prison camp alone is reported to have detained half the South's male population at one time or another between 1982 and 1985, when it was closed.[33] But it was not merely the high number of detainees that escalated resistance activity, but the wretched conditions of their imprisonment and their treatment as hostages with no prisoner-of-war rights. Moreover, the internment of detainees outside Lebanon in Israel's Atlit prison, in violation of the Geneva Convention (relating to the Treatment of Prisoners of War),[34] along with their torture in the notorious Khiyam prison in the South, further ignited the resistance's ardour.

However, the Islamic resistance factions did not single-handedly confront the Israeli occupation, but were assisted by other secular groups such as the LCP, OCA and, as of 1984 Amal, all of which united to form the Lebanese Resistance Front. However, after 1985, the reconstituted Islamic Resistance was virtually alone in fighting Israel and its Lebanese proxy, the South Lebanon Army (SLA). It was also during that year that Israel unilaterally withdrew from those parts of the South it had annexed to the existing security zone.

Nevertheless, its reenactment thereafter of the 'Iron Fist' policy that it had applied to the Occupied Territories militated against the potential of the withdrawal to defuse the conflict. Abetted by the

SLA, Israel stepped up its campaign of terrorising the southerners not only by escalating its bombardment of Shi'ite villages, but by imposing curfews, sealing off entire villages and disconnecting the water and electricity supplies of villages suspected of sympathising with the Resistance.

The Iranian-Syrian Role

While Hizbu'llah was influenced by Sadr's political movement, insofar as many of its cadres were drawn from Amal, the origins of the party do not actually lie in it. In point of fact, the fountainhead of Hizbu'llah was not even located in Lebanon but in the religious academies of Najaf in Iraq where hundreds of young Lebanese Shi'ites studied in the early 1960s and 1970s under the tutelage of radical Shi'ite ideologues such as Khumayni and Muhammad Baqir as-Sadr.[35]

Upon the Ba'ath party's assumption of power in 1968, however, dozens of Lebanese students were expelled,[36] a deportation policy which reached its peak in 1977 when over 100 clerics were compelled to return to Lebanon.[37] Along with other devout Shi'ites, the Najaf graduates, including several potential Hizbu'llah officials, set about recreating the Iraqi-based Da'wa Party in Lebanon,[38] while others established the Lebanese Muslim Students' Union in the early 1970s.[39] A political current co-extensive with Sadr's was thus born.

A leading figure behind this current was al-Sayyid Fadlu'llah whose religious authority underwent a considerable expansion after Sadr's disappearance.[40] But rather than establish an organisation of his own to rival Amal, Fadlu'llah preferred to reform the increasingly secular movement from within.[41] In fact, Fadlu'llah upheld this view to the very end. Even when Hizbu'llah was eventually established, 'he was not involved nor did he join in the meetings and the initial work carried out during Hizbu'llah's formation', according to former Hizbu'llah secretary-general, Shaykh Subhi al-Tufayli.[42] The advancement of Fadlu'llah's status to pre-eminent *mujtahid* (a cleric who can practice legal rationalism, known as *ijtihad*) of the '*Hala al-Islamiyya al-Shi'iyya*' (Islamic State of Affairs) carried a much higher social and political value than any association he might have had with a particular political party. If anything, his organisational affiliation with Hizbu'llah would have undermined his independence and alienated many of his followers who did not identify with the party.[43] In effect, his role was deliberately confined to 'the socialisation and education of this generation [the Shi'ite youth of the 1970s]'.[44]

Thus, Fadlu'llah was able to woo a significant portion of Amal's membership, especially its younger activists.[45] Along with other members of the *Hala al-Islamiyya*, these Amal adherents came to identify themselves with the Committee Supportive of the Islamic Revolution, a cultural organisation founded in 1979 in the run-up to the revolution in Iran. Since the committee is considered by Hizbu'llah as its 'prospective nucleus', party members emphasise that its birth preceded the Islamic Revolution. The committee's staging of a mass demonstration in support of the revolution prior to its actual triumph is cited as proof of the spontaneous nature of the Islamic movement.[46]

However, it is highly unlikely that the Islamic resistance would have been launched, and the party subsequently formed, without a revolutionary paradigm to inspire it. Moreover, without Iran's political, financial and logistical support, its military capability and organisational development would have been greatly retarded. Even by Hizbu'llah's reckoning, it would have taken an additional 50 years for the movement to score the same achievements in the absence of Iranian backing.[47]

Most significantly, it was Iran's dispatch of 1,500 Revolutionary Guards (*Pasdaran*) to the Biqa' in the wake of Israel's 1982 invasion, which played a direct role in the genesis of Hizbu'llah. In a bid to export its Islamic Revolution, Iran had initially sought to propagate Khumayni's pan-Islamic ideology by infiltrating existing Shi'ite organisations such as Amal.[48] When these efforts bore little fruition,[49] Iran seized the opportunity provided by the Israeli invasion to organise the sundry resistance groups into a single organisational framework.

However, it was only with Syrian consent that Iran was able to enter the Lebanese political arena, which has been under Damascus' control since 1976. In need of a strategic ally who could help ward off the Israeli and American threat through the Islamic Resistance, Syria facilitated the guards' entry into the Biqa' by granting them direct access to its borders with the region.[50]

Another factor conducive to the formation of Hizbu'llah was the schism within Amal engendered by the participation of its leader, Nabih Berri, in the National Salvation Committee. Established by president Elias Sarkis in June 1982, the declared aim of the committee was to replace the PLO in West Beirut with the Lebanese Army and included an array of leaders, one of whom was Bashir Gemayel, the pro-Israeli Maronite leader of the Lebanese Forces militia. Berri's involvement in what was perceived as an American orchestrated plan, coupled with the fact that he sat at the same table as Gemayel, was viewed by Amal's religiously disposed members as a deviation from Sadr's Islamic line.[51] Consequently, Amal officials such as Hassan Nasru'llah, Subhi al-Tufayli, Muhammad Yazbek, Husayn al-Khalil, Na'im Qasim, Muhammad Ra'id, 'Abbas al-Mussawi and Ibrahim al-Amin al-Sayyid split from the movement, as did Husayn al-Mussawi, who went on to found Islamic Amal.

Thus, the split in Amal constituted the first stage of Hizbu'llah's inception. The second stage was marked by the participation of several Islamic groups in resistance activities against Israel, at the forefront of which was the Association of the 'Ulama of Jabal 'Amil (comprising solely clerics from the South). Although there was some co-ordination amongst the various groups, they were not bound initially by any organisational links, nor did they share a single strategy.[52]

The coalescence of all of these resistance elements into a single institutional framework signalled the third and final stage of Hizbu'llah's establishment. With the assistance of the 300–500 *Pasdaran* who remained in the Biqa' town of Ba'albakk after the bulk of them had returned to Iran, the defectors from Amal joined forces with other Islamists to establish the 'Committee of Nine', which could properly be called Hizbu'llah's first *Majlis al-Shura* (the party's supreme decision-making council).[53] The committee incorporated three ex-Amal representatives, three clerics and three members of the Committee Supportive of the Islamic Revolution.[54] While they were not represented in the *Shura*, all of the factions that resisted Israel were absorbed by the fledgling organisation.

In effect, Hizbu'llah represented an umbrella movement which banded together alienated Amal members, Islamic Amal, individual clerics along with their followings, the Lebanese Da'wa, the Association of Muslim 'Ulama in Lebanon and the Association of Muslim Students.[55] Since membership in these organisations overlapped with membership in the Committee Supportive of the Islamic Revolution, Hizbu'llah can be considered the political and military outgrowth of this broad cultural movement. Thus, what originated as a religious current in the early 1970s, metamorphosed into a relatively disorganised resistance movement, which in turn, transformed itself into a structured political party.

1 Political Accommodation and Violence in Non-Islamic States

The cornerstone of Hizbu'llah's intellectual structure is the Islamic state ideal. However, the realisation of this fundamental tenet is not actively pursued by the party regardless of its feasibility as a political scheme. Due to the absence of certain social and political circumstances, Hizbu'llah has adopted a strategy of self-preservation, which entails indefinitely postponing the establishment of an Islamic state in Lebanon. Accordingly, much of Hizbu'llah's political thought focuses on the religious and moral bases for political accommodation and political violence in non-Islamic states.

While the concept of political violence refers to a wide range of politically motivated violent acts, which are perpetrated by states as well as groups and individuals, the form of political violence I refer to here is insurgency. This chapter, therefore, deals with Hizbu'llah's views on revolution, *coups d'état*, guerrilla warfare and various forms of terrorist violence practised by groups against secular and un-Islamic domestic regimes.

Despite the debate over whether all violent acts which target unarmed civilians constitute acts of terrorism, for simplicity's sake, terrorist violence will be treated as one strategy of insurgency which is distinguished from other strategies by its deliberate attempt to terrorise a civilian population for political ends. Accordingly, Hizbu'llah's views on all forms of insurgency, both terrorist and otherwise, will be examined.

The Oppressors versus the Oppressed

Central to Hizbu'llah's notion of political action is the division of the world, formulated by Khumayni, into 'oppressors' (*mustakbirin*) and 'oppressed' (*mustad'afin*). So pivotal is this conceptual dichotomy to Hizbu'llah's political thought that it is invoked in almost every official's speech. Moreover, both the Open Letter of 1985 and Hizbu'llah's 1992 electoral programme are addressed to the 'oppressed'.[1] Borrowed from Marxist theory and the Qur'an, Khumayni's theoretical construction is infused with a sense of moral dualism and millenarianism in its division of humankind into good and evil forces[2] which are pitted against each other in an apocalyptic battle, from which the oppressed emerge victorious.[3]

However, a clear distinction must be made between Khumayni's dichotomy and the division of the world by other Islamic theorists into 'Dar al-Islam' (the Abode of Islam) versus 'Dar al-Harb' (the Land of War) which sets Muslims against non-Muslims. This is precisely the error committed by James Piscatori, who confuses this peculiarly Sunni formulation with the Shi'ite oppressor/oppressed division.[4] The oppressors do not represent the non-Muslims and the oppressed the Muslims, but rather those who are socially and economically deprived, politically oppressed and culturally repressed[5] vis-à-vis those who practise this oppression, regardless of their religious identity. More apposite would be the analogy between Dar al-Islam and the Shi'ite notion of 'Hizbu'llah' (the party of God) and Dar al-Harb with 'Hizbu'shaytan' (the party of Satan), which has some religious connotations as well as humanistic ones. Nevertheless, this classification of Hizbu'llah's does not constitute the basis of its theory on political action, which is based purely on humanistic criteria.

Although the concept of oppression is derived from the Qur'an, its usage in the Qur'anic context is essentially humanistic and does not refer to the Muslim believers as such but to all 'those who were being oppressed on earth' (28:5). While this religious reference is devoid of any economic implications, it is conjoined with the secular designation of the oppressed as Frantz Fanon's 'wretched of the earth', whose exploited status as Third World peoples adds a secular class dimension to the concept.[6] Thus, the juxtaposition of exploitation with oppression renders the concept applicable to poor Muslims and non-Muslims, especially those belonging to the oppressed non-Western world.

However, the secular origins of the class criterion are underplayed in Khumayni's and Hizbu'llah's conceptualisation of oppression, resulting in the Islamicisation of class analysis whose defining elements, exploitation and poverty, become Islamic virtues.[7] As articulated by Khumayni, 'Islam originates from the masses not from the rich.'[8] More significantly, the Prophet Muhammad valued 'the sweat of a worker' more than 'the blood of a martyr'.[9] The glorification of the underdog is echoed by Hizbu'llah's characterisation of Imam 'Ali as one who 'loved the poor and deprived'.

Not only is deprivation a moral asset for those who happen to be afflicted with such a status, it is apotheosised as a virtue to be emulated by religious leaders. Against this backdrop, Imam 'Ali is claimed to have abstained from life's luxuries and chose instead to lead a humble life like his followers.[10] So ubiquitous is this theme in Hizbu'llah's political thought that it has become institutionalised as a norm to which Hizbu'llah officials must adhere. Thus, asceticism is a predominant feature of the lifestyles of Hizbu'llah's leadership, in accordance with the party's self-designation as 'the first party to oppose deprivation'[11] and as the champion of the 'peasants and farmers, the labourers and the poor, the oppressed and deprived, the workers and homeless'.[12]

It is important to note, however, that the homeless Hizbu'llah is referring to are those who have been displaced by the Israeli occupation – the Shi'ite southerners. At first glance, this appears to contradict the aforementioned distinction between the Muslim believers and the oppressed. Hizbu'llah's depiction of the Islamic *umma* (community of Muslim believers) as 'oppressed, poor and deprived',[13] only underlines this apparent contradiction. On closer inspection though, two qualifications can be made regarding the conjunction of Shi'ites and oppressed. First, the inclusion of Shi'ites or Muslims in Hizbu'llah's oppressed category does not *ipso facto* exclude other religious groups from this category.

Second, the classification of the Shi'ites as oppressed does not stem from the Qur'an but from the Israeli occupation of South Lebanon and the cultural division of labour typifying Lebanese society, whereby class and community overlap. As mentioned in the previous chapter, the Shi'ites constituted a 'community-class' by dint of their low educational, occupational and economic status. Therefore, any designation of the Shi'ites as oppressed necessarily emanates from a class analysis perspective as opposed to an Islamic one.

This observation is substantiated by Hizbu'llah's identification of the Muslims, and more specifically the Shi'ites, with the oppressed who, prior to the early 1980s, did not have access to the 'elite' universities in the country which were monopolised by the 'wealthy classes'.[14] This reference not only reveals the class origins of Hizbu'llah's concept of oppression, but also demonstrates the humanistic aspect of the concept which is unrelated to class.

According to Hizbu'llah, those privileged enough to attend elitist universities such as the American University of Beirut and the Saint Joseph University – presumably the Christians – desperately try to imitate the West in all spheres of their lives. This mimicry extends to the realm of thought, as evidenced by their espousal of 'arrogant, materialistic ideas'. Through this myopic Western vision, they view their oppressed Muslim counterparts with disdain.[15] Accordingly, economic status alone does not seem to be a sufficient criterion of oppression. Only those who identify with the West are deemed oppressors. The fact that they generally belong to the upper classes of society is coincidental, as is their religious identity.

It is not poverty per se which determines whether one is oppressed, but deprivation and exploitation. It is only when poverty is the result of state discrimination, negligence and abuse that it becomes synonymous with oppression. Otherwise, poverty is merely a social description. Furthermore, economic deprivation and exploitation are not the only criteria of oppression, as attested to by Khumayni's and Hizbu'llah's significant middle-class support base. The incorporation of all social classes into the oppressed category is based on the Qur'anic portrayal of the oppressed as those who are economically, politically or culturally 'weak' vis-à-vis the 'arrogant' oppressors, a bifurcation which is enshrined in the constitution of the Islamic Republic of Iran.[16]

Since neither weakness nor arrogance is intrinsic to any religious community, it follows that the Qur'anic notion of oppression is even more universal than the Marxist one. Not only do all social classes represent the oppressed, but all religious denominations too. Moreover, the category of oppressors includes Shi'ites, as well as other Muslims and Christians. As expressed by al-Sayyid Ibrahim al-Amin al-Sayyid at the height of the civil war: 'We do not discriminate between Muslim and Christian in our rejection of oppression.'[17]

The common denominator between the oppressed Muslims and Christians is their 'humanitarianism'[18] and their rejection of oppression as reflected in their political stands, behaviour and intellectual identity.[19] More specifically, it is the attitude to Zionism and the West – America in particular – that differentiates the oppressors from the politically and culturally oppressed. Anyone who is 'free', who 'resists Zionism' and who 'may be exposed to danger' as a result of his beliefs, qualifies as an oppressed person.[20] Conversely, all those who side with the 'greatest abominations in our era',[21] America and the Zionist 'enemy', are the oppressors who must be confronted by Hizbu'llah.[22] Even the initial stages of the Lebanese civil war are perceived through the oppressor/oppressed lens. Rather than a conflict between leftist Muslims and rightist Christians, the war is construed by Ibrahim al-Amin al-Sayyid as 'a conflict between oppressed and oppressor',[23] in view of the latter's association with Israel and America.

In light of America and Israel epitomising oppression according to Hizbu'llah, the prioritisation of the party's abominations by some scholars appears markedly disordered. The ordering of the 'infidel Satans' (America and Israel) at the bottom of the execration scale flies in the face of Hizbu'llah's notion of oppression. Moreover, the vanguard of the 'sinful world' is definitely not represented by the 'secularised Shi'ite Muslims', and the Sunni Muslims are certainly not considered sinful by the party, let alone the second most sinful category.[24]

Unlike many Islamic 'fundamentalist' groups who, according to As'ad Abu Khalil, deem those Muslims who do not subscribe to their Islamic vision as 'infidels', and who view secularist Muslims as 'apostates' who ought to be punished by death,[25] Hizbu'llah has no such *takfir* (declaring the infidelity of adversaries)[26] discourse. Above all, it is the oppressors who are anathematised, regardless of their religious identities, political leanings or religiosity. Furthermore, the party does not equate secularism with oppression or sin. As underlined by Hizbu'llah MP Muhammad Fnaysh, only the secularist who 'disavows Islamic principles and sanctities' or who enforces secularism as a state religion is considered hostile to Islam and an oppressor.[27]

The distinction between the Sunni Islamist deprecation of secularism as a profanity and Hizbu'llah's more tolerant view is also exemplified by their perspectives on secular Syrian Ba'athism. While Sunni Islamists depict the Ba'ath Party as a 'Crusader party ... hellbent upon subverting Islam',[28] Hizbu'llah tries to mitigate the sacrilege associated with Syrian secularism by claiming that Hafez al-Assad 'is not an atheist'.[29] But more significantly, it is Syria's unyieldingness towards Israel and its safeguarding of Arab rights,[30] which not only indemnify it from Hizbu'llah's rebuke, but also render it an oppressed state. The same case can be made for the PLO whose secularism did not prevent Hizbu'llah from condemning Amal's 'War of the Camps' against the organisation or from actively intervening on behalf of the Sunni Palestinian refugees – a course of action which also refutes Hizbu'llah's alleged odium for Sunni Muslims.

Lest this be construed as an indication of Hizbu'llah's countenance of Arab secularists only, on account of their stance towards Israel, it must be stressed that any oppressed secular group or state is not only condoned but also morally supported by the party. Hizbu'llah sympathises with secular Christian and even Marxist Third World Leaders such as Nelson Mandela, Daniel Ortega and Fidel Castro[31] because of their countries' oppressed status. Castro, for example, is 'respected' for preserving Cuba's independence from US influence and for confronting the US' hegemony over South America.[32]

Mandela is esteemed for his role in resisting the oppressive apartheid regime in South Africa. This sympathy extends to non-Third World movements such as Northern Ireland's Republicans (though not to the IRA as such) whose resistance to Britain's 'oppression, aggression and occupation' is reminiscent of the Palestinian and Lebanese situation.[33] So oppressed are the Irish Catholics perceived to be, that Khumayni even went so far as to name a Tehran street after imprisoned IRA hunger-striker Bobby Sands.

Occupation of one's land by Israel or any other foreign power emerges as a principal determinant of oppression and, like all oppressed people, those whose land is occupied will be afforded Hizbu'llah's 'automatic' support.[34] But even an oppressed people whose land has been subjected to foreign occupation does not win Hizbu'llah's total sympathy if its rejection of oppression hinges on Western support. According to this logic, the Afghan *mujahidin*'s recourse to American aid in their resistance to the Soviet occupation detracted from their moral integrity as an oppressed people. By compromising their independence, they became the 'American *mujahidin*',[35] a highly pejorative epithet in Hizbu'llah's lexicon.

It is upon this basis that Hizbu'llah's address to the 'Free Downtrodden Men' is made, the operative word being 'free'. Also employed by Husayn al-Mussawi in his delineation of the oppressed, the term refers to the refusal of the downtrodden to succumb to American domination, even if this means that the rule of their indigenous oppressors will continue indefinitely. As tyrannical as the Saddam Husayn regime is, the Iraqi opposition should not rely on American support, or it will remain politically indebted to the US.[36]

Apart from Israel, whose demonisation by Hizbu'llah renders it the ultimate oppressor, the US occupies the most 'sinful' category of Hizbu'llah's enemies. The second most oppressive are the various occupiers of the lands of the oppressed, but whose occupation cannot be compared with Israel whose very existence is perceived as illegitimate. Third are the tyrannical regimes governing the oppressed whose subservience to the West, and the US especially, in addition to their inherent injustice as dictatorships (regardless of the foreign powers which bolster their rule) translates into oppression.

Accordingly, the 'oppressed of the world'[37] are the victims of these three classes of oppression, which fall under the Qur'anic designation of 'the arrogant'. Along with those whose economic deprivation is thrust upon them by a neglectful state, these 'friends'[38] of Hizbu'llah are urged to form a common 'international front' to fight oppression.[39] Thus, Hizbu'llah fundamentally strives for the 'unity of humanity'.[40]

Justifications for Political Violence and Accommodation in Relation to State Oppression

The exemplary just state for Hizbu'llah is the Islamic republic. However, with the exception of Iran, where such a state exists, the realisation of such an ideal by Shi'ite Islamists has been virtually impossible. Moreover, when the appropriate circumstances for the establishment of the Islamic republic do not obtain, any revolutionary activity that strives in this direction will result in chaos – a much abhorred outcome for both Sunni and Shi'ite Islamists. In view of this likelihood, and bearing in mind Hizbu'llah's conceptualisation of oppression, the conditions under which Islamists may resort to political violence or political accommodation with un-Islamic Muslim and secular states can be readily discerned.

Contrary to 'Abbas Kelidar's assertion that the Shi'ite community is predisposed to rebellion because of its 'belief that the authority of Muslim rulers, with the exception of Imam 'Ali's, could not be recognised as legitimate',[41] only rarely has the denial of legitimacy actually translated into rebellion or revolution.[42] As noted by Sartori, anti-system is not equivalent to outside the system or revolution.[43] And legitimacy has not been withheld from regimes not related to 'Ali's descendants. In fact, legitimacy has been conferred on secular states (such as post-Ta'if Lebanon) and withheld from Muslim ones (such as Saudi Arabia). It follows that the overthrow of secular states is not the underlying purpose of *jihad* (holy war).

The cornerstone of Hizbu'llah's doctrine on political violence is the principle of the non-compulsion of Islam.[44] Thus, there is no religious sanction for rebellion against secular states such as Lebanon just because they are not 'governed by divine laws'.[45] This belief is grounded in Hizbu'llah's reading of the Shari'a (Islamic law) which deems rebellion and civil disobedience 'unacceptable'.[46] In light of this Islamic precept, the party feels duty-bound to 'preserve public order'[47] and consequently views civil peace as a 'red line' which cannot be crossed.[48]

This maxim applies not only to the secular state, but also to the oppressive secular state. According to Husayn al-Mussawi's exegesis of the Shari'a, 'an oppressive government is preferable to chaos because chaos is even more oppressive',[49] a prioritisation which is rooted in two distinct but related sources. First is the Shari'a which conceives of public disorder as an even greater 'evil' than oppressive rule,[50] because of its own ineluctable culmination in civil war. The fact that the Prophet Muhammad did not resort to violence during twelve years of oppression in Mecca is cited as an example of this Islamic reasoning.[51] Second is the ease with which external enemies, with particular reference to Israel, can penetrate a lawless society, especially in a civil war. It was for these reasons that Hizbu'llah exercised extreme restraint in the face of the government's killing of several Hizbu'llah protesters who took part in a demonstration against the Oslo Accord, on 13 September 1993, otherwise known as the 'September Massacre'.[52]

But the Islamic proscription of civil war and Israel's certain infiltration of the Lebanese arena if civil war did break out, are not the only grounds for Hizbu'llah's aversion to chaos. By focusing all efforts on the removal of an oppressive regime, Hizbu'llah believes that attention would be deflected from the 'liberation priority', which takes precedence over all other concerns. In contrast to Sunni Islamists, who view their local regimes as the immediate enemy,[53] Hizbu'llah perceives Israel as a much greater threat than the oppressive policies of the Lebanese government and the unjust sectarian configuration underpinning it.[54] Thus, Israel emerges as the unparalleled oppressor, while oppressive states and regimes are again cast as the least abominable oppressors.

The category of oppressive regimes covers a wide spectrum of governments with varying degrees of oppression and legitimacy. Although the Lebanese government is deemed oppressive, it is not perceived 'as though it is not doing anything' in terms of infrastructure and education.[55] Moreover, the nuance between oppression and illegitimacy is evident in Hizbu'llah's conferral of legitimacy[56] or constitutionality[57] upon the oppressive Lebanese government. Although the party cannot deem other oppressive Arab regimes to be legitimate – since their political authority is derived neither from God nor from the people, it does not advocate the use of violence against them.

Indeed, Hizbu'llah urges Islamic groups to adopt 'internal dialogue'[58] and to 'reconcile'[59] with states such as Turkey, Algeria and Egypt, which are considered illegitimate and far more oppressive than the Lebanese state. The Algerian people 'are oppressed'[60] by the Algerian regime, which not only nullified the results of the parliamentary election and dissolved parliament, but which is implicated in the massacres beleaguering Algeria. Nonetheless, Shaykh Na'im Qasim, Hizbu'llah's deputy secretary-general, 'disapproves of the use of violence by some Islamists'.[61] Nasru'llah even claims that Hizbu'llah 'does not know anyone from the FIS [Islamic Salvation Front] in Algeria',[62] an organisation which most Hizbu'llah officials normally distinguish from the GIA (Armed Islamic Group), which is generally considered to be one of the perpetrators of violence.[63]

Similarly, the party exhorts Egyptian Islamists to refrain from taking up arms against the state,[64] and calls for a dialogue between the two.[65] Rather than target the Egyptian state headed by Husni Mubarak, the 'tyrant',[66] Islamists' weapons should be used against Egypt's 'fundamental enemy', Israel.[67] Coupled with the fear of civil war,[68] this is the same rationale behind all of Hizbu'llah's entreaties to Islamists to reconcile with illegitimate and oppressive regimes.

The party professes that its religious references not only legitimise, but sometimes enjoin participation in oppressive political systems, if that participation 'averts the causes of evil' or 'secures interests'.[69] According to Husayn al-Mussawi, 'it is not right to shun an impure system', when political, or more specifically, parliamentary participation could serve the 'Islamic interest'.[70] This reasoning is not confined to states whose oppression is tempered by their legitimacy, such as Lebanon, but also to illegitimate and oppressive political systems such as Egypt, Jordan and Turkey.[71]

Although Turkey is vehemently condemned for its institutionalisation of secularism and its attempts at effacing the Islamic identity of Turkish society,[72] Hizbu'llah extols the Islamic Welfare Party's democratic course.[73] Only when participation results in 'an even greater evil' than political exclusion is it proscribed by Shi'ite jurists,[74] as in the case of participation in the Palestinian National Authority, led by the much despised Yasser 'Arafat, with whom even dialogue is discouraged.[75]

In those instances where participation and dialogue are barred, violence is permitted. When 'the cause of corruption is so great that there is no other solution', political violence becomes warranted.[76] Thus, neither government illegitimacy nor oppression alone suffice as a justification for civil disobedience, nor does the co-existence of both factors in one state. What does justify it is the practice by the state of an insufferable and draconian form of oppression, which either subjects people to pro-Zionist rule or which otherwise threatens the very existence of the Islamists. States that fit this description are viewed as a much greater evil than any chaos that may result from Islamists' attempts to overthrow them.

As the archetype of oppression in its harshest form, Israel represents the state with which co-operation is beyond the pale. Accordingly, any regime that is part of the 'Israeli scheme' is perceived as iniquitous and the resort to violence against it becomes fully condonable and even imperative. It is on the basis of this moral logic that Hizbu'llah repeatedly declared its intention to destroy the Amin Gemayel regime. Unlike the post-Ta'if Hariri regime, which was merely oppressive and therefore not deserving of destruction, the 'hypocrisy, oppression and blasphemy' of the Gemayel regime, which were the products of its association with Israel warranted its destruction.[77]

In a similar vein, the 'authoritarian' Palestinian leadership under 'Arafat is looked upon as an intolerably oppressive rule that must be overturned. As the custodian of Jerusalem and the 'sacred' Palestinian cause, 'Arafat's capitulation to Israel, by dint of his successive accords with the detested state, renders him a 'traitor' who 'must be executed'. By expressing its desire for 'a Palestinian Khalid Islambuli' (assassin of Anwar Sadat) to emerge, the party insinuates that 'Arafat ought to be assassinated for selling out Palestine.[78]

The threat of eradication by a highly repressive state is the other instance of oppression that vindicates the use of violence.[79] Although Hizbu'llah has repeatedly condemned the course of violence adopted by the Algerian Islamists, it regards the FIS' initial militant response, which it later abandoned, to the military coup as a legitimate act of self-defence.[80] As enunciated by Yussef Meri', self-defence is the only Qur'anic justification for taking up arms against an oppressive state.[81] Political violence is therefore morally and religiously legitimised as defensive *jihad* if its paramount aim is self-preservation.

Political Accommodation with the Lebanese State

Accommodation with the Political System

As a form of political accommodation, Hizbu'llah's agreement to abide by the reformulated Lebanese constitution, and its decision to participate in the parliamentary election of 1992, in the post-Ta'if political order, must be viewed within the framework of its moral bases for political violence and accommodation in oppressive secular systems. Although one cannot ignore the party's customary rationale for its accommodation with the Lebanese state, which relates to the end of the civil war in 1989 and the establishment of its resistance priority in 1990,[82] its changing perception of this state, from one which warranted revolutionary rejectionism to one which merited political accommodation, provides a deeper insight into the transformation of its political stand.

Aside from the Gemayel regime itself, which was branded 'an oppressive, hypocritical and blasphemous' rule, the political system within which it operated, and with which it was closely identified, was viewed in equally iniquitous terms. This perception did not stem from the un-Islamic nature of the Lebanese state, but from its 'fundamentally oppressive' configuration[83] which was founded on the Maronite community's political supremacy. Its depiction by the party as 'a rotten sectarian system'[84] was therefore a product of the institutionalisation of this hegemony.

By implication, Hizbu'llah's opposition to the sectarian underpinnings of this system was as much an opposition to the principle of political sectarianism as it was a rejection of the Maronites' monopoly of the 'sectarian privileges'[85] the system had to offer. While Hizbu'llah's disparagement of the political system issued from its repudiation of political sectarianism per se, it was partially rooted in the system's underrepresentation of the Shi'ite community.

There was no way that the party could reconcile itself to a system that was not only unjust by dint of its sectarian essence, but also because it apportioned its sectarian shares on an entirely inequitable basis. Because such a system could not lend itself to the possibility of political reform, but required a revolutionary overhaul to extirpate its very roots, any opposition to it had to come from outside its constitutional boundaries, or it would be 'protecting and safeguarding the constitution currently in force'.[86] In effect, Hizbu'llah's opposition to the pre-Ta'if political system rendered it not only an 'anti-system' party, to borrow Sartori's terminology, which sought to change the very system of government, but a revolutionary one, which sought to change it from 'outside the system'.[87]

With the formulation of a new constitution under the Ta'if Agreement of 1989, Hizbu'llah's perception of the state underwent a significant transformation. Correspondingly, the party metamorphosed from a revolutionary 'total refusal' anti-system party, into a 'protest' anti-system party.[88] Yet even as an anti-system protest party, its political alienation from the state could not be classified under Milbraith and Goel's 'normlessness' category – which denotes a rejection of both the principles and institutions underpinning the political system[89] – as it rejected the sectarian essence of the system but not its institutional structure. By the same token, it could not be classified in the 'cynicism' category either – which refers to distrust of the government and political leadership of a country, without questioning the political order within which they operate – as it did reject the political order. Although the party's perception of the state underwent a transformation, its attitude to it remained ambivalent.

On the one hand, the party criticised the Ta'if accord for merely 'amending' the former constitution, and hence 'preserving the sectarian substance' of the political system to the extent that sectarianism had become 'totally constitutional'.[90] Moreover, despite the 50–50 formula stipulated by the accord, which divides power equally between Muslims and Christians, the Maronites would continue to play a 'hegemonic' role in the system by means of their politically 'unaccountable' president, as well as their cabinet ministers and parliamentary representatives. [91] By contrast, the Muslims would be politically accountable, yet without any real power. [92]

For this reason, the Maronites would be disinclined to abolish political sectarianism. Thus, although the accord calls for the phased abolition of political sectarianism by means of a national council headed by the president, the cabinet approval and two-thirds parliamentary majority required for the ratification of such a scheme could never be achieved.[93]

On the other hand, Hizbu'llah does not view the Ta'if Accord as 'completely evil',[94] as suggested by Magnus Ranstorp's claim that the party's rejection of the accord is a 'uniform' one.[95] Certain positive features of the accord, such as its termination of the civil war[96] and its stipulation of the necessity of abolishing political sectarianism (notwithstanding the unfeasibility of this goal) in the future, mitigate its negative aspects and make it more palatable to the party.[97]

It is on this account that the party does not regard its infiltration of a system, whose total destruction it formerly called for, as being incongruous with its pledge to abolish political sectarianism.[98] Not only does the constitution's intent to uproot sectarianism from the political system distinguish it from the previous constitution, but its more equitable distribution of power among the sects further differentiates it from the pre-Ta'if state. Despite the political unaccountability of the Maronite president, the party admits that much of the power he wielded in the past has in fact been transferred to the multi-sectarian cabinet.[99] Along with other redistributions of power within the state's structures which have served to erode the Maronites' political dominance, the diminution of the president's power has meant that, although the politically sectarian 'foundations' of the system have remained intact, the 'structure' of the system has undergone significant change.[100] In turn, these structural changes are conducive to the eradication of political sectarianism from 'within the system' insofar as the scope for political participation by those who oppose sectarianism (i.e. the Muslims) has been expanded.[101]

Although the party's adjustment to the post-Ta'if sectarian system is attributable to the relatively egalitarian diffusion of power among the sects, it still rejects the sectarian basis of the system. While the Ta'if Accord has expanded the scope of Shi'ite political participation and accorded the post of Speaker of the House, which is still reserved for Shi'ites, greater powers, this does not detract from the need to eradicate sectarianism.[102]

Therefore, the Ta'if Agreement cannot be 'accepted as a conclusive formula',[103] but must be dealt with as a provisional arrangement open to modification. However, the fact that the party recognises that the abolition of political sectarianism will be extremely difficult, in light of the large Christian presence in the cabinet and parliament, signifies that though the agreement is not conclusive in theory, it is in actuality.

As an agreement which is conclusive in theory but not in reality, which represents more than a mere reform of the previous system but less than a radical change, and which for those reasons is 'neither completely evil nor completely good',[104] Hizbu'llah will co-exist with it 'without according it legitimacy'.[105] The party will work from within the confines of this basically 'corrupt' or illegitimate system in order to change it.[106] In other words, it will oppose this system on a de jure basis, but will grant it de facto recognition.

Underlying this decision to observe the 'continuation of this system despite its oppression' is the party's aversion to chaos.[107] As stated above, a central tenet of Hizbu'llah's political thought is the avoidance of public disorder. Husayn al-Mussawi's assertion that 'an oppressive government is preferable to chaos' can therefore be extended to the political system as a whole. The 'sectarian discrimination' that inheres in the current system clearly denotes that it is oppressive,[108] but unlike the pre-Ta'if system, it is not oppressive enough to warrant civil war. Even if the party was not fully immersed in resistance to the Israeli occupation – from which attention would be deflected if it pursued the overthrow of the system – the positive features of the system obviate the need for its total destruction.

Political Accommodation with Post-Ta'if Regimes

Hizbu'llah's attitudes to post-Ta'if governments cannot be considered prototypical instances of political accommodation on account of their oppositional nature. However, when compared with the party's anathematisation of the Gemayel regime, both the form and content of this opposition represent such radical departures from that stand, that no term short of accommodation can be used it to describe it.

As a regime associated with Israel, which in turn threatened the very existence of Hizbu'llah, the Gemayel government fulfilled the two aforementioned criteria that designate it an ultimate oppressor necessitating politically violent or revolutionary responses to it. To oppose such a regime from within the system would therefore be both morally and religiously proscribed, as well as fruitless, as it would be 'a superficial opposition that will ultimately agree with the existing regime', and which would also serve to legitimise the oppressive political system.[109] Over twelve years later, this rationale is still echoed by Muhammad Muhsin, who contends that any political force which wanted to confront the Gemayel regime from within the political system, had to acquiesce to the Maronites' political hegemony.[110]

While the principal factor which licensed Hizbu'llah's participation in the post-Ta'if system was its changed perception of the Lebanese political system, the fact that the Rafiq al-Hariri government was not viewed as being oppressive enough to warrant destruction, facilitated this participation. Furthermore, in contrast to the Gemayel regime, which was directly associated with the unjust political system, government and system became dissociated from each other in the post-Ta'if order. This enabled Hizbu'llah to retain the ideological purity of its opposition to the Hariri regime and afforded it a politically non-violent and a morally legitimate means of channelling this opposition.

What is more, this opposition did not assume the form of a 'boycott' that opposed the government on every conceivable issue, but was one which selectively opposed or supported various government policies according to 'rational' criteria.[111] It was, as Hizbu'llah describes it, a 'constructive' opposition,[112] which criticized the government and its policies in a responsible manner, with the general interest in mind, as opposed to a 'disruptive' one that would 'disrupt' the work of government solely on account of its hostility towards it.[113] Thus, although Hizbu'llah twice raised a vote of no confidence in the Hariri governments of 1992 and 1995, its parliamentarians have, in the words of Augustus Richard Norton, 'behaved responsibly and cooperatively' in voicing their opposition to the Hariri government.[114]

Rather than uniformly oppose the government, or focus its parliamentary activity on peculiarly Islamic issues,[115] Hizbu'llah's opposition was an 'inclusionary' and 'issue-based'[116] social, economic and political critique of the government, which pursued (and still pursues) the implementation of such secular issues as the abolition of political sectarianism, social justice for the oppressed, public freedoms, the diffusion of political power and political transparency. Accordingly, its castigation of the government revolved around the popular themes of political corruption, administrative inefficiency, overspending on large-scale reconstruction projects and the underdevelopment of deprived areas.[117]

Despite the fact that the party's opposition is not limited to the government, but extends to the very system of government, the responsible and constructive nature of its opposition makes its political behaviour more akin to a 'constitutional opposition' than an 'anti-system opposition'.[118] According to Sartori, parties falling into the former category assent to the 'fundamentals' of the political system, whereas those in the latter category reject those fundamentals.[119]

While such categories may have been mutually exclusive in the mid-1960s when Sartori coined them, the recent emergence of issue-based, and hence constructive, anti-system parties, which focus their participatory efforts not so much on changing the system as on producing a more responsible government, challenges this view. Islamic parties such as Hizbu'llah and Turkey's Refah,[120] in addition to the various Communist parties in Europe, represent a new breed of party – anti-system in substance, but constitutional in form.

Not only is Hizbu'llah's opposition to the Lebanese government constructive in form, it is also politically mature in content. Though the party depicts the government as an 'oppressive' one which has come to power by means of the 'exploitation of circumstances', the 'falsification of the general will' and electoral 'forgery', and as such does not truly represent the Lebanese people,[121] it admits that the government is still theoretically legitimate.[122]

For this reason, the party disagreed with the civil disobedience campaign or 'the Hunger Revolution', launched by Hizbu'llah's former secretary-general, Shaykh Subhi al-Tufayli, arguing that though his demands for improved living conditions in the Biqa' were justified, the means he used to fulfil them were ill-conceived.[123] Clearly, the party did not believe that the use of violence against an oppressive but legitimate government was religiously or morally justifiable, especially when public disorder was the most probable outcome.

While unrelated to the actual legitimacy of the government, the party's changing stand on participation in the Hariri regime was another indication of the party's political maturation. Although its refusal to participate in the Hariri government was initially based on the grounds of principle, those who objected to this participation later came to reject it on political grounds.[124] This shift was largely attributable to the party's distinction between a government that was only theoretically participating in negotiations with Israel, and one that was technically negotiating with it.[125] In turn, Hizbu'llah's ability to make this distinction was greatly facilitated by the diminishing likelihood of a Lebanese-Israeli peace during Hariri's second tenure in office, and hence the theoretical nature of his government's negotiations with Israel.

In short, 'the party was no longer of the opinion that participation in government was illegitimate', thereby enabling some party members to advocate such participation, while others objected to it solely on account of the Hariri regime's social and economic policies.[126] Hizbu'llah's refusal to participate in government on principled grounds would be confined to one which had already concluded a peace agreement with Israel, was already in negotiations with it, or was about to enter negotiations with it.

But Hizbu'llah's participation in a government that was neither negotiating with Israel, nor about to, could still not be guaranteed, as exemplified by the case of the second Hariri government. That socio-economic and political considerations are as great an obstacle to participation, and hence full political accommodation, as are ideological ones, is further demonstrated by Hizbu'llah's refusal to participate in the favourably viewed Salim al-Hus government, which was not about to enter peace negotiations with Israel.

As portrayed by the party, the regime led by Prime Minister Hus and President Emile Lahhud, which was instituted at the end of 1998, took an unprecedented stand towards the Resistance and displayed an unparalleled 'concern and vision of balanced development for the deprived regions'.[127] It was a regime 'distinguished' by such 'positive qualities' as the 'qualifications' and 'integrity' of its cabinet ministers,[128] and the 'honesty' of its president.[129] Moreover, the party had nominated Hus for the premiership, which was also indicative of its support for this government.[130]

Yet despite this vocal show of support, the party declined to pass a motion of confidence in the Hus government, and chose instead to abstain from voting, claiming that it could not vote for a government, no matter how favourable, before viewing its actual performance.[131] As it turned out, the economic legacy left by Hariri's overambitious reconstruction project had left the new government with little room to manoeuvre and therefore prevented it from implementing many of its development schemes. The party claimed that, even it had been afforded the opportunity to join such a government, it would have declined from doing so. Not only would the party's presence in a government over whose policies it had little control not be 'beneficial' to people's needs and demands and thereby render it an 'uninfluential' actor in the decision-making process, but it would have caused the party to 'bear responsibility for mistakes' that it had not made.[132]

The upshot of all this is that Hizbu'llah's participation in any future government is not only governed by developments in the peace process, and the consequent likelihood of the conclusion of a Lebanese-Israeli peace accord, but is also contingent upon the state of the economy. While the party could, quite conceivably, join a government such as the present one, and then withdraw from it once it was about to partake in peace negotiations, it could not participate in it to begin with, without assessing the ultimate feasibility of its economic goals. Undoubtedly, the party is not oblivious to the invidiousness that comes with being in power under dire economic straits, or to the luxury of being out of power in such circumstances.

In the final analysis, the extent of Hizbu'llah's political accommodation with Lebanese governments has as much to do with political considerations as with ideological ones, related to the peace process. This juxtaposition of the ideological and the political has enabled the party's opposition to the Hariri regime, and its semi-support for the Hus administration, to assume a politically constructive form and a politically mature content – the requisites for any party's institutional longevity.

2 The Islamic State and Democracy

The Islamic State Ideal

With the exceptions of the brief period of rule of Imam 'Ali and the even briefer duration of Imam Hassan's caliphate, Hizbu'llah does not consider any other Shi'ite government, whether dynasty or empire, as worthy of emulation. What is more, the party does not regard any period in Shi'ite history as a 'Golden Age' to which it aspires to return. This is the principal difference between the Sunni and Shi'ite exemplary Islamic state. While the Sunnis seek to recreate the Golden Age comprising the first three Caliphs, the Shi'ites do not strive to return to 'the historical period in which the Prophet lived or the periods that followed'.[1]

As the Shi'ite conceptualisation of the Islamic state has no historical precedent, it can best be described as a Utopia which has yet to be fulfilled. Only with the reappearance of the *Mahdi* or 'Hidden Imam' – the Twelfth and last of the Shi'ite Imams who is believed to have been in occultation (*ghayba*) since 874 CE and whose eventual return (*raj'a*) to institute the rule of justice on earth is anticipated — can the Utopian Islamic state be established. However, the party does not elaborate much on the pan-Islamic Mahdist state, save to portray it as one in which there will be no room for non-believers.[2] Accordingly, Hizbu'llah's theoretical formulations on the ideal Islamic republic relate to the pre-Mahdist Islamic state. Since the Islamic Republic of Iran 'represents the only Islamic government in our era',[3] which most closely approximates this ideal, much of the party's state theory is borrowed from Ruhu'llah Khumayni, in addition to Islamic scholars such as Sayyids Muhammad Baqir as-Sadr and Muhammad Husayn Fadlu'llah.

The Means of Establishing the Islamic State

As unviable as the establishment of an Islamic state is, the Islamic republic ideal remains the bedrock of Hizbu'llah's intellectual structure. Thus, while much of the party's political thought is borrowed from secular humanism, Hizbu'llah is quintessentially an Islamic movement that staunchly adheres to 'the fundamentals'[4] of 'the genuine Muhammadan Islam'.[5] The Israeli occupation may have been its initial *raison d'être*, but its overriding purpose is to serve the 'Islamic aim'.[6]

Since the political and the spiritual are inseparable for 'Islamic totalists'[7] such as Hizbu'llah who perceive Islam as a 'complete and comprehensive system for life',[8] this aim necessarily entails the formation of an Islamic state. By 'complete' and 'comprehensive', the party means the diverse social, political and economic laws embodied in the Shari'a which, according to Khumayni, presuppose the existence of an Islamic state for their execution.[9] Likewise, Khumayni's depiction of the establishment of an Islamic state as a religious duty[10] is echoed by Hizbu'llah.[11] Thus, although the implementation of an Islamic state is contingent upon its feasibility as a political scheme, it is still viewed as a religiously ordained necessity by the party.

In fact, the very notion of an Islamic movement that does not aspire to this goal is inconceivable to Hizbu'llah,[12] not only because its implementation is a religious duty incumbent upon every Muslim, but also because Islam represents the only 'right system for mankind'.[13] As the sole belief system capable of effectuating the society of perfect justice, equality and freedom, any society that is not founded on the basis of Islam will be fraught with adversity, deprivation and oppression, as exemplified by Lebanon.[14] While this appears to contradict the aforementioned assertion that secularism cannot be equated with oppression, and hence injustice, one must recall that the Islamic state is regarded as the best, though not necessarily the only, means of attaining justice.

Therefore, all countries in the region should unite to form an 'all-encompassing Islamic state', of which Lebanon would be an intrinsic part.[15] Failing this, an Islamic republic should be established within Lebanese borders, in anticipation of the rise of the *Mahdi* who would institute the rule of Islam in the entire world.

However, even this limited goal has been relinquished because of the perceived difficulty of implementing an Islamic state in Lebanon. Such a scheme would not only be rejected outright by Lebanese Christians, Sunnis and Druze, but even by a significant portion of the Shi'ite community. According to Judith Harik's 1992 study, only 13 per cent of Shi'ites lent their support to the creation of an Islamic republic in Lebanon.[16] Accordingly, the order of execution has been inverted: only after Islam envelops the entire region under the auspices of the Twelfth Imam, will Lebanon be subjected to Islamic rule, unless of course the Lebanese people choose to establish an Islamic state before that time.[17] In effect, the party's theory on the Islamic state is based on the premise that the great bulk of Lebanese society would consent to the establishment of an Islamic republic in Lebanon.

Pending the establishment of the pan-Islamic Mahdist state, the ideal of an Islamic state in Lebanon will remain a permanent fixture of Hizbu'llah's intellectual structure and political thought but will not feature in its political programme.[18] Yet this should not be construed solely as a compromise dictated by Lebanese reality, but should also be comprehended as a keen observance of a central article of the Islamic faith – and therefore a component of the party's intellectual structure – which posits that Islam cannot be enforced upon followers of other faiths. Hizbu'llah's reference to the Qur'anic injunction, 'Let there be no compulsion in religion' (2:256), both in its Open Letter of 1985[19] and 14 years later as articulated by Shaykh Na'im Qasim,[20] is indicative of the tenacity with which this conviction is held. Moreover, the party's constant reassurance that it has no intention of forcibly 'imposing' an Islamic state on the Lebanese people, from as far back as 1985 to the present, is further testimony to this point.[21]

Thus, while the Prophet Muhammad's formation of an Islamic government and appointment of a successor provides contemporary Islamists with the rationale for the enduring necessity of an Islamic state,[22] it is not incumbent upon Muslim believers to coerce others into accepting an Islamic state. And the Islamic state that is established by armed force does not even deserve to be called an Islamic state[23] as its means of attaining power would be inherently unjust.

For Nasru'llah, forceful imposition is highly incongruous with the Islamic state, because the Islamic state is not an end in itself, but a means of fulfilling justice. The precondition of its existence is justice, defined as the general population's endorsement of the Islamic republic.[24] By 'general' Nasru'llah does not mean a mere 50 per cent parliamentary majority, nor the election of an Islamist prime minister, but the 'overwhelming' adoption of the Islamic state by the people.[25] Accordingly, a mass majority, as opposed to a simple majority, is the extent of popular support that Hizbu'llah envisions for the implementation of an Islamic scheme. The party's call for a referendum (with a two-thirds or more majority, implicit in such a system of voting) on the issue reflects its insistence upon a sweeping popular embrace of the Islamic state.[26]

Martin Kramer's contention that 'the will of the majority was of no consequence' for Hizbu'llah is an unfounded one. Even if we are to believe his supposition that the Open Letter's clauses on freedom of choice were the work of Fadlu'llah and not Hizbu'llah,[27] we could not dismiss of all of the above-cited views promulgated by the party as mere lip service to this principle.

As noted earlier, the confinement of the Islamic state ideal to the realm of political thought has a firm doctrinal basis which the party staunchly adheres to. Moreover, the fact that Hizbu'llah is under no religious obligation to impose an Islamic state further undermines the credibility of Kramer's allegation. According to former Hizbu'llah secretary-general Shaykh Subhi al-Tufayli, it is not Hizbu'llah whom God will call to account for the non-fulfilment of an Islamic state, but those who obstructed its creation.[28] The only religious obligation upon the party is that it actively pursues justice, regardless of whether or not this culminates in the creation of an Islamic state.

It would be tempting at this point to conclude that, since Hizbu'llah does not believe in the imposition of Islam 'from above' as maintained by *étatist* or statist Islamists, it strives to Islamicise society 'from below' as do civil or societal Islamist groups.[29] Muhammad Fnaysh's assertion that the Islamic republic is contingent upon the emergence of an Islamic society[30] would tend to support such an inference. However, neither this asseveration, nor the party's insistence that the precondition to the Islamic state is its endorsement by an overwhelming portion of the population, as in the case of Iran, denote that Hizbu'llah is actively engaged in the propagation of Islam so as to ensure the creation of an Islamic society amenable to the notion of an Islamic state. Notwithstanding Fnaysh's conviction that the Islamist society[31] should precede the Islamic state – or that personal piety and the moral community are the prerequisites of the Islamic state[32] – the party does not place precedence on the theological over the political as do societal/civil groups.

Moreover, Hizbu'llah would not disagree with the statist Islamists' thesis that the Islamic state is the condition of personal piety and the moral community.[33] Like Khumayni, Hizbu'llah believes that the 'moral refinement' of the people is one of the goals of the Islamic state.[34] Clearly, this is one intellectually inconsistent area that has not been fully resolved by the party. Although it may be difficult to rationalise why Islamicisation is not a priority for Hizbu'llah, and to comprehend its ambivalence on the issue of the moral community and the Islamic state, there may be two possible explanations for these inconsistencies.

First is the perceived futility of attempting to proselytise a religiously heterogeneous society. Not only would non-Muslims be impervious to an Islamic *da'wa* (call), but so would many secularist Shi'ites. But that is not to say that the party has no moral discourse. On the contrary, it has an extensive Islamicisation programme. Nonetheless, the ultimate end of its Islamicisation efforts is not the highly improbable creation of an Islamist society, which would construct the ideal Islamic state, but rather, the fulfilment of the Islamic imperative to spread the word of Islam, without any ulterior political motives. Since the political is the master of all concerns for Hizbu'llah, Islamicisation is not accorded the same weight as the political and military resistance to oppression.

Even if Islamicisation were conducive to the creation of an Islamic state, Hizbu'llah would still have focused its attention on resisting Israeli oppression, which is viewed as a far greater injustice than the secularism of society. In other words, liberation from Israeli occupation is considered a far greater attainment of justice, and hence a greater imperative, than the Islamicisation of society. This does not contradict Hizbu'llah's conviction that Islam is the most suitable means of realising justice. If anything, it proves the contrary since it was Hizbu'llah, a quintessentially Islamic party, which achieved this just goal.

Second, the party's predication of two seemingly contradictory theories of Islamic state and society may not be so paradoxical after all. The Islamic state is a means of fulfilling justice and the precondition of its existence is justice, which is defined as the adoption of the Islamic republic by a predominantly Islamist society. It follows that the moral and pious (Islamist) society is both the precondition and product of the Islamic state. Hizbu'llah therefore believes that the moral community is the condition of the Islamic state, which in turn reinforces the piety of the moral community. Although Hizbu'llah concurs with both the civil and statist Islamists' perspectives on Islamic state and society, it retains the belief that the Islamic state must originate from below.

Sovereignty

The theory of the Islamic state, as articulated by both Sunni and Shi'ite Islamists, rests on an essentially pessimistic view of human nature. As an intrinsically evil creature who is 'even worse than other animals',[35] man's 'egotism, sloth, greed, obtuseness, domination and oppression'[36] render him incapable of legislating for himself. Only God possesses the right to legislate for man. Consequently, any legislation that is not divine in source remains inherently 'deficient'[37] and will most likely result in 'unbelieving tyranny'.[38] This bleak prognosis is not confined to dictatorships, which in any case are intuitively rejected by human sentiment (*al wijdan al-insani*), but extends to democracies which human sentiment generally accepts.[39] Hizbu'llah's vindication of the Islamic state is based on the diminution of the compatibility between human sentiment and the concept of popular sovereignty. Specifically, three features of democracy make it inferior to Islamic government.

First is the oppression implicit in the much-vaunted principle of majority rule. The supremacy of the majority's opinion necessarily entails the 'suppression' of the minority's view, the same argument raised by the British philosopher, John Stuart Mill. The tyranny of the majority is even more pronounced when the minority in question repudiates not just the majority's opinion, but the social contract as such. The failure of the democrats to adequately resolve this predicament is considered a significant flaw in democracy.[40]

Second is the tendency of democratic systems to be dominated by the will of the minority, which ostensibly appears as the will of the majority. The existence of certain social, economic, political and religious elites in society often culminates in the manipulation of the system. The vast capabilities at the disposal of this minority enables it to hold sway over the majority, either by buying votes or distorting public opinion, thereby negating the very purpose of democracy.[41]

Third is the defectiveness and injustice of a system that only claims to represent the current generation of voting age and completely disregards the rights and interests of those who are currently under age and of future generations. In the first place, the present population cannot designate itself as the representative of future generations without their consent. In the second place, it cannot be assumed that future generations can later change the law to their advantage simply by constituting a majority, when the damage inflicted by many of these laws is irrevocable. For example, a population may deplete its oil reserves without giving much thought to future generations who cannot undo the laws that led to the depletion of this vital resource.[42]

The basic weakness of democracy lies in its investiture of sovereignty in the 'people' (the current generation of voting age), whose 'ignorant' and 'capricious' nature hinders their ability to know where their true interests lie, let alone the interests of future generations. By entrusting a group of sagacious experts with the task of deliberating the true interests of present and future generations, Islam ensures that all decisions express the 'invariable will' of the *umma* (the present and future generations) rather than the transient whims and desires of the parliamentary majority.[43]

But this seemingly elitist solution does not deny the 'people' a role in the decision-making process. Although the concept of *shura* (consultation) is not identical to democracy,[44] it provides Islamic Shi'ite scholars such as Muhammad Baqir as-Sadr and Ruhu'llah Khumayni with the necessary justification for popular representation.

Based on the interpretation of the Qu'ranic concept of 'caliphate' as the vicegerency of the entire Muslim community, Sadr maintains that the *umma* was accorded the right to partake in the management of the social and political affairs of the Islamic state.[45] Thus, although the Shari'a-based constitution did not necessitate popular involvement, Sadr was able to spell out two areas of Islamic law where some degree of popular participation could take place: the 'indeterminate sphere' and the 'discretionary sphere'.[46]

In the first instance, people could indirectly effect the outcome of certain unresolved religious issues by means of their elected consultative council representatives who would vote for specific juristic options. In the second instance, the existence of several gaps in Islamic law, related primarily to socio-economic issues, which needed to be filled by human legislation, also afforded people the opportunity to impinge upon the legislative process.[47]

However, this popular role is significantly undercut by its subjection to 'constitutional supervision'[48] or in Khumayni's words, the Council of Guardians, whose task it is to ensure that all legislation conforms to Islamic principles,[49] in addition to their aforementioned discernment of the invariable will. Thus, even though it is the people who choose their representatives, the supervisory role of the Council of Guardians vests sovereignty in the *umma* rather than the people.[50] Legislation may well be the result of consultation with the majority, but it does not reflect their wishes. Rather, it reflects the truth (*al-haqq*)[51] which God exemplifies.

In effect, both the Shari'a-based constitution and the Islamic precepts to which all legislation must conform, ultimately place sov-

ereignty in God, who in turn, has left a margin of space in which
the *umma* can exercise its derived sovereignty. Other than the parliamentary arena, this space also includes the presidency, the
Council of Experts who select the *Wali al-Faqih* (leader jurisprudent)
or Leadership Council[52] and other political councils.[53] But again,
the responsibility of the Council of Guardians, half of whose
members are appointed by the *Faqih*,[54] to supervise the elections of
these institutions, by screening all prospective candidates, circum-
scribes the latitude of the *umma*'s sovereignty in that it severely
limits its choice of representatives. It also detracts from the
democratic character of the system, which is implied by the very
existence of institutions such as parliament, president and cabinet,
and the checks and balances regulating relations between them.[55]

Political Pluralism

According to Fadlu'llah, Islam does accord people the right to
choose, 'but this does not mean unlimited choice'.[56] The political
options available to people must fall within the ideological
parameters of Islam and the framework of the *Wilayat al-Faqih*
(Guardianship of the Jurisconsult/Governance of the Jurisprudent).[57]
But this is not the same as saying that the legitimisation of political
pluralism is restricted to Islamic parties and organisations. According
to Principle 26 of the Iranian constitution, parties as well as religious
societies, 'whether Islamic or pertaining to one of the recognised
religious minorities', are permitted so long as they do not 'violate ...
the criteria of Islam or the basis of the Islamic Republic'.[58]

   Non-Islamic political forces may participate in the Islamic state
on condition that they respect the domination of Islam over state
and society. But one caveat must be inserted here: the constitutional
permission granted to non-Islamic organisations in Article 26 only
extends to those representing religious minorities, as there is no
mention of any other type of party. Implicit in this intentional
oversight is the assumption that ideological parties cannot co-exist
with the Islamic state or with the concept of the *Wilayat al-Faqih*.
Parties representing religious minorities do not fall into this category
because the ultimate end of their political role is to represent and
protect the rights of their constituencies – a goal that is not incom-
patible with the supremacy of Islam over the legislative process or
with the *Faqih*'s rule.

On the other hand, parties representing counter-ideologies are *ipso facto* excluded from the legislative process. The condition that all legislation conforms to Islamic principles leaves ideological parties with no legislative role to play. Moreover, since the notion of an ideal socio-political order inheres in all ideological parties, they cannot possibly consent to the domination of Islam over state and society and the *Faqih*'s supreme authority. Consequently, the sole purpose of political pluralism in the Islamic state is to ensure a fair degree of religious pluralism and little else.

It is against this background that Kramer's citations of Fadlu'llah's views on political pluralism seem to be of spurious origin. As paraphrased by Kramer, Fadlu'llah allegedly believes that 'non-Islamic parties and organisations can have no role in Islamic society or the Islamic state' because such a role would enable them to 'overthrow the Islamic order'.[59] It is very doubtful that a religious scholar as intellectually consistent as Fadlu'llah would hold such a conviction and concurrently propose (as cited by Kramer) that all state offices, with the exception of the highest decision-making authority, would be open to non-Muslims.[60] Moreover, if Fadlu'llah's purported justification for banning non-Islamic parties was that they posed a threat to the existence of the Islamic state, then surely he could have qualified this prohibition by countenancing those parties which agreed to respect the supremacy of Islam over state and society, such as those representing religious minorities.

Thus far, the party's views on political pluralism have been inferred from the model provided by the Islamic Republic of Iran. To the extent that Hizbu'llah can be taken as a microcosm of the ideal state it envisages, a study of its internal structure and dynamics provides another valuable insight into the party's conceptualisation of political pluralism. While the party admits to some internal 'disagreements', and even grants that that it would be 'unnatural' for all members to think alike,[61] it is adamant in its objection to the possibility of there being more than one ideological current within the party.[62]

As reasoned by 'Ali Fayyad, the Islamic party (or any party for that matter) can only withstand political disputes that do not digress from its intellectual 'givens', or it would defeat the whole purpose of its existence.[63] Since the terms 'moderate' and 'radical' denote ideological tendencies, Muhammad Ra'id refuses to classify party members in this way. Far more appropriate, he believes, is the classification of members along a non-ideological continuum ranging from 'flexibility and realism' to 'less flexibility and realism'.[64]

According to some party observers, however, even this limited degree of political pluralism is non-existent. According to one anonymous source, the party is an 'iron entity' which proscribes even mere differences of opinion. For this observer, the party's usage of terms like 'unanimous' to describe the general atmosphere of its fifth party congress is demonstrative of the pervasiveness of the themes of 'obedience and loyalty'.[65] Though it may be difficult to test the veracity of this claim, and hence the exact extent of internal political pluralism, there can be no denying that obedience is a much-valued asset for party leaders. Both Hizbu'llah's secretary-general and its deputy secretary-general refer to the resolution of disputes within the *Majlis al-Shura* by the *Wali al-Faqih* whose decisions are 'binding' on all party members.[66]

But most debates do not require external arbitration. Only those that centre on strategic issues necessitate the *Faqih's* intervention. One such example was when Hizbu'llah's leadership was divided over the issue of participating in the parliamentary election of 1992. The *Faqih's* subsequent ruling in favour of those who advocated partici-pation had the effect of compelling those who opposed this course of action to acquiesce to the *Faqih's* verdict. But this compulsion is self-imposed in that all *Shura* members request the intervention of the *Faqih* in the first place. In fact, the belief in the *Faqih's* supreme authority is a prerequisite for membership in the party.

Since the *Wilayat al-Faqih* concept is also the foundation of the Islamic state, it follows that those who do not respect this principle would be politically marginalised. Moreover, just as the Islamic party cannot withstand ideological differences, the Islamic state cannot encompass more than one ideological orientation or it too would defeat the whole purpose of its existence. Accordingly, parties and individuals would have to be distinguished from one another purely on the basis of political flexibility and realism. The only exception to this rule would be parties representing small religious minorities whose participation in the legislative process would be conditional upon their acquiescence to the Islamic foundations of the state.

By analogy, Muhammad Fnaysh suggests that, just as the American constitution would not sanction the presence of groups that sought to overthrow the capitalist system, as demonstrated by the McCarthy era, the Islamic state cannot countenance the existence of ideological groups seeking to overturn it.[67] Accordingly, the Islamic state is perceived to be no less politically pluralistic than the US democratic system, which also restricts political participation to groups that respect its foundations.

Religious Pluralism

It has already been established that political pluralism applies exclusively to those organisations and parties representing religious minorities, which respect the domination of Islam over state and society. According to Fnaysh, Hizbu'llah believes that 'there must be a Christian role [in the Islamic state] so long as there are Christians in society'. The example of Iran is invoked to delineate the extent of religious pluralism envisaged by the party.[68] As stipulated by Article 64 of the Iranian constitution, Zoroastrians, Jews and a number of Christian minority groups are all entitled to parliamentary representation commensurate with their numbers in the population.[69]

This thinking represents a significant departure from the classical interpretation of the *dhimma* – the contract between the Muslim community and non-Muslim minorities, which accords the latter religious recognition and protection in return for their submission to the Islamic state – which originated in the seventh century when there were no representative political structures such as parliament.

Another substantial difference between the Iranian model and the *dhimma* is the absence of the *jizya* (poll tax), which was imposed on religious minorities in return for their non-conscription in the army. While religious minorities are not conscripted into the Iranian army, there are no constitutional clauses which bar them from volunteering their services. Article 144 of the constitution specifies that the army as a whole must be 'committed to Islamic ideology', but it does not require that army recruits have faith in Islam, but merely in 'the objectives of the Islamic revolution'.[70]

Regardless of the actual treatment of minorities in Iran, they are afforded, in theory at least, greater scope of authority than Sunni Islamists are willing to grant. According to Emmanuel Sivan's analysis of the sermons of several radical Sunni clerics, all preachers upheld the view that Christians could not 'become full-fledged members of the polity'. The *dhimmi* status bestowed upon them would prohibit them from military service and positions of authority such as judges, ministers and top civil servants.[71]

Although the state judicial system in Iran is only open to Shi'ite *mujtahids*, and the Iranian president must belong to the Shi'ite denomination,[72] there are no constitutional provisions which stipulate that ministers must adhere to Shi'ite Islam, even though there has not been a single non-Shi'ite minister to date. As stated earlier, Fadlu'llah shares a similar view in so far as he is willing to grant minority groups access to all state offices except the presidency.[73]

Although Hizbu'llah's political thought is greatly influenced by Fadlu'llah's theoretical formulations, its stand on the issue of the inclusion of minority groups in the executive branch of the Islamic state does not mirror his. If we are to infer the party's views on the issue from its internal composition, the absence of any Christians in any of its apparatuses could be taken as an indication of its refusal to permit minorities to partake in Islamic government. The justification given by several Hizbu'llah officials for the exclusion of Christians from its political structures lends further credence to such an inference.

Like any ideological party, Hizbu'llah can only recruit those who espouse its ideology.[74] But while secular ideological parties can claim adherents from all religious denominations, the inseparability of Islam and politics means that membership in Hizbu'llah is confined to Muslims.[75] What is more, the fact that 'ideology is not hereditary' means that affiliation to the party is restricted to Islamist Muslims who adhere to the party's political thought and Islamic ideology.[76] The central place this ideology gives to the belief in the *Faqih's* supreme authority confines party membership even further to Shi'ite Islamists.[77]

It can therefore be surmised that Hizbu'llah does not foresee any role for non-Shi'ites in the executive apparatus of the Islamic state. This conclusion is substantiated by Husayn al-Mussawi's assertion that non-Muslims 'would not be part of the [Islamic] government', and would only enjoy the rights they were entitled to earlier in Islamic history.[78] While not as unequivocal as Mussawi, Fnaysh's vindication of the historical exclusion of non-Muslims from the military on the grounds that they could not have been expected to defend an essentially 'ideological' state[79] seems to point in a similar direction.

Perhaps the rationale behind this reasoning is that the participation of minority groups in parliament does not pose a threat to the security of the Islamic state, whereas their inclusion in the military, and in government could culminate in the state being overthrown.

It could also be that, while the precondition to parliamentary participation is a respect for the *Faqih*'s authority, inclusion in government necessitates belief in his supremacy.

Equally likely though, is the explanation posited by Ra'id: Based on the Islamic principle of non-compulsion, it is supposed that any Islamic state must have been consented to by the overwhelming majority of Lebanese people (which would presumably be the case if the Muslims came to constitute an overwhelming majority, or if society became Islamicised). Consequently, the absence of any significant religious minorities in the Islamic state would deem their inclusion in government unnecessary. Theoretically, the Iranian constitution's non-designation of the religious denomination of cabinet ministers could grant religious minorities governmental representation, but Ra'id is more inclined to believe that the framers of the constitution found it redundant to specify this. The negligible size of minority groups would only entitle them to parliamentary representation.[80]

The Endorsement of Democracy

The Endorsement of Democracy in Relation to the Islamic State Ideal

Despite Hizbu'llah's commitment to the Islamic Republic ideal, its acknowledgement of the unfeasibility of implementing such a scheme in Lebanon culminated in its 'Lebanonisation' or '*infitah*' (openness)[81] towards Lebanese state and society, which was epitomised by its decision to participate in the parliamentary election of 1992. After winning twelve seats in the 128-member parliament (eight party members and four non-Shi'ite supporters), which rendered it the largest parliamentary bloc, it went on to win ten seats (seven party members and three supporters) out of 128 in the 1996 election. Two years later, the party participated in the first municipal elections to be held in Lebanon in 35 years, winning almost half of all municipal council seats in the South, the overwhelming majority of seats in the Biqa', and all of the seats for the Shi'ite districts of the southern suburbs of Beirut.

Some political observers, such as Nizar Hamzeh and As'ad AbuKhalil, have attributed Hizbu'llah's parliamentary participation, and its policy of *infitah* generally, to the shifting balance of power within the Iranian leadership. The 1989 victory of the moderate faction led by former Iranian president Hashemi Rafsanjani over the hard-line clerical group led by Hujjat u'l-Islam 'Ali Akbar Muhtashemi, Iran's former interior minister, is reputed to have been mirrored within Hizbu'llah's ranks.[82] According to Hamzeh's rationale, the politically accommodationist stand maintained by al-Sayyids Husayn al-Mussawi and 'Abbas al-Mussawi, in addition to Shaykh Subhi al-Tufayli, who represented the Rafsanjani faction, triumphed over the politically exclusionist and radical position advocated by al-Sayyids Hassan Nasru'llah and Ibrahim al-Amin al-Sayyid, who represented the Muhtashemi group.[83]

Two essential flaws characterise this reasoning. First is the erroneous assumption that Nasru'llah opposed the notion of political accommodation, and second is the gravely mistaken categorisation of Tufayli as an exponent of parliamentary participation. That Nasru'llah espoused such a view on participation seems highly unlikely when one bears in mind that it was during his tenure as secretary-general that the party rolled its electoral campaign machine into motion, months before the elections. Paradoxically enough, Hamzeh later affirms that Nasru'llah was in fact an advocate of parliamentary participation, in contradistinction to Tufayli, whom he quite rightly accuses of calling for the burning of voting centres in his home village of Brital, in protest at the party's decision to contest the election.[84] What is more, so ideologically averse to the notion of participation was Tufayli, that the party's determination to pursue parliamentary representation prompted him to resign from the Hizbu'llah hierarchy.[85]

This does not mean that the internal dynamics of the Iranian leadership had no impact on Hizbu'llah's decision to join the political system, only that such an account provides a superficial explanation for Hizbu'llah's internal dispute over political participation. Both Fnaysh and Nasru'llah admit that there was an 'extensive' and 'fiery' debate within the party,[86] which could have quite conceivably corresponded to the views of the two factions within the Iranian leadership. But both Tufayli's resignation from the party and Fnaysh's assertion that the debate was initially 'an intellectual and theoretical' one which questioned the very principle of participation[87] cry out for a detailed analysis of the ideological grounds of this debate, and an examination of the political and intellectual considerations which induced the party leadership to opt for participation.

The party's deliberation of the moral bases for political accommodation in oppressive political systems, discussed in the previous chapter, provides a partial exposition of the ideological grounds of Hizbu'llah's debate on participation in the Lebanese state. However, the party's decision to integrate into the democratic political system must also be viewed within the framework of its theory on the Islamic state. By viewing Hizbu'llah's parliamentary participation from this ideological perspective, the political factors and religious and moral issues, which prevailed upon the party to become a legitimate player in this political system, can also be discerned.

Religious and Moral Considerations

While it may be tempting to ascribe Hizbu'llah's democratic participation to the few strands of democratic thought that inhere in its theory of the Islamic state ideal, such an endeavour would be ill-founded. Several features of the Islamic state, such as the prohibition on non-Islamic ideological parties from joining the political system, the exclusion of religious minorities from the executive apparatus of the state, the centralisation of power in the *Wilayat al-Faqih* and the Council of Guardians, and the derived nature of the *umma*'s sovereignty which is vested ultimately in God, render the Islamic state devoid of any real democratic substance.

It could be argued that the Islamic Republic of Iran's extensive borrowing of Western democratic concepts and procedures, including elections, public referendums, political parties, parliament, cabinet and presidency, gives it a semblance of democracy.[88] Yet although the Iranian model espoused by Hizbu'llah may resemble a democracy in its general structure, the sharply delimited ideological parameters that govern this structure attest to its quintessentially Islamic foundations. Only if it is propounded that the concept of democracy need not be measured by Western standards, as do John O. Voll and John Esposito, could the synthesis between democratic structure and Islamic foundations be designated a democracy, or an 'Islamic democracy' to be more precise.[89] The roots of Hizbu'llah's democratic participation cannot be claimed to lie in its Islamic state ideal, unless one is prepared to classify the Islamic Republic of Iran as a fully-fledged democracy that affords people a wide ideological spectrum of choices.

Even if one is prepared to do this, and to thereby underscore the correlation between the democratic character of Hizbu'llah's Islamic state ideal and the party's assent to abide by the democratic rules of the game, this linkage alone does not provide a sufficient explanation for the party's parliamentary participation. The few strands of democratic thought that characterise the party's state theory, as exemplified by the aforementioned democratic features of the Iranian state, may have facilitated the party's transition into a democratic political player, but they did not necessitate it. Thus, in order to discern the reasons which impelled Hizbu'llah to endorse participatory politics, other aspects of Hizbu'llah's state theory, such as the conditions it posits for the establishment of the Islamic state, must also be examined.

First among these conditions is the Islamic principle of non-compulsion, discussed previously, which dictates that Islam cannot be imposed on the followers of other faiths. By extension, an Islamic state cannot be forcibly imposed on a religiously diverse society such as Lebanon's. As expounded by Fnaysh:

> Since [Lebanese] society is not an Islamic one and Hizbu'llah is part of this society, it has to demand of itself what it demands of others. No one can impose a state on others and expect to succeed. If an Islamic state were established by force, then it would no longer be Islamic and would lose all legitimacy.[90]

Since the Islamic state is not an end in itself but a means of fulfilling justice, the precondition of its establishment is justice, which Hizbu'llah defines as the general population's endorsement of an Islamic republic. Lebanon's sectarian diversity would therefore preclude the implementation of Hizbu'llah's Islamic state ideal, in light of the religious and moral constraints that govern the party's political thought. These constraints necessitate that the Islamic political project closely interacts with socio-cultural reality. In other words, both the Islamic principle of non-compulsion and the party's conceptualisation of justice require Hizbu'llah to formulate its political strategy within the framework of a multi-sectarian Lebanon.[91]

Not only will an Islamic political scheme that is formulated in a contextual vacuum generate an inherently unjust pseudo-Islamic state, but it will most likely be a precarious one that will necessarily result in the much-abhorred outcome of anarchy. The certainty of this outcome is borne out for Hizbu'llah by the experience of civil war, which proved that no sectarian group could succeed in instituting its particular religious political vision through revolutionary or violent means.[92] Therefore, the party will not force the Lebanese people to choose between 'an Islamic state or *fawda* (anarchy)'.[93]

Neither does Hizbu'llah believe that it is compelled to 'either get everything or nothing'.[94] The alternative to an Islamic state need not be 'political withdrawal' which would effectively 'leave the nation's destiny to others', but could be replaced by political participation.[95] Thus, although Hizbu'llah conceives of the Islamic state as the most suitable means of fulfilling justice, its non-materialisation should not be replaced with a complete absence of justice, which would presumably result from a Hizbu'llah boycott of the democratic political system.

By participating in such a system and promoting communal co-existence, civil peace and general freedoms, the party could secure 'the greatest possible extent of justice', which is clearly preferable to a limited extent of justice or no justice whatsoever.[96] In effect, the party strives for 'possible justice', which is 'open to others', rather than 'absolute justice', which is equated with 'the coercive despotism' that comes from 'the imposition of one's personal conception of justice on everyone else'.[97]

The 'absolute justice'[98] represented by the Islamic state would remain a central pillar of Hizbu'llah's intellectual structure, but the indefinite postponement of its implementation would exclude it from the party's political discourse.[99] Conversely, the 'greatest possible extent of justice', which could be secured through a democracy, would feature prominently in the party's political discourse, but would not be elevated to the status of intellectual structure.[100] Thus, Hizbu'llah would integrate itself into the political system, but its intellectual commitment to the concept of the Islamic state would prevent it from imbibing the democratic basis of that system and from being politically assimilated by it.

Political Considerations

As seminal as these religious considerations are for Hizbu'llah's relatively recent endorsement of democracy, one cannot overlook the central role played by the logic of survival in contributing to its overall 'Lebanonisation'. Revolutionary activity is not only shunned in principle, but is also eschewed out of purely rational considerations related to the unlikelihood of such activity succeeding.

Prior to the end of the Gulf war between Iran and Iraq in 1988, Hizbu'llah had made the establishment of an Islamic state in Lebanon contingent upon Iran's victory in the war. As envisaged by the party, an Iraqi defeat would have led to the inevitable overthrow of the secular Ba'athist regime and the institution of Islamic rule in its place. This would have paved the way for the creation of an all-encompassing Islamic state in the region, of which Lebanon would have been an intrinsic part.[101]

After the implementation of UN Resolution 598, which called for a permanent ceasefire, Hizbu'llah had to reformulate its political strategy. However, that is not say that the party would have contravened its religious principles and compelled the Lebanese people to accept Lebanon's incorporation into a pan-Islamic state. While inconclusive, the party's repeated assurances in its Open Letter of having no intention of imposing an Islamic state on the Lebanese people,[102] at a time when the Gulf war was still in progress and the prospect of an Iranian victory still conceivable, imply that the institution of Islamic rule in Lebanon was not a foregone conclusion. In all probability, Iran's triumph in the war would have facilitated the establishment of such a state, but it would not have constituted a sufficient condition for this eventuality. The end of the war without an apparent victor rendered the possibility of an Islamic republic in Lebanon even more unlikely, and the resort to revolutionary means to impose it ultimately counter-productive.

Within a local and regional context that was not conducive to the establishment of an Islamic state in Lebanon, Hizbu'llah was faced with a choice between indefinite political isolation and political inclusion in a democratic system. The realisation that the party would have to wait 'a hundred years' at the very least for the emergence of the religious, moral and political groundwork required for the creation of an Islamic republic in Lebanon, impelled it to adopt the democratic route to power.[103] It was precisely this awareness that the party 'could not sit on its hands without being active in an arena that allowed it to take part in changing the situation', that distinguished it from other Islamic movements which did not share the party's realism.[104]

Yet it could also be argued that, even if the movement did choose to sit on its hands and withdraw from the political arena until such time that the circumstances for establishing an Islamic republic were ripe, its recognition of Syria's stranglehold over Lebanon would have obstructed such a course of action. Although Syria had initially assisted in the creation of Hizbu'llah by granting Iran unfettered access to the Biqa', it was not willing to countenance the unchecked growth of an Islamist movement which, with Iranian backing, had the potential to install Islamic rule in Lebanon. Not only would such a scheme thwart Syria's ambitions in Lebanon, but it would also serve to embolden the Alawite regime's internal Sunni Islamist opposition.

The exact extent of the Assad regime's strong aversion to the prospect of an Islamic state in Lebanon became evident in 1987 when Syrian troops clashed with Hizbu'llah fighters in West Beirut over the movement's refusal to hand their bases to Syrian forces.[105] Twenty-three Hizbu'llah fighters were killed in the process, in what the party dubbed the 'brutal' Fathu'llah 'massacre'.[106] But even then, the inchoate movement possessed the necessary political acumen to 'lick its wounds' and prevent the occurrence of 'a great battle in Beirut'.[107]

Syria's intervention in 1988 in the 'War for Supremacy of the South' between its ally, Amal, and Hizbu'llah, was another indication of its intent to curb the growth of the movement. After its expulsion from the South, Hizbu'llah relaunched its offensive against Amal later that year, at which point Iran caved in to Syria's desire to see the war ended and Hizbu'llah's expansion reined in. The upshot of this was a modus vivendi between Iran and Syria known as the 'Damascus Agreement', whereby Hizbu'llah was permitted to continue its military operations against Israel from the South, while relinquishing its stronghold of the southern suburbs to Syrian forces. In this manner, Syria was able to exert some control over Hizbu'llah and to simultaneously benefit from the threat it posed to Israel and its role as a counterbalance to Amal.[108]

For its part, Hizbu'llah followed Iran's suit and acceded to Syria's domination over Lebanon, and by implication, resigned itself to the impracticability of the institution of Islamic rule under Syrian political custodianship. This reality was made all the more poignant by the consecration of Syria's role as the supreme authority over Lebanese affairs in the internationally recognised Ta'if Agreement of 1989, which effectively ended the Lebanese civil war, and the Treaty of Brotherhood, Co-operation and Co-ordination between Syria and Lebanon of 1991.

Not only did the Ta'if Agreement necessitate a reformulation of political strategy for Hizbu'llah, it threatened the very survival of the movement insofar as it called for the disarmament of all Lebanese militias, without making the Islamic Resistance an exception to the rule.[109] Hizbu'llah and Syria eventually came to the understanding that the movement would be allowed to retain its arms in the South in order to continue its resistance against Israel, which was also to Syria's advantage in that it provided it with a potential bargaining tool in future negotiations with Israel.

But the party still felt that its resistance needed to be legitimised on the popular, and to a lesser extent, international levels. Only by integrating into the political system could the party 'convince the majority of Lebanese people of the logic of the Resistance',[110] and receive international legitimisation as 'a popular current' as opposed to 'an artificial or alien current imposed by political, regional or international equations'.[111]

But resistance was not the only role that the movement sought to preserve through its parliamentary participation. If Hizbu'llah confined itself to resisting the Israeli occupation, it would outlive its utility once an Israeli withdrawal was in the offing. The party could only ensure its political survival in the aftermath of such an eventuality by carving out a political role for itself for the post-withdrawal future. The fact that it had nurtured an extensive support base among the Shi'ite community, by dint of its decade-long resistance activity and rapidly expanding social services network, greatly facilitated the party's quest for such a role.

Hizbu'llah's political integration was therefore necessitated by the 'urgent demands and needs of its social base' which called for popular representation,[112] in addition to the dictates of political survival. This point is accentuated by May Chartouni-Dubarry, who rightly argues that the party's infiltration of the political system was not only attributable to the aforementioned regional developments, but was also a product of its 'strong domestic roots'.[113]

It was precisely because of these roots that Hizbu'llah's embrace of democracy should not be considered an abrupt volte-face, but a 'natural development' over its decade of existence.[114] Its metamorphosis over those ten years from a narrow resistance group into a broad social movement necessitated that it play the role of 'the party of general political and social resurrection' as well as 'the party of the Resistance'.[115] Parliament was not only viewed as a podium through which the 'voice' of the Resistance could be heard,[116] but also as a platform from which the political and material demands of its supporters could be made.[117] To that effect, Hizbu'llah has made full use of its presence in parliament, from 1992 until the present, to champion the cause of the oppressed and to actively pursue the abolition of political sectarianism.

But even as the largest parliamentary bloc and the most vociferous government critic, Hizbu'llah has had to limit its opposition to the confines of the 'saqf al-Suri' (Syrian ceiling),[118] which the party 'does not accept', yet has had to observe in order to protect its Islamic Resistance.[119] Thus, for example, although the party could have gained a larger number of parliamentary seats had it run its own independent list in the southern constituency, Syria's 'unhidden desire' to see it forge an electoral alliance with Amal[120] compelled it to do so in both the 1992 and 1996 parliamentary elections.

Notwithstanding the party's rationale that it was compelled to join forces with Amal in order to protect its resistance priority, the party's rank and file has found such compromises hard to digest, to the extent that Nasru'llah had to personally call on the party's supporters to 'put their emotions aside'[121] after the party leadership succumbed to Syria's request for it to join Amal's electoral list in 1996. Yet despite the loss of its political integrity, Hizbu'llah has been able to emerge from all this with its ideological integrity relatively intact for two central reasons.

In the first place, although Hizbu'llah's supporters resent the leverage Syria is able to exert over the party, they are fully cognisant of the fate of those political forces that do not subscribe to the 'rules of the game' assigned by Syria. Hizbu'llah's deference to Syria's wishes is construed as a survival mechanism necessary for safeguarding the continuation of the Resistance and the party's representational role.

In the second place, as astutely observed by Dubarry, Hizbu'llah's participation was not the result of its co-option by the state (or in other words, Syria), but a product of the party's independent assessment of the costs and benefits associated with participation and withdrawal. Thus, in contrast to the Islamist movements in Egypt and Jordan which were co-opted 'from the top', and hence deemed unfaithful to their Islamic cause, Hizbu'llah's entirely voluntary participation is not perceived as a betrayal of its Islamic principles.[122] Even if it has had to make political concessions, these are viewed as self-imposed and calculated measures designed to preserve its other intellectual pillars, namely the Resistance and the cause of the oppressed.

The Commitment to Democracy

Precisely because Hizbu'llah's decision to participate in the democratic system was motivated in part by rational considerations related to the party's survival, it could be argued that Hizbu'llah is only using democracy to preserve its political status and is therefore not genuinely committed to it as an ideological principle. In fact, Hizbu'llah makes no pretence at embracing democracy as a central pillar of its intellectual structure. As stated earlier, Hizbu'llah confines the concept of democracy to the political realm, as opposed to the realm of 'intellectual thought', which is reserved exclusively for the Islamic state.[123]

However, it does not necessarily follow that the party does not genuinely endorse democracy as 'a system of government', but merely advocates its use as 'a procedure of transition to power',[124] which Abdel Salam Sidahmed and Anoushiravan Ehteshami believe to be the case for all participatory Islamists.[125] To believe in democracy as a system of government, one need not believe in it as the best system of government, just as the non-idealisation of any principle need not mean that it is rejected out of hand. By the same token, Hizbu'llah's embrace of democracy as a system through which the greatest possible extent of justice can be fulfilled means that, although it is not viewed as the ideal system capable of fulfilling absolute justice, as Islam is, it is accepted, and even championed, as the next best system to Islam. Thus, although Hizbu'llah does not endorse democracy as the best system of government on the intellectual level, it endorses it as a system of government on the political level.

This endorsement is not only evident from the party's discourse on justice, but can also be discerned from the party's views on public freedoms, which for the most part were responses to the Hariri government's attempt to curb them. As perceived by the party, the government's ban on demonstrations[126] and the broadcasting of news by non-state-owned television media constituted a violation of the public's right to free expression. In a similar vein, the government's unlawful attempts at obstructing the re-election of the Greater Labour Confederation's former leader, in its bid to replace him with a pro-government candidate, was construed by the party as an encroachment upon the public right to freedom of choice,[127] which it views as a fundamental 'constitutional and human right'.[128]

In short, the former government was castigated by the party for only subscribing to democracy in 'appearance',[129] and therefore for not being committed to it in principle. Thus, although Hizbu'llah does not espouse democracy as an intellectual construct, it does expect the government to. Moreover, to the extent that it invokes the Israeli state as a democratic exemplar, inasmuch as it 'respects the will of its people' and illustrates the indispensability of democracy to 'the resolution of [internal] disputes',[130] the party exhorts the government to emulate such democratic qualities. Thus, the genuineness of the party's political endorsement of democracy is further underscored.

In addition to such indicators of the party's democratic credentials, Hizbu'llah's goal of 'deconfessionalising'[131] Lebanese politics is also demonstrative of its sincere commitment to the implementation of democracy. While it could be contended that Hizbu'llah's intent to abolish political sectarianism is an intrinsic part of its plan to establish an Islamic state in Lebanon, insofar as the party's extensive popularity amongst Lebanon's Shi'ites would give it an advantage over all other political forces in a majority system,[132] it is not difficult to repudiate such an argument, in view of two factors.

In the first place, the party's aspiration to deconfessionalise the political system is an essentially secular and democratic demand for equality of opportunity. No bona fide democrat could dispute Hizbu'llah's call for the replacement of 'a sectarian democracy' with 'a citizen's democracy where representation would be based on citizenship and not on sectarian considerations'.[133] Even if such a demand was ultimately conducive to the establishment of an Islamic state, this would not detract from the democratic substance of this demand.

In the second place, Hizbu'llah does not match its demand for the abolition of political sectarianism with a call for the replacement of the current system with a majority one. While the party advocates the constituency system, it does not require that this system be established on a majority, first past the post, basis, which would necessarily exclude the sizeable Christian minority. Rather, the party favours a proportional representation basis, which would guarantee the inclusion of all Lebanese sects, and prevent any one from monopolising the executive branch of the state.[134]

The corollary of this is that Hizbu'llah does not pursue the concept of a non-sectarian citizens' democracy as a means of monopolising political power and instituting Islamic rule, but values it as an end in itself. Accordingly, Hizbu'llah would not overturn democracy if it attained a parliamentary majority under a non-sectarian proportional representation system. As maintained by several party officials, if Hizbu'llah were ever able to form a government on its own, it would 'accept' the dissolution of this government if the popular will later chose to replace it with another one.[135] The party would assent to this reversal of power, but would 'strive to regain people's trust, so that it could reinstate its government democratically and not through revolution'.[136]

To some extent, such discourse is a product of the 'pragmatising' effect of political pluralism, which compels participants in the democratic system who constitute less than a 51 per cent parliamentary majority to negotiate and bargain with other participants and thereby adopt a more moderate and inclusive political tone.[137] But it is also a product of the party's conviction that a simple 51 per cent majority would not provide a sufficient popular basis for the establishment of an Islamic state,[138] even in a religiously homogeneous Muslim state.[139] Thus, even if Hizbu'llah did secure a parliamentary majority of 51 per cent of the popular vote, it would still have to operate within the confines of the democratic political system in order to accommodate the 49 per cent or so of Lebanese society who do not favour the establishment of an Islamic state.[140]

Yet as strong an indicator of Hizbu'llah's political endorsement of democracy as this is, and as reassuring as it may be to secular democrats, one is reminded here of the precondition Hizbu'llah posits for the establishment of the Islamic state.

In the final analysis, the party would institute Islamic rule if the overwhelming majority of Lebanese people demanded the establishment of an Islamic state. By implication, Hizbu'llah would overturn the democratic system that brought it to power if it obtained such a large parliamentary majority and would consequently not afford people the opportunity to oust it, or any other Islamic party that might succeed it. This would necessarily be the case because the Islamic state does not contain a mechanism for its own overthrow, as does the exemplary democratic state.[141] As stated earlier, there would not be any non-Islamic parties that espouse counter-ideologies in the Islamic state, and therefore the electorate would not be able to vote for a party that advocates the reinstitution of the secular democratic system.

In effect, there is a seeming incongruity between Hizbu'llah's expressed intent to preserve democracy and the undeclared potential it has to subvert it. However, this becomes less of an incongruity when one recalls that the party's preference for an Islamic state over a democratic state does not make its commitment to democracy in the absence of an Islamic state a disingenuous one. The party's intellectual commitment to the Islamic state is profound, but this does not render its political commitment to democracy hollow.

This incongruity has been shrouded by the ultimate unfeasibility of Hizbu'llah ever amassing such a large extent of popular support for the implementation of an Islamic state in a religiously and politically diverse society. This has enabled it to pledge its sincere commitment to the cause of democracy in Lebanon, whilst preserving its Islamic state ideal.

3 The Concept of the Guardianship of the Jurisprudent

Insofar as adherence to the concept of the *Wilayat al-Faqih* constitutes a criterion for admission to Hizbu'llah and a prerequisite for participation in the executive branch of the ideal Islamic state, it is a fundamental element of Hizbu'llah's intellectual structure. Accordingly, the concept merits further explication, not only in relation to the political thought of Hizbu'llah, but also as a theological abstraction as formulated by Khumayni.

The Origins of the Concept of the *Wilayat al-Faqih*

Khumayni's theory of the *Wilayat al-Faqih* is predicated on his belief in the necessity of establishing an Islamic republic. From Khumayni's perspective, the notion of awaiting the *Mahdi*'s return for the institution of justice on earth was nonsensical. According to his logic, God could not possibly have limited the validity of his laws to 200 years, i.e. from the rule of the Prophet Muhammad until the Lesser Occultation,[1] when the very existence of these laws posits the existence of an Islamic government for their enforcement. Moreover, 'the necessity of government to spread justice, to teach and educate, to preserve order, to remove unrighteousness and to defend the frontiers' is also taken by Khumayni as an indication of the exigent need for an Islamic state which could not have been simply overlooked by God.[2]

Having established the compelling need for an Islamic state governed by the Shari'a, Khumayni goes on to argue that it can only be led by someone as well versed in the Shari'a as the expert in Islamic jurisprudence – the faqih.[3] On the basis of several religious sources, he claims that the religious erudition of the jurists authorises them to inherit the political, as well as the religious, authority of the Prophet and Imams during the Greater Occultation.[4]

One such source is the Qur'anic injunction to 'Obey God and the Messenger and those in authority among you' (4:62),[5] which Khumayni construes as a divine proclamation of the *fuqaha*'s (plural of *faqih*) right to rule. To further bolster this claim, he also quotes from a number of *hadiths* (sayings) of the Prophet and Imams, which refer to the jurists as 'the heirs of the prophets', 'the fortress of Islam' and 'the trustees of the emissaries [of God]'.[6] In a similar vein, Imam 'Ali's instruction to his followers 'to obey his successors', whom he defined as 'those who transmit my statements and my traditions and teach them to the people', is also cited by Khumayni as doctrinal proof of the Prophet's and Imams' devolution of authority to the jurists.[7]

Of particular significance is Khumayni's interpretation of the tradition attributed to the Twelfth Imam in which he responds to a question on who was responsible for the community's guidance in his absence: 'As for the events which may occur, refer to the transmitters of our sayings ...'.[8] The operative phrase here is 'events which may occur', which Khumayni expounds as meaning social and political issues, as opposed to unprecedented legal issues.[9] In effect, the jurists' political authority emanates directly from the Hidden Imam.

Notwithstanding the delegation of the Hidden Imam's political authority to the *fuqaha*, the role of 'de facto functional Imam'[10] can also be seen as a culmination of the historical development of the *Na'ib al-'Amm* (General-Delegate) concept, which was advanced by the prominent Shi'ite scholar, Shaykh Zaynu'd-Din ibn 'Ali al-Juba'i, known as *Shahid ath-Thani* (the Second Martyr), in the sixteenth century. As propounded by this Shi'ite scholar, the *'ulama* (religious class) were the rightful inheritors of the Hidden Imam's religious authority, and as such, they were entrusted with the Imam's religious prerogatives such as the collection and distribution of religious taxes and the declaration of defensive *jihad*. However, it was not until the late eighteenth century when the *Usuli* school of jurisprudence, which championed the practice of *ijtihad* (legal rationalism) in Shi'ite jurisprudence, triumphed over the conservative *Akhbari* school which opposed it, that the theoretical functions of the *Na'ib al-'Amm* were finally assumed by the jurists.[11] With the consolidation of *ijtihad* as a juristic principle, the *mujtahid* or *faqih* was thereby enabled to deliver *fatwas* (religious edicts) on almost any social or personal issue, which were to be adhered to by the *muqallid* (follower).

In fact, the expansion of the social role of the jurist was conceptualised centuries before the *Usuli* victory. As far back as the thirteenth century *Nasiru'd-Din Tusi* (d.1273), the Shi'ite scholar whom Khumayni greatly admired, postulated the Platonic-inspired concept of the 'Perfect Teacher' who would guide the community during the Hidden Imam's occultation.[12] Other advocates of an enlarged juristic role include al-Karaki, known as *Muhaqqiq ath-Thani* (d.1534),[13] Ahmad Naraqi (d.1829)[14] and Murtada Ansari (d.1864).[15] Still, Khumayni's assertion that these scholars conceived of an enlarged political role for the *Wali al-Faqih* is somewhat of an exaggeration in that they did not put forward the claim that the *faqih* should replace the temporal ruler as Khumayni does.

The widest scope of political authority these scholars were willing to grant the *fuqaha* was their occasional intervention in political affairs so as to redress injustices and protect the community's moral and religious standards.[16] Some scholars even legitimated the jurists' right to carry out religious penalties (*iqamat al-hudud*),[17] but within the confines of their role as legal agents who acted on behalf of the people, rather than as governors over the people.[18]

It is through this lens that the *fatwa* issued by one of the first universally recognised *maraji' at-taqlid* (models of emulation), Ayatu'llah Muhammad Hassan Shirazi, against the Qajar government's tobacco concession to the British in 1892, should be viewed. This oppositional political stand did not stem from Shirazi's belief that the political authority inherent in the deputyship of the *fuqaha* was his right to claim. The underlying purpose of Shirazi's political intervention was merely to rectify an injustice committed by the government – not to overturn the government.

In effect, only some of the politically relevant functions of the Imam were delegated to the *fuqaha*. Khumayni's major contribution to the field of jurisprudence was to extend that delegation to all of the Imam's political functions, including the executive function. Based on this extension of authority, Khumayni concluded that the *fuqaha* ought to concern themselves with the 'political, economic and legal problems of Islam' rather than to focus exclusively on 'ritual matters', as had been the case in the past.[19]

The active pursuit of the Islamic state therefore becomes a 'duty incumbent upon just *fuqaha*',[20] unless of course such action is deemed futile, in which case the jurists reserve the right to wield power – a right which intimates the de jure illegitimacy of temporal rulers.[21] Only the deputy of the Twelfth Imam, the *Wali al-Faqih*, has the legitimate right to rule.

Khumayni's Conceptualisation of the *Wilayat al-Faqih*

The Twelfth Imam provides the doctrinal backdrop against which Khumayni's theory of the *Wilayat al-Faqih* is set. As enshrined in

Principle 5 of the Iranian constitution: 'During the Occultation of the *Wali al-'Amr* (Lord of the Age), the *wilaya* [guidance] and leadership of the *umma* devolve upon the just and pious *faqih*.'[22] Implicit in this stipulation is that the duration of the Faqih's rule is to persist indefinitely until the *raj'a* (return) of the Twelfth Imam (also known as Lord of the Age).

Nonetheless, neither this nor the designation of the *Wali al-Faqih* as the 'Imam' equates the *Wilayat* with the Imamate.[23] While the *Faqih* shares in the political and legal authority of the Imam on account of his overall competence to rule, the fact that he is not endowed with *'isma* (infallibility) renders him unable to partake in the Imam's spiritual authority.[24] Khumayni thereby distinguishes between the existential or divine authority (*wilaya al-takwiniyya*) of the infallible Prophet and Imams, and the relative, functional and extrinsic authority (*wilaya i'tibariyya*) of the fallible *fuqaha*.[25]

Unlike the Prophet – and by extension, the Imams – who, 'is more entitled to the believers than their own selves' (33:6), the *Faqih* does not retain the right to control all aspects of the believers' lives. Even if Khumayni does have frequent recourse to this verse, as asseverated by one researcher,[26] this is clearly not what is understood by his followers who do not accord him the right to intervene in matters of personal interest.[27] As elaborated by Fayyad, the only exception to this rule is when such intervention is perceived as benefiting the general good, as is the case when the interests of the individual clash with the interests of the community.[28] Only the infallible are empowered with the spiritual authority to command the blind obedience of the believers.

But the term 'spiritual' should not be confused with the term 'religious' in this context, for although the *Faqih* does not share the Imam's spiritual authority, the Imam's religious prerogatives are devolved upon him in his capacity as the *Na'ib al-'Amm* (General Delegate). Moreover, the *Faqih*'s status as *marja' at-taqlid* (model of emulation) empowers him to issue religious injunctions, which in theory would be binding on the entire community if he emerged as the sole *marja'*, in light of the doctrinal obligation upon the Shi'ite believer to subscribe to the rulings of one prominent *mujtahid*. Nevertheless, the multiplicity of *maraji'* (plural of *marja'*) at any one time, which has been the case ever since the death of Ayatu'llah Burujirdi in 1961,[29] serves to delimit the religious authority of the *Faqih* to his *muqallids* (followers).

While the *Faqih*'s commands that pertain to well established religious precepts (*al-hukum al- kashif*) are not binding on the entire community, his discretionary directives based on his assessment of the general good (*al-hukum al-wilayati*) are.[30] In other words, although the multiplicity of *maraji'* precludes the paramountcy of his religious authority as a *marja' at-taqlid*, the binding force of his political authority over the entire *umma* as *Wali Amr al-Muslimin* (the Legal Guardian of the Muslims), remains unparalleled. So supreme is this political authority that all other *fuqaha* must bury their dissent to ensure the survival of his regime and to preserve the unity of the community.[31] Thus, while juristic pluralism characterises the religious sphere, juristic autocracy typifies the political sphere.

This juristic autocracy is also evident in the *Faqih*'s authority to appoint and dismiss the *fuqaha* who comprise the Council of Guardians, the *faqih* who constitutes the supreme judicial authority of the country,[32] and members of the highly influential Nation's Expediency Council.[33] Moreover, his domination over the political system as such also serves to augment his political authority over the *fuqaha*. As stipulated by Principle 110 of the Iranian constitution, his role empowers him to declare (defensive) war and peace, to screen presidential candidates, and to delineate the general policies of the Islamic Republic after consulting with the Expediency Council.[34]

For the advocates of the *Wilayat al-Faqih* however, the *Faqih*'s hegemony over the executive, judicial and legislative branches of government does not equate it with a dictatorship[35] in light of the following institutional safeguards. In the first place, all of the *Faqih*'s directives are based on the divine law and the general good, and accordingly cannot be considered arbitrary opinions (*istibdad bi'l-ra'i*).[36] Second, is the 'wide space' allocated to the *umma* in which to pursue its political role.[37] In addition to the limited popular sovereignty inherent in the system, the *Faqih*'s recourse to technocrats in the administrative and management functions of the state[38] also detracts from the authoritarian nature of such a system. Third, are the *Faqih*'s unique attributes of justice and piety, as required by the constitution, which preclude the possibility of despotism.[39]

In fact, all constitutional provisions outlining the essential qualifications of the *Faqih* pertain to the three posts he is entrusted with. The requirements of knowledge of the divine law, justice and piety, and social and political competence correspond to the post of *ifta'* (the formulation of formal legal opinions), the dispensing of justice and the supreme administration of the state, respectively.[40] These qualities are not only necessary for his post as head of state, but also as leader of the *umma*, insofar as his post of *ifta'* relates to religious and political issues that transcend national boundaries. The incorruptible *Wali al-Faqih* therefore emerges as a Platonic philosopher-king who epitomises the absolute Good, by virtue of his unmatched justice and knowledge.[41]

It is precisely this preoccupation with 'who' should rule and the special qualities of the ruler that distinguishes Shi'ite political thought from Sunni.[42] While the Sunnis are more inclined to view the state as an institutional manifestation of the Shari'a, the Shi'ites tend to perceive it as 'a prophetical phenomenon'.[43] Thus, although the concept of the *Wilayat al-Faqih* embodies some populist undertones – to the extent that the *Faqih* must be recognised as such by the majority of people[44] and insofar as they play an indirect role in his election by the Council of Experts – the principle of divine selection remains at its core.

The Role of the *Wilayat al-Faqih* in the Political Thought of Hizbu'llah

From the inception of Hizbu'llah to the present, the status and role of the concept of the *Wilayat al-Faqih* has remained an integral part of the party's intellectual foundations. Despite the fact that several Shi'ite personages – including Ayatu'llahs Khu'i and Muntazari, Shaykh Murtada Mutahhari, and Sayyid Fadlu'llah – have called the concept into question,[45] the envisagement of the *Faqih*, and Khumayni in particular, as a divinely ordained and inspired ruler of the *umma* has continued to pervade the political thought of Hizbu'llah. Like Khumayni, the party acknowledges the *Faqih* as the designated deputy of the Twelfth Imam during his Occultation. It also views the *Wilayat al-Faqih* as an extension of the *wilayat* of the Prophet and Imams, and as such, accords it a sacrosanct character: 'He who rejects the authority of the *Wali al-Faqih*, rejects God and Ahlu'l-Bayt [this refers to the descendents of Imam 'Ali and his wife Fatima, the Prophet Muhammad's daughter] and is almost a polytheist.'[46]

Although Nasru'llah made this declaration over twelve years ago, when revolutionary sentiments were still high, it still provides a fair reflection of the party's conception of the *Wilayat* today, notwithstanding the fervid language used. Rather than demonise those who repudiate the supreme authority of the *Faqih*, today's Hizbu'llah is more likely to refer to the 'fatality' of differences which overstep the conceptual boundaries of the *Wilayat*,[47] or to imply that dissent on this issue will result in expulsion from the party.[48] But despite the difference in terminology, the underlying theme remains one: the party cannot countenance a negation of the sacred concept of the *Wilayat al-Faqih*.

The continued primacy of the *Wilayat* is also evident in the perception of the *Faqih* as 'the continuity of Muhammad's message after his death'[49] and the depiction of Khumayni as 'the Hussein of the era',[50] 'the sacred man' and 'descendant of the Prophet'.[51] More significantly, his role as architect of the Islamic Revolution earns him the revered title of 'the *Mujaddid al-Din* (the Renewer of Religion) in this era'.[52] According to Shi'ite tradition, an eminent figure arises during each Islamic century to revitalise the religion – the *Mujaddid*.[53] Conferring this epithet on Khumayni therefore puts him on a par with the Fifth (or Sixth) and Eighth Imams, who were also designated as *Mujaddids* in the second and third Islamic centuries, respectively.[54]

Despite the veneration of Khumayni's revolutionary role and his incomparable stature as *Wali al-Faqih*, the sanctity of the concept of the *Wilayat* has not been undermined during the post-Khumayni era. Although Khumayni's successor, 'Ali Khamini'i, did not occupy the post of *marja' at-taqlid* when he was selected as *Faqih*,[55] his *Wilayat* is considered as sacrosanct as Khumayni's, since he too is accorded the title of '*Wali Amr al-Muslimin*' (the Legal Guardian of the Muslims).[56] Although he is not cast as the 'instigator' of the Islamic Revolution as Khumayni was,[57] he is depicted as 'the reminder' of its victory.[58] Moreover, after Khamini'i emerged as a *marja' at-taqlid* in 1997, Hizbu'llah officially pledged its loyalty to his religious authority or *marja'iyya*, even though its individual members are free to emulate another *marja'*, as some of its adherents do.[59]

However, there is no denying that Khumayni commanded a much wider following than Khamini'i both in the Shi'ite world and within the ranks of Hizbu'llah. Although the Shi'ite believer is only obliged to comply with the *Faqih's* political authority,[60] the majority of Hizbu'llah's adherents chose to subject themselves to Khumayni's religious authority in spite of the wide variety of other *maraji' at-taqlid* to emulate at the time.[61] What is more, his 'path' and teachings are considered 'jurisprudential givens' which together comprise a 'constitution' for Hizbu'llah,[62] although following a dead *marja'* is barred in Shi'ite jurisprudence.[63]

Bearing the religious significance of Khumayni's *Wilayat* in mind, and the sanctity of the *Wilayat* as a religious and political institution, it becomes easier to comprehend Hizbu'llah's repeated assertion that the party's commitment to the *Wilayat* does not represent a 'political' commitment to a national head of state. It is an 'intellectual' commitment to a sacred Islamic figure and his successors whose commands are considered 'fixed truths'.[64]

Hizbu'llah's unswerving loyalty to the *Wali al-Faqih* is symptomatic of its general pan-Islamic proclivity. To the extent that the term 'Islamic Republic' connotes a pan-Islamic frame of reference and the term 'Iran' refers to a geographically limited political entity, the almost invariable use of the former appellation in lieu of the latter attests to this pan-Islamic disposition. It also shows that the party's pan-Islamic allegiance is owed primarily to the *Faqih*, and only secondarily to Iran, the state.

Thus, although Iran represents the 'nucleus of the world central Islamic state',[65] its people are subject to the same authority as other Shi'ite believers – the 'Imam of all Muslims in the world'.[66] Thus, the *Wilayat* is the ultimate repository of pan-Islamic affiliations, while the Iranian state, which most closely resembles the Islamic state ideal, is the penultimate source of allegiance. Accordingly, when Hizbu'llah depicts the Islamic Republic as 'our religion, our *Ka'ba* [the Muslim Holy of Holies], our blood and our veins',[67] it relates to the *Wilayat al-Faqih*, and not to the Iranian government. By the same token, the reference to 'Islamic thought'[68] or 'Islamic decision-making' should be construed as a euphemism for the *Wali al-Faqih*, and not for Iran as Martin Kramer alleges.[69]

However, it would be erroneous to conclude, as some scholars have done, that the pan-Islamic implications of the doctrine of the *Wilayat al-Faqih* are tantamount to Hizbu'llah's rejection of the idea of nationalism.[70] Aside from Hizbu'llah's accommodation of the notion of nationalism, and the pan-Arabist element of Hizbu'llah's political identity (see the following chapter), it should be repeated that the *Wilayat* is not a political project for the party.

Since the political power wielded by the *Faqih* is exclusive to Iran – in view of the fact that the Republic represents the only Shi'ite Islamic state in the world – he is only able to exercise political authority over other Shi'ite believers who are subject to the rule of other political powers. Consequently, the *Faqih* is a national leader in the first instance, and a pan-Islamic leader of the *umma* in the second instance. In its turn, the *umma*, Hizbu'llah included, is politically (or practically) beholden to nationalism and only intellectually (or theoretically) bound to pan-Islamism.

Even the political authority exercised by the *Faqih* is relatively circumscribed. The party's claim that the *Faqih* only issues 'general guidelines' for political action[71] is indicative of the limited political authority that he exerts. According to one Hizbu'llah official, the generality of the *Faqih*'s proposals leaves the party with a wide space for decision-making.[72] His authority is confined to strategic issues such as *jihad*, political rule and the classification of 'friends and enemies'.[73]

A case in point is the *Faqih*'s ruling on the non-recognition of Israel. Although Hizbu'llah's intense animus towards Israel stems from an independent ideological and political basis, it is prone to attributing its rejection of UN Resolution 425 – which presupposes a recognition of Israel – to the Faqih's ruling on the issue.[74] Presumably, if the *Faqih* declared a *fatwa* calling for Israel's destruction after an Israeli withdrawal from South Lebanon, Hizbu'llah would be obliged to enforce it.

Another example is the *Faqih's* stand on politically motivated suicide. Hizbu'llah could not have adopted the martyrdom mission as a military strategy had the *Faqih* not officially sanctioned the use of such a tactic. As affirmed by Ibrahim al-Amin al Sayyid, those responsible for the bombing of the US Marines' compound 'martyred themselves because the Imam Khumayni permitted them to do so'.[75] Had the *Faqih* not deemed such an act religiously justifiable, it is highly improbable that the party would have endorsed it as a policy.

The permission of the *Wali al-Faqih* is also sought in matters pertaining to political participation and rebellion. As noted earlier in the chapter, rebellion is religiously proscribed and is only legitimised in cases of extreme oppression. Accordingly, a religious justification of the issue requires the *Faqih*'s jurisprudential deliberation.[76] On the other side of the coin, the question of political accommodation and participation in non-Islamic systems is also subject to jurisprudential examination. If the *Faqih* judges participation to 'avert the causes of evil' and to promote Islamic interests, then it becomes religiously sanctioned.

This was the same conclusion reached by the *Faqih* with respect to Hizbu'llah's proposed participation in the Lebanese parliament, whereby Khamini'i 'blessed' its decision to contest the 1992 general election.[77] Implicit in the term 'blessed' is the notion that the *Faqih* did not spontaneously issue a *fatwa* on the issue, as was the case for the non-recognition of Israel or the death warrant against writer Salman Rushdie. It was Hizbu'llah's indecision, or internal 'debate' as described by Fnaysh, over a religiously problematic issue that necessitated the *Faqih*'s arbitration.[78]

It therefore emerges that the *Faqih* only initiates directives on matters that concern the entire *umma*, such as the classification of 'friends and enemies'. But in matters specific to particular states, like the issue of *jihad* and political participation, he awaits a request for his intervention before delivering any rulings. All of this points to the *Faqih*'s recognition of the national boundaries dividing the *umma* and the consequent limits of his *Wilayat*. Hizbu'llah's claim that it is 'enlightened enough to decide for itself'[79] on other political issues which are not religiously problematic, such as its vote of confidence in the government or its promulgation of laws,[80] further limits the scope of the *Faqih*'s political authority. Thus, the party is able to balance its intellectual commitment to the concept of the *Wilayat* with its allegiance to the Lebanese state.

4 Islamic Universalism and National Identity

Underlying the Utopian Mahdist state envisaged by Hizbu'llah and the concept of the *Wilayat al-Faqih*, to which it is resolutely committed, is the principle of Islamic universalism. In fact, insofar as the concept of the *umma* refers to the collectivity of all Muslims, pan-Islamism is a feature of almost every pillar of Hizbu'llah's intellectual structure and as such merits closer inspection as a pillar in its own right.

The Pan-Islamic Concept of Hizbu'llah

Islamic universalism is inherent in the very concept of Hizbu'llah or the Party of God. As a Qur'anic derivation, the usage of the term 'Hizbu'llah' in *sura* 5, *aya* 56 and *sura* 58, *aya* 22, refers to the generality of 'those who turn [for friendship] to Allah, and His Messenger, and the Believers' and who 'believe in Allah and the Last Day', respectively.

According to Hizbu'llah, this is the precise meaning intended by its self-designation as the Party of God:

> The party of God is an expression for describing the multitude of believers generally. It is definitely not a closed group within this multitude who claims for itself the honour of affiliation to the Party of God, at the exclusion of other believers.[1]

In a similar vein, Tufayli defines the Party of God as anyone who follows the path of the Qur'an and who wins God's favour,[2] thereby denoting the generality of Muslim believers. Diametrically opposed to this 'army of Muslims' is the 'army of unbelievers',[3] which is synonymous with the Qur'anic concept of the 'Party of Satan' (*Hizbu'shaytan*)[4] (58:19). As prophesised by the Qur'an (5:56), these forces of good and evil are locked together in a perpetual battle, which will result in the ultimate triumph of the former over the latter.

It therefore becomes apparent that in neither the Qur'an's nor Hizbu'llah's conception is the Party of God identified with an exclusive 'regimented party'[5] or 'narrow political framework', which can single-handedly defeat the equally universalistic Party of Satan. Therefore, Hizbu'llah represents an intellectual and political orientation that governs the lives of all those who affiliate themselves with it, irrespective of the organisational framework within which they operate.[6] In other words, Hizbu'llah does not have a monopoly over the Qur'anic concept of 'Hizbu'llah'.

Correspondingly, the Lebanese Hizbu'llah are viewed as an extension of the Hizbu'llah *mujahidin* (those engaged in *jihad*) in the Islamic world[7] who are characterised as 'all the oppressed Muslims who struggle under the *Wali al-Faqih's* leadership'.[8] By the same token, the party's military wing, the Islamic Resistance, is regarded as an intrinsic part of the Islamic Resistance in the world, which is led by Khumayni.[9]

While the insertion of the concept of the *Wilayat al-Faqih* in the definition of Hizbu'llah betrays a sense of Shi'ite particularism, it does not appear in all of the party's expositions of the term 'Hizbu'llah'. According to one Hizbu'llah official, 'every Muslim is automatically a member of Hizbu'llah'.[10] Moreover, the party claims in its Open Letter to be 'a nation tied to the Muslims in every part of the world by a strong ideological and political bond, namely Islam'.[11] In this specific context, Hizbu'llah's '*umma*'[12] encompasses both Shi'ite and Sunni Muslims, regardless of their adherence to the concept of the *Wilayat al-Faqih*.

A discrepancy therefore emerges between the delimitation of Hizbu'llah's *umma* to the Shi'ite adherents of the *Wilayat al-Faqih* on the one hand, and the enlargement of the *umma* to include all Muslim believers, on the other hand.

There are only two viable explanations for this discordance: First is the possibility that there are gradations of Islamic solidarity within Hizbu'llah's *umma*. The party considers all Muslim believers an inseparable part of its *umma*, but its intellectual kinship with the (mainly Shi'ite) devotees of the *Wilayat al-Faqih* locates this latter group at the very centre of the *umma*, while the former group remains at the periphery. 'Abbas al-Mussawi's assertion that the *Pasdaran* (Iranian Revolutionary Guards) were not perceived by the party as 'a normal part of our Islamic body, but as the head',[13] lends support to this observation. It could well be that Hizbu'llah's *umma* is a Shi'ite *umma* in the first degree and an Islamic *umma* in the second degree.

Second is the explanation proffered by Fayyad: from its very inception, the party has been divided over the definition of Hizbu'llah. For some party members, Hizbu'llah represented the entire Islamic *umma* or *'hala al-Islamiyya'*. Others in the party confined the concept of Hizbu'llah not only to the adherents of the *Wilayat al-Faqih*, but more specifically, to the organisation's active members, without relinquishing their belief in pan-Islamism as a religious and political principle. However, events on the ground have now rendered this debate meaningless. Hizbu'llah has metamorphosed from a pan-Islamic movement to a regimented party which retains the notion of Islamic cultural and political unity as an intellectual construct.

The Universalism of the *Wilayat al-Faqih* and the Islamic Republic of Iran

Hizbu'llah's supranational commitment to the concept of the *Wilayat al-Faqih* and to the Islamic Republic of Iran epitomises the party's pan-Islamist leanings. Although Hizbu'llah's pan-Islamic allegiance is directed first and foremost at the *Faqih*, on account of his transnational authority, his role as spearhead of the Islamic Revolution in Iran and founder of the Islamic Republic means that much of the pan-Islamic allegiance channelled to him trickles down to the revolutionary state he officially heads. The relationship with the *Faqih* 'transcends Iran as a state',[14] but because of this the Islamic Republic is designated by the party as 'our *marja'iyya* (religious authority).' In addition, the occurrence of the 'Husayni, Kerbala'i Revolution'[15] in Iran imparts a sacred character to the Iranian state which is described by the party as 'the genuine Islamic Muhammadan Iran'.[16]

The inextricable bond between the *Wilayat al-Faqih* and the Iranian state on the one hand, and the Islamic Revolution and the Iranian state on the other, serves to consecrate the relationship between Iran and Hizbu'llah. The various shorthand references to Iran as the 'Islamic Republic', 'Muslim Iran', the 'Islamic state', or the 'Islamic Revolution', in common use among party officials, cloud the distinction between the *Wilayat*, the Islamic Revolution and the Iranian state, and correspondingly, render Iran a pan-Islamic symbol for Hizbu'llah.

It is against this background that the many cultural symbols imported by Hizbu'llah from Iran should be viewed. The portrait of

Khumayni on the masthead of Hizbu'llah's newspaper *al-'Ahd* (as observed by Kramer),[17] as well as the portraits of both Khumayni and Khamini'i, which are plastered all over the walls of the southern suburbs of Beirut and the town of Ba'albakk, are not considered to be Iranian symbols. When asked once about their ubiquity in these Hizbu'llah strongholds, Nasru'llah affirmed that these were pictures of 'our religious *maraji*',' and not of Iranian leaders as such.[18] In addition, the party does not perceive the wearing of the *chadur* (the black, tent-like Islamic dress, normally identified with Iranian culture) by some women in the southern suburbs as an Iranian cultural import, but as an assertion of 'Islamic' identity which is manifest in other Arab countries too.[19]

By the same token, Hizbu'llah's declaration that 'Iran and Lebanon are one nation',[20] and that the party is not 'part of Iran' but 'Iran in Lebanon and Lebanon in Iran'[21] is also a function of the pan-Islamic symbolism of the Iranian state, which is partly attributable to the Islamic Revolution. The conceptual interchangeability between the Iranian state and the Islamic Revolution, and the pan-Islamic implications of both terms, are also demonstrated by the party's self-description as 'the Islamic Revolution in Lebanon'[22] – a variation of the 'Iran in Lebanon' theme.

The Islamic Revolution was therefore identified with Iran but not exclusive to it – Khumayni implanted the revolutionary spirit in the 'Muslim nation in Iran' first, but from there it spread to 'all corners of the Islamic world'.[23] This expansion was in line with Khumayni's logic, which stipulated that the Islamic character of the Revolution necessitated its export to other countries in light of the universality of the Islamic message.[24] It was precisely the 'universal [Islamic] slogans' championed by the fledgling Islamic Republic that facilitated the export of its Revolution to Afghanistan, Lebanon and Palestine, where ordinary Muslims were transformed into '*mujahidin*'.[25]

The Pan-Islamic Dimension of the Palestinian Cause

If the Islamic Republic of Iran represents the 'head' of Hizbu'llah's *umma*, then Palestine, and Jerusalem specifically, typifies its body. This epitomisation is not unique to Hizbu'llah, but applies to Islamic movements generally. According to Hamas, the Palestinian cause is an essentially Islamic one, by virtue of the historical sanctity of Jerusalem. As expressed in the Hamas charter:

Palestine is an Islamic land which has the first of the two Qiblas (the direction to which Muslims turn in prayer), the third of the holy Islamic sanctuaries, and the point of departure for Mohammed's midnight journey to the seven heavens (i.e. Jerusalem).[26]

In light of its pan-Islamic characteristics, Hizbu'llah perceives Jerusalem as the 'sacred religious symbol' of the *umma*.[27] The cause of Jerusalem is considered a pan-Islamic cause as opposed to a Palestinian cause – it is the cause of 'all Muslims' and the 'responsibility of the entire *umma*'.[28] Khumayni's inauguration of 'Jerusalem Day' (*Yawm al-Quds*) in 1980, which is celebrated annually by Hizbu'llah, reflects this pan-Islamic thinking.

Over and above this, the sanctities Jerusalem contains, such as the al-Aqsa mosque, are 'our *umma*'s sanctities', and by extension, the land where the *umma's* sanctities are located becomes the possession of the *umma*.[29] Accordingly, no one can determine the fate of a land that belongs to an entire *umma* which consists of present and future generations of Muslims.[30] The only acceptable fate for Jerusalem, in Hizbu'llah's conception, is its liberation from Israeli occupation by the pan-Islamic 'Jerusalem Army'.[31]

Israel's occupation of Palestine therefore becomes 'an occupation of an Islamic land'[32] on account of the sacrosanct character of Jerusalem. Consequently, the liberation of Jerusalem is a euphemism for the liberation of Palestine in its entirety. This explains why the party considers the liberation of all of Palestine 'an Islamic duty' rather than a Palestinian duty.[33] It also accounts for the party's invariable reference to the Palestinian people as 'our Palestinian people'[34] or 'the Muslim Palestinian people',[35] or more common still, 'our Muslim people in Palestine'.[36]

But this solidarity with the Palestinian people is as much a product of the their active struggle against Israel, the 'enemy of the *umma*',[37] as it is of the pan-Islamic symbolism of Jerusalem. The portrayal of Hamas and Islamic Jihad, the *Intifada* and the Palestinian people generally, as 'Husayni' and 'blessed'[38] is not a mere attempt at Sunni-Shi'ite ecumenism on the part of Hizbu'llah – which would have been the case had the party's solidarity with the Palestinian people been solely attributable to the occupation of sacred Jerusalem – but is an intrinsic part of Hizbu'llah's political thought. The declaration of the party's affinity with 'its prisoners of war in Palestine', in the same breath as Khumayni and the Hidden Imam,[39] is indicative of Hizbu'llah's apotheosis of the Palestinian people.

Thus, it is the martyrdom, imprisonment, displacement and overall struggle of the oppressed Palestinian nation to liberate its land from the oppressor, Israel, which earns it Hizbu'llah's utmost respect and camaraderie. The pan-Islamic dimension of the Palestinian cause is therefore partially reducible to the humanistic and secular concept of oppression.

Solidarity with the Muslim *Umma*

Aside from the very use of the term '*umma*' and its Islamic ecumenical connotations, there is much evidence which attests to Hizbu'llah's attempts at Sunni-Shi'ite reconciliation. As early as 1985, the party was exhorting Muslims to thwart 'imperialist' plots that sought to sow discord within the ranks of the Islamic *umma*.[40] For 'Abbas al-Mussawi, the bid to separate Hizbu'llah from 'Muslims generally' was as much a 'crime' as it was to its separate the party from its 'Iranian brothers'.[41]

The import of such declarations lies not only in their endeavour to forge Muslim brotherhood, but more significantly, in their refusal to attribute the blame for the disunity of the *umma* to any doctrinal or ideological differences between Sunni and Shi'ite Islam. By attributing internal fragmentation to external forces, the blame is deflected from either sect and the potential for reconciliation enhanced. Moreover, the creation of a scapegoat or extraneous threat, whether real or imagined, serves to promote Islamic unity.

Bearing in mind the non-materialisation of Sunni-Shi'ite unity, the '*umma*' Hizbu'llah frequently refers to is actually a non-existent *umma*, which the party aspires to create. The only real *umma* is 'Hizbu'llah's *umma*', which consists of all those who defy Israel and the hegemonic West – namely, Iranian, Palestinian and Lebanese Shi'ite Islamists. The universal *umma* which comprises all Muslims is currently 'useless', 'weak' and 'without a will'.[42] In other words, its political passivity renders it a 'dead *umma*'.[43]

The underlying premise here is that the *umma* is not merely a religious community of passive believers who abide by the Qur'an and observe Islamic rituals, but a political community of Islamic activists who fight in God's cause. As interpreted by Fayyad, when Tufayli defines the *umma* as those who follow the path of the Qur'an and who win God's favour, he means those who are willing to actively defend this path as dictated by the 'genuine Muhammadan Islam'.[44]

According to this understanding of the concept, the *umma* is essentially purposive. By implication, the call for Islamic unity is a strategy devised to confront the *umma*'s enemies. Only the 'unity of Muslims as an *umma*' can defeat the imperialist designs of 'world arrogance'.[45] Furthermore, the unity of the Muslims is 'the hammer that crashes the plots of the oppressors',[46] chief of which is Israel. Since Israel does not differentiate between Muslims, Muslims should unite to fight it collectively rather than as separate territorial entities.[47] This exhortation is also based on the logic that 'the Muslim bears a religious legal responsibility [*wajib shari'*]' towards his brother in faith, irrespective of his geographical location.[48]

Having said that, Hizbu'llah does not deny the existence of an incipient 'Islamic identity',[49] which has emerged as a result of the growth of the Islamic current in the region.[50] The party cites a whole array of Sunni Islamic movements whose oppression by internal or external forces has won them Hizbu'llah's sympathy and show of solidarity.

According to this categorisation, the 'oppressed' status of Muslims in the Philippines, Burma, Bosnia, Somalia,[51] Azerbaijan[52] and Chechnya,[53] where Muslim minorities are struggling for regional autonomy, generates much sympathy for them on the part of Hizbu'llah. Conversely, it is the secessionist struggle waged by the Sudanese Christian minority and the joint American-Israeli assault on Sudan – which 'has based its system of government on the Qur'an and has refused to be brought into line by the Americans' – which warrant Hizbu'llah's support for the beleaguered state.[54]

Support is also afforded to Sunni mainstream movements such as the Muslim Brotherhood in Jordan[55] and Egypt, where Islamists have been barred from true political representation.[56] In Turkey too, the Islamists are 'very oppressed' in light of 'the West's interference in Turkey's affairs' and the repression inflicted upon the Welfare Party by the Turkish army.[57] Additionally, the party considers the FIS 'an Islamic front' whose 'general path' it supports,[58] and whose 'total extermination' by the Algerian army and government it strongly condemns.[59] The massacres are explained away by the party as 'tribal' conflicts – between the families of soldiers killed by the FIS and other splinter groups and the families of Islamists who have been killed by government forces – which have spiralled out of control.[60]

However, it would be overly presumptuous to classify these movements and states as an intrinsic part of 'Hizbu'llah's *umma*' for several reasons. In the first place, these movements do not feature regularly in the public speeches of party officials as do the Iranian and Palestinian Islamists. In the second place, when Hizbu'llah specifies the locale of its *umma*, only Lebanon, Iran and Palestine are cited as instances of 'our *umma*'.

Still, the varying degrees of political activism and oppression characterising these movements means that they cannot be relegated to the 'dead *umma*' category either. Perhaps they would be better categorised as an *umma* in the making, or an embryonic *umma*, whose potential unity as a community of *mujahidin* has yet to unfold. In other words, the classification of these movements by the party in the 'our *umma*' category is largely contingent upon their future ability to prove their pan-Islamic credentials, which can only be gauged by their willingness to shoulder the responsibility of liberating Jerusalem – the pan-Islamic symbol *par excellence*. In effect, the only true criterion for becoming a member of Hizbu'llah's *umma* is to confront the enemy of the *umma*, Israel, and to a lesser extent its patron, the US, as Islamists in Iran, Lebanon and Palestine have done.

The Primacy of Islamic Identity

As a universal message for mankind that encompasses all national identities, Islam necessarily demands the subordination of racial, tribal and kinship affiliations to it. The supremacy of the Islamic identity is therefore a requirement of the Islamic faith, which Hizbu'llah staunchly upholds. The tenacity with which this conviction is held is evinced by the primacy Hizbu'llah places on the *umma* over the Lebanese state.

The following statement by Tufayli exemplifies the prioritisation of the Islamic identity over national affiliations: 'We do not consider ourselves a Lebanese party but an Islamic party and the Lebanese problem is but one aspect of our concerns.'[61] For Ibrahim al-Amin al-Sayyid, the primacy of the Islamic identity over the Lebanese identity is not only dictated by religious doctrine, but also by logic. 'Lebanonism' cannot vie with Islam for the loyalty of the Muslim in Lebanon because it is nothing more than a 'geographical expression', while Islam is a cultural, intellectual and political expression which transcends geography.[62] Accordingly, Hizbu'llah believes in the 'geography of land' but not in the 'geography of the individual'.[63]

Put more concretely, the party does not recognise 'territorial boundaries',[64] especially those that separate the Islamic *umma* and obstruct the creation of an authentic Islamic identity. The national borders between Palestine and Lebanon are therefore considered 'artificial'[65] and 'unnatural'[66] by-products of colonialism. In fact, Hizbu'llah has repeatedly voiced its rejection of the Lebanese entity, which it refers to as a 'French architectural box'.[67] Even today's 'Lebanonised' Hizbu'llah still professes its 'rejection of the Lebanese entity in terms of the present boundaries'.[68]

Even on the unconscious level, the party discusses the *umma* in a manner that is oblivious to geography. Thus, when Hizbu'llah speaks of 'the Muslim *umma* in Iran',[69] or 'the *umma* in Lebanon',[70] the underlying assumption is that the Muslim community constitutes an identity, which happens to be dispersed throughout the world, like any expatriate community. This also applies to the party's reference to 'the Islamic situation in Lebanon'[71] or the 'Islamic Resistance in Lebanon',[72] as opposed to the 'Lebanese Islamic situation' or the 'Lebanese Islamic Resistance'. What all this implies is, not only that the *umma*, the Islamic situation and the Islamic Resistance in Lebanon are all extensions of a wider Islamic community, but more importantly, that the party refuses to sub-categorise the Islamic identity into national types. Hence Husayn al-Mussawi's assertion: 'Some say we are Lebanese Muslims ... No! We are Muslims of the world and we have close links with other Muslims.'[73]

Not only does the party reject the classification of Islam into national categories (i.e. Lebanese Islam), but also its classification along racial lines (i.e. Arab Islam versus Persian Islam). Hizbu'llah rejects the notion of Arab supremacy in Islam[74] and asseverates that it does not follow the 'Arab nation'.[75] This view mirrors Khumayni's belief in the incompatibility between Islam and Arabism, which for him represented the 'pre-Islamic age of ignorance' (*'Ahd al-Jahiliyya*).[76]

While Hizbu'llah refrains from equating Arabism with paganism, it has no qualms about deriding Arab culture, which the party describes as 'the culture of weakness, passivity and surrender'.[77] It was precisely because the Arabs accorded primacy to their Arab identity over their Islamic identity that this defeatist culture governed their struggle against Israel. The triumph of the 'Arab mentality' over the Islamic mentality will therefore lead to 'dangerous results' in the Arab-Israeli conflict.[78]

Hizbu'llah seeks to instil in all Muslims an Islamic identity which would override all of their national affiliations, and which would be conducive to the creation of an *'umma mujahida'* (combative community)[79] capable of defeating Israel. Only once such an *umma* emerges will the establishment of a 'greater Islamic state'[80] – of which Lebanon would be an indivisible part[81] – become a reality.

National Identity and Nationalism

Arab Identity and Nationalism

Despite the Islamic universalism of Hizbu'llah and its conceptualisation of the Islamic *umma*, Arab nationalist overtones characterise much of its recent political discourse. To some extent, these overtones are a product of its overall pragmatisation, and hence a carefully crafted move to gain popular legitimation in the predominantly Sunni Arab world. The party has attempted to obtain this legitimation by presenting itself as a distinctly Arab movement, as evinced by its self-designation as an Islamic, Lebanese and 'pan-Arabist' Resistance,[82] which fights for 'the cause of all Arabs and Muslims' rather than that of the Shi'ites alone.[83]

Yet the Arabisation of Hizbu'llah was just as much a product of the party's attempt to forge a 'united Arab front'[84] which could confront Israeli designs in the region,[85] as it was a product of the party's desire to expand its popular base in the Arab world. While the appropriation of Arab nationalism for such a purpose appears to be at variance with the party's attribution of the Arabs' defeat vis-à-vis Israel to the primacy accorded to their national identity, this discrepancy can be explained by two developments in the party's political thought.

First was the party's awareness of the potentially formidable task of politically mobilising the 'dead *umma*' – with its numerous racial and national varieties of Islam – to partake in the struggle against Israel. Since Hizbu'llah's limited *umma* was ultimately incapable of defeating Israel single-handedly, the party soon realised that Arab support was indispensable to its confrontation with the Israeli state.

Accordingly, Hizbu'llah embarked on an endeavour to portray the cause of Jerusalem as a peculiarly 'Arab Islamic'[86] one by underlining its 'Arab Islamic' identity.[87] All Muslims and Arabs had to assert their right to the Arab Islamic land of Jerusalem,[88] including Palestinian Christians who had both a national and a religious claim to the land.[89] Jerusalem therefore belonged to Arab and non-Arab Muslims, as well as non-Muslim Arabs. But despite the pan-Islamic symbolism of Jerusalem, the religious diversity that characterised its Palestinian inhabitants rendered it an essentially Palestinian, and hence Arab, cause.

By extension, the conflict with Israel was primarily a struggle between the Arab world and Israel, and only secondarily a struggle between the Islamic *umma* and Israel. This classification is further supported by the fact that the other territories occupied by Israel, such as South Lebanon and the Golan Heights, in addition to Palestine in its entirety, are Arab rather than Islamic lands. Therefore, the chief protagonists in the conflict with Israel are Arab states and not non-Arab Muslim ones which, with the exception of Iran, are far removed from the scene of the conflict, both geographically and politically.

It is in light of these considerations that Hizbu'llah perceives the conflict with Israel as an Arab-Israeli conflict, which can only be successfully concluded by Arab states. Thus, although the party derided the Arabs for their successive defeats in their wars with Israel,[90] and denounced them for having 'stood by as onlookers' during the 1982 Israeli invasion of Lebanon,[91] Arab unity was viewed as a sine qua non for the defeat, or at the very least, isolation of Israel.

This acknowledgement was greatly facilitated by various regional developments, of which the Palestinian *Intifada* was but one. While Islamic groups such as Hamas and Islamic Jihad led the popular Palestinian uprising against Israel, the considerable role played by Christian and Muslim secular nationalists in the *Intifada*[92] was demonstrative of the political efficacy of Arab nationalism, especially when conjoined with Islam.

Another factor which paved the way for Hizbu'llah's recognition of the utility of Arab consciousness and solidarity in the struggle against Israel was the Arab boycott of the fourth US-sponsored MENA (Middle East and North Africa) economic conference, which sought to normalise relations between Israel and the Arab world. The conference, held in November 1997 in Qatar's capital, Doha, was boycotted by several Arab states, including Algeria, Bahrain, Morocco, the Palestinian National Authority, Syria and Lebanon, as well as traditional Hizbu'llah foes, Saudi Arabia, Egypt and the UAE. Hizbu'llah praised Arab states for the 'defiance' they displayed by not attending the conference,[93] while Egypt was commended not only for boycotting the conference, but for 'inciting' other Arab states to do so,[94] as accused by Qatar. Thus, although several other Arab states such as Djibouti, Jordan, Kuwait, Mauritania, Oman, Qatar, Yemen and Tunisia, attended the conference, the party viewed the non-attendance of other Arab states as an indication of the Arabs' hidden potential to 'stand together and fight back'.[95]

This view was confirmed by the Arab reaction to Israel's attack on Lebanon's civilian infrastructure in February 2000. Although the Arab world had condemned Israel's assault of 1996 and provided the Lebanese government with material aid, its reaction to Israel's recent assault was unprecedented for it and unmatched by the remainder of the Muslim world. In a rare show of support, the Arab League decided to relocate its venue from Cairo, where it customarily meets, to Beirut. Aside from its call for an Israeli withdrawal from Lebanon, the most prominent outcome of the ministerial meeting was its appeal to Arab states to cease normalising relations with Israel until progress had been made on the Palestinian-Israeli peace track.

Not only did the Israeli assault foster a strong sense of Arab solidarity with Lebanon, it served to fully legitimise the Islamic Resistance on the official state level. This process of legitimation was epitomised by Saudi Crown Prince 'Abd'ullah bin 'Abdul 'Aziz's depiction of the Resistance as 'heroic', and by the subsequent meeting between him and several Hizbu'llah parliamentarians.

As pertinent as the party's new-found conviction in the political efficacy of pan-Arabism was to its re-appropriation of Arab nationalism as a means of confronting Israel, the evolution of the party's intellectual discourse on the relationship between nationalism and Islam also accounts for this re-appropriation. In contrast to the party's former belief that nationalism and Islam were mutually exclusive, because of the secular nature of Arab nationalism and the perceived impediment it posed to the universalism of Islam, the party came to believe in the reconcilability of the two.

Thus, parallel to the party's acknowledgement that pan-Arabism could play a role in the struggle with Israel was its admission that Islam could both 'recognise and embrace' different cultures and nationalities.[96] This view is echoed by Fnaysh, who argues that Arab nationalism can only be considered antithetical to Islam insofar as it is espoused as a system of 'managing social affairs'.[97] So long as Arab nationalism is not elevated to the status of ideology, it can be encompassed by Islam. Therefore, Hizbu'llah does not view its quest for Arab unity as an obstacle to the universalism of Islam.[98]

The culmination of this reasoning is Hizbu'llah's professed affiliation to an 'Arab-Islamic' world,[99] over and above its allegiance to the universal Islamic *umma*. Thus, although Islamic civilisation represents the 'broadest level of cultural identity' for Hizbu'llah, to borrow Samuel Huntington's terminology,[100] Fayyad's admission that Islam can be categorised into cultural types, such as 'Arab-Islam, African-Islam and Indo-Islam',[101] is a tacit acknowledgement of the existence of 'subcivilisations' within Islam.[102]

While the party's recognition of Islamic subcivilisations represents a radical departure from its earlier refusal to categorise Islam into national types, it does not actually contradict the party's belief in the universalism of Islam. This is revealed by the 'sub' prefix, implicit in which is the notion of subordination or secondariness. The party's conceptualisation of Islamic subcivilisations is therefore entirely compatible with its belief that various cultures and nationalities can be subsumed under Islam. Furthermore, insofar as these cultural types all fall under the generic civilisational category of Islam, the ideological supremacy of Islam remains intact.

In effect, the Arab Islamic world is one which is intellectually committed to Islam, but which retains a unique cultural character that constitutes the basis of its politically motivated unity. Thus, while Islamic civilisation is defined by shared values, institutions and beliefs,[103] the Arab Islamic subcivilisation is bound together by 'a shared fate and history',[104] in addition to common 'language, customs and dress'.[105]

It follows that non-Muslim Arabs are part of this subcivilisation by dint of their Arab identity. In fact, Hizbu'llah had advanced this theory several years before its 'Lebanonisation' or '*infitah*' towards Lebanese society. Cognisant of the fact that the Lebanese Christians identified themselves with Western civilisation, and were therefore only 'physically here but spiritually elsewhere', Tufayli called on the Christians to be both 'physically and spiritually part of the [Arab-Islamic] region' as early as 1986.[106]

Over a decade later, Nasru'llah declared that all Lebanese, irrespective of their religious identity, 'belonged to a single *umma* and civilisation'.[107] Although Huntington sub-classifies Islamic civilisation into racial and national types, it is highly unlikely that his Arab Islam category includes Maronite and Greek Orthodox Christians, when he implies that the Lebanese Maronites are part of 'Catholic' civilisation.[108] Based on such a classification, one could postulate that he would also categorise the Lebanese, and other Levantine, Orthodox Christians as part of the 'Orthodox' civilisation, centred in Russia,[109] rather than as a constituent unit of the Arab Islamic subcivilisation.

These assumptions are further substantiated by Huntington's affirmation that 'people who share ethnicity and language but differ in religion may slaughter each other, as happened in Lebanon', as proof of his claim that 'the major civilisations in human history have been closely identified with the world's great religions'.[110] Clearly, Huntington does not believe that ethnicity, language or other cultural attributes can constitute a civilisation or subcivilisation in the absence of the religious criterion.

Conversely, Hizbu'llah maintains that 'while religion is one aspect of civilisation, it need not be the only aspect. Ethnicity can also provide the basis for civilisation.'[111] Thus, even though Islam is the predominant aspect of Islamic civilisation, Arab non-Muslims can be considered part of this civilisation insofar as their Arabism renders them members of the Arab Islamic subcivilisation. By extension, the Lebanese Christian is part of the Arab Islamic subcivilisation, and therefore 'part of the Islamic *umma*'.[112]

Lebanese Identity and Nationalism

Co-extensive with Hizbu'llah's embrace of Arab nationalism, or Arabisation, is its 'Lebanonisation' or '*infitah*' towards Lebanese state and society, the predominant manifestation of which is the party's accentuation of its Lebanese identity and its self-designation as a nationalist movement. In large part, this proto-nationalism is a product of the party's desire for popular legitimation across all sectors of Lebanese society, as revealed by its public political discourse.

Fully aware of the delegitimising impact of its transnational ties with the *Wali al-Faqih* and the Iranian state with which he is associated, Hizbu'llah has sought to overturn the once pervasive popular perception of it as an Iranian surrogate organisation, devoid of any national identity or loyalty. To that effect, the party has publicly striven to harmonise its Islamic identity, of which its affiliation to the Islamic Republic and the concept of the *Wilayat al-Faqih* is an intrinsic part, with its national identity.

As argued by Nasru'llah, just as the affiliation to Christianity, Communism or any other belief system does not conflict with one's

Lebanese identity, Hizbu'llah's affiliation to Islam, and by implication its allegiance to the *Wilayat al-Faqih*, does not undermine its 'Lebanese identity or patriotism'.[113] In a similar vein, just as other Lebanese groups are not deemed any less nationalist on account of the political and material support they once received from foreign powers, Iran's support for Hizbu'llah does not render the party any less nationalist than these other groups.[114]

Thus, although Iran played a cardinal role in the establishment of the movement, Hizbu'llah underlines the fact that the Islamic Resistance was founded by Lebanese, not Iranian, Shi'ites and that, as such, Hizbu'llah's decision-making issues directly from the party's Lebanese leadership.[115] Furthermore, the party emphasises that it is not Iranian land that it is fighting to liberate, but Lebanese territory.[116] If, in the process of this resistance, other political forces such as Iran or Syria benefit from its 'results', then this 'does not detract from its nationalism and Lebanonism', since the party did not launch the resistance on their behalf, but on behalf of the Lebanese nation.[117]

Accordingly, Hizbu'llah does not believe that its religious commitment to the *Wilayat al-Faqih* and its ties with Iran 'clash' with Lebanon's national interest.[118] In fact, Nasru'llah implies that, in the event of a conflict of interest between the Lebanese and Iranian states, Hizbu'llah would pursue Lebanon's interests at Iran's expense.[119] Implicit in such a declaration is the intellectual, as opposed to political, nature of Hizbu'llah's allegiance to the *Wali al-Faqih*. Empowered only with the ability to initiate rulings that relate to the *umma* as a collectivity of states, the *Faqih's* limited political authority permits the party to pledge its political allegiance to the Lebanese state, and to thereby uphold the concept of nationalism.

All this flies in the face of Magnus Ranstorp's oversimplistic claim that because 'Hizbu'llah subjects itself to authority from outside its own nation state, it rejects the very idea of nationalism'.[120] Not only does this affirmation ignore the essentially intellectual nature of the party's allegiance to the *Wali al-Faqih*, it also completely disregards the nationalist dimension of its Islamic Resistance, as well as the party's endeavour to reconcile its Islamic identity and universalism with its nationalism, as revealed in its nationalist political discourse.

From Hizbu'llah's perspective, the greatest indication of nationalism is the readiness to sacrifice oneself for one's nation, as epitomised by the Islamic Resistance martyrs and fighters who both lose and risk their lives in order to liberate national territory.[121] Not only does this confirm Hizbu'llah's nationalist credentials, but coupled with the fact that 'others have forsaken' the task of resistance, it renders Hizbu'llah the 'most patriotic' of all Lebanese movements.[122] Accordingly, 'it is not for others to measure Hizbu'llah's patriotism; it is for Hizbu'llah to measure theirs'.[123]

The resistance to the Israeli occupation therefore emerges as a 'national cause', 'goal' or 'duty', as well as a religious one,[124] which is waged on behalf of 'all Lebanese and Arabs' as well as all Muslims.[125] By extension, Hizbu'llah's Resistance is not only an Islamic one, as its name suggests, but also a 'Lebanese' and 'nationalist' resistance,[126] 'whose *jihad* is Lebanese'.[127] To substantiate such a claim, in late 1997 the party established the 'Lebanese Brigades of Resistance to the Israeli Occupation', a multi-sectarian military adjunct to its Islamic Resistance forces.

Although this could not be replicated on the political level, on account of the ideological prerequisite for institutional affiliation, the party still sought to portray itself as both a Lebanese Islamic Resistance and a Lebanese Islamic party.[128] It attempted this by incorporating the new synthesis it had forged between its Islamic and Lebanese identities into its political ritual. In a radical break with past practice, the party hoisted the Lebanese flag next to its own flag at its public speeches and rallies,[129] and played the national anthem before holding prayers for its martyrs.[130]

A corresponding shift occurred in the party's political discourse. In a complete reversal of the party's earlier refusal to identify itself as a Lebanese party, Hizbu'llah now depicts itself as a party which represents all Lebanese. Thus, for example, while the party had previously distinguished itself from Amal solely on the basis of its Islamic identity and Amal's Lebanese identity,[131] it now sets itself apart from the movement by claiming the opposite. Unlike Amal, which pursues Shi'ite interests exclusively, as a Lebanese party, Hizbu'llah seeks to realise the interests of 'all Lebanese citizens'.[132]

While such developments in the party's political discourse are primarily a product of its desire for popular legitimation, they are also attributable to the maturation of its intellectual discourse on the compatibility between national identity and nationalism, on the one hand, and Islamic identity and universalism, on the other. As in the past, the party still maintains that Islam and the nation state are not comparable, since Islam stands for an entire civilisation, of which certain nations are merely constituent parts.[133] Moreover, the fact that Islam is a comprehensive intellectual system, which overarches all other cultural identities, further renders Islam and nationality incomparable.[134]

Yet despite this view, the fact that the nation state is no longer reduced to little more than a 'geographical expression',[135] but is designated as a culture in its own right, represents a significant departure from the party's earlier thought on national identity. According to this reformulated conception, the Lebanese nation state is bound together not only by geography, but also by race, language and history.[136] Insofar as such ties produce a distinctive 'cultural identity', it is natural that the Muslim develops 'an emotional bond' with his nation.[137] According to Qasim, just as the emotional bond with one's brother is impervious to ideological differences, the strong sense of kinship felt by the Hizbu'llah adherent towards his compatriot is unaffected by his religious affiliation.[138]

Thus, despite the strong intellectual bond between the Lebanese Shi'ite and the Iranian or Iraqi Shi'ite, the shared 'traditions, mentality, practices and norms' of the Lebanese Shi'ite and Christian, would render the Lebanese Shi'ite 'culturally different' from the Iranian or Iraqi Shi'ite.[139] Fayyad notes that the same holds true for Iran, Hizbu'llah's exemplary Islamic state. The geographically delimited boundaries between it and Iraq betoken the distinctly national affiliations and loyalties of their people.[140]

In fact, several researchers of Islam have observed Khumayni's implicit acceptance of the nation state.[141] This acceptance was implied by the essentially territorial war between Iran and Iraq, which was defined as such by Khumayni,[142] as well as his constant reference to the 'Iranian fatherland', 'the Iranian nation' and 'the Iranian patriot'.[143] It is even institutionalised in the Iranian constitution which stipulates that 'the official and common language and script of the people of Iran is Persian',[144] and which also requires that the president of the country be 'of Iranian origin' and 'nationality'.[145] By the same token, only Iranians can enlist in the army and security services.[146]

The subtext here is that, with all its pan-Islamic implications, even the exemplary Islamic Republic both recognises and encourages the preservation of territorial boundaries and national identity. More than this, by confining participation in all branches of the state to Iranian nationals, the Islamist framers of the constitution rendered the Iranian nationality not only a social identity, but also a political one.

Clearly, Khumayni and his Islamist counterparts did not view political nationalism as being antagonistic to Islam, as does the Islamist researcher, Falzur Rahman. According to Rahman's line of reasoning, while Islam can appreciate 'social nationalism', which he defines as the cultural cohesiveness of a group, it cannot countenance 'political nationalism' which entails political loyalty to a nation state.[147]

Hizbu'llah would disagree with this theorisation on two different levels. In the first place, rather than view Islam as averse to political nationalism, Hizbu'llah believes that it nourishes it insofar as the defence of one's nation is a *wajib shari'* enjoined by Islam.[148] This is demonstrated by the fact that the resistance to the Israeli occupation was not launched by Lebanese secularists, who are not bound to such an obligation, but by Lebanese Islamists who are.[149] It is in light of this intellectual distinction that Qasim affirms that 'had I not been a committed Muslim I would not have had this perception of nationalism'.[150] In effect, the party believes that its Islamic identity or 'Islamism' serves its national affiliation or 'Lebanonism'.[151]

In the second place, so long as nationalism is no more than an expression of one's social and political identity, it cannot be deemed antagonistic to Islam. It is only when nationalism becomes an intellectual identity that vies with the Muslim's intellectual affiliation to Islam that it can be considered *'asabiyya* (tribalism or fanaticism), and hence, antithetical to Islam.[152]

But what this also implies is that, although Lebanonism does not contradict Islamism, its exclusion from the intellectual realm renders it ultimately inferior to it. It follows that the Hizbu'llah adherent would identify himself more with a fellow Shi'ite Muslim of different national origin, with whom he has a strong intellectual bond, than with his non-Muslim or non-Shi'ite fellow countryman, as admitted by Qasim.[153]

While this may appear to be inconsistent with the party's professed intent to back Lebanon's interests if they were ever to clash with the interests of another state, such as Iran, on closer inspection, Qasim's assertion does not actually discredit this claim. Just because the party's paramount intellectual identification lies with the pan-Islamic symbol of Iran, the primacy of this identification does not flow to the political sphere. One is again reminded here of the intellectual, as opposed to political, nature of Hizbu'llah's allegiance to the *Wali al-Faqih*.

Thus, despite the fact that the concepts of the *Wilayat al-Faqih* and the Islamic Revolution serve to consecrate the intellectual bond between Hizbu'llah and Iran, the Iranian state does not command the party's paramount political loyalty. In effect, although the intellectual bond is ultimately stronger than all other bonds for Hizbu'llah, the party does not confuse it with the political bond, which is reserved for the Lebanese nation state. By consigning the Islamic identity to the intellectual realm and national identity to the political realm, the party is able to reconcile nationalism with Islam, as epitomised by Ra'id's self-designation as a Lebanese 'affiliated to Islam intellectually'.[154]

5   The Struggle with the West

Another fundamental component of Hizbu'llah's political thought is its general antagonism towards the West. Some scholars have attempted to downplay this animus by refusing to attribute it to 'cultural differences' or to a 'civilisational struggle' with the West and by depicting it instead as a 'defensive reaction' to the West's 'hostile' policies in the region.[1] In a similar vein, others claim that the anti-Westernism of political Islam does not stem from 'some intrinsic antipathy or animosity to all things Western', but from 'differences over specific domestic, regional and foreign policies with select Western states'.[2]

Although there can be no denying that the US' biased regional policy and political intervention in Lebanon greatly aggravated Hizbu'llah's hostility towards the West, and that it consequently constituted a necessary condition for the party's anti-Westernism, it is not a sufficient condition. As averred by Na'im Qasim, there is a 'cultural conflict between us and the West'[3] and not merely a political or ideological conflict. What is more, the animosity that is rooted in this conflict does appear to be 'intrinsic' or inbred insofar as Hizbu'llah 'raises its youths to be hostile to the US'.[4]

Accordingly, Samuel Huntington is not far off in his assertion that it is not political Islam that is 'a problem for the West', but Islam, the civilisation, 'whose people are convinced of the superiority of their culture'.[5] 'Abbas al-Mussawi's declaration that 'Islamic civilisation is desired as an alternative to all civilisations' corroborates this view.[6] By the same token, Islam's antagonism towards the West is not confined to the CIA or to the Department of Defense, but to the West as a civilisation which is convinced of the universality of its culture and the necessity of propagating it throughout the entire world.[7]

It is the Western attempt to subordinate Lebanon in the 'civilisational, cultural and intellectual' realms, as well as the 'political and economic' spheres,[8] which underlies Hizbu'llah's virulence towards it. To all intents and purposes, Hizbu'llah is engaged in a 'civilisational struggle' with the West,[9] inherent in which is a rejection of the 'values, beliefs, institutions and social structures'[10] of Western society.

The Origins of Hizbu'llah's Anti-Westernism

As maintained by Hizbu'llah, this rejection of Western civilisation is rooted in the 'historic' confrontation between Islam and the West,[11] which dates back to the early spread of Islam in the seventh century. By the late eleventh century, this confrontation intensified with the launch of the Crusades by Roman Catholics from the West who sought to forcibly impose Christianity on the Near East and, by some Islamist accounts, to annihilate the Muslims there.[12] As anathematised as the Crusaders are,[13] European colonialism of the nineteenth and twentieth centuries is an even greater object of execration in light of its attempts to 'civilise' the Muslims.[14] The Western incursion into the Muslim world during this period was not only political and military, but also 'accompanied by a dangerous intellectual invasion, the most important means of which was the Orientalist movement and the Evangelist missions'.[15]

The West was therefore initially identified with European Christendom – which America was opposed to[16] – and by extension, the civilisational confrontation with it was restricted to European Christendom. In the twentieth century, however, America came to affiliate itself with Western civilisation, which thereby represented 'Euroamerican' Christendom.[17] Correspondingly, Islam's confrontation with the West in the twentieth century became a civilisational struggle against American and European political and cultural hegemony over the Middle East.

At the forefront of this struggle is Hizbu'llah, which singles out Britain, France and the US as the principal Western powers whom it regards as its enemies,[18] on account of their colonial and neo-imperial roles in the region. Although the term 'world arrogance'[19] is often used as a synonym for the US, the party's reference to the 'arrogant West' as a totality,[20] coupled with its identification of 'the forces of arrogance' as Britain and France, as well as the US,[21] is demonstrative of its antipathy towards the West as a hegemonic civilisation. Furthermore, the delineation of the West as a 'blasphemous'[22] 'world of infidels',[23] characterised by 'evil',[24] also attests to the party's inveterate bitterness towards Western civilisation.

However, the diatribe against the West is levelled first and foremost at the US, and only secondarily at Britain, France and the rest of the Western world. This is evidenced by the designation of the US as the 'pioneer of evil', which 'steers the materialist [i.e. Western] world towards the subjugation of the oppressed peoples of the world'.[25] The 'great imperial powers' are therefore 'led by America',[26] which typifies 'the first root of vice' and the 'source of all malice' on account of its ultimate responsibility for all Muslim catastrophes.[27] Over and above this, its characterisation as the 'greatest abomination' in the present era renders it comparable to Yazid, who represented the 'greatest abomination' during Imam Husayn's era.[28] In short, it is the 'Great Satan'[29] who (because of the reasons cited below) will 'always be hated' by Hizbu'llah.[30]

Precisely because the US is depicted as a 'Great Satan', while Britain and France are merely branded as 'evil', there is much more room for political discourse with the latter than there is with the former. Nonetheless, the political, cultural and intellectual confrontation with the West as a collectivity of states remains an essentially civilisational struggle, which can only be classified as an invariable component of Hizbu'llah's intellectual structure.

The Western Conspiracy Against Islam

Notwithstanding the historical origins of the confrontation between Islam and the West, Hizbu'llah's struggle with contemporary Western civilisation, at the helm of which is the US, is largely shaped by its conception of American and European designs in the region and the US' consideration of Islam as its 'principal rival'.

According to the party's reading of events, this Western perception of Islam, and the region in general, preceded the downfall of the Soviet Union, with whom the West was supposedly preoccupied.[31] Although Hizbu'llah acknowledges the earlier existence of an 'ideological' conflict between 'East and West',[32] it believes that the two sides put aside their differences in the wake of the Islamic Revolution in Iran.[33] Thus, although the ex-Soviet Union or the 'East' represented an alternative 'Orthodox' civilisation to the West,[34] it was confronted as an ideological system rather than as a civilisation. Islam, however, emerged as an even greater threat to both powers insofar as it represented a civilisational, as opposed to an ideological, adversary.[35]

Contemporary Islamists accuse the West of harbouring 'plots and designs to subordinate, humiliate and undermine Islamic institutions and culture'.[36] Likewise, Hizbu'llah believes that the West is embroiled in a 'great conspiracy'[37] or 'arrogant scheme' to hegemonise the region[38] and to 'confront Islamic civilisation'.[39]

This conspiracy was first conceived in the colonial period when 'world arrogance' inaugurated its 'divide and rule' policy by dividing the Muslim world into separate nation states in order to dominate the region.[40] Having accomplished this feat, the West is now intent on subdividing Muslim nations even further, by creating internal strife and aggravating existing religious and sectarian sensitivities,[41] as in the cases of Egypt, Iraq, Syria and Lebanon.[42]

For Hizbu'llah, the case of Lebanon is particularly illustrative of the 'colonial plot' to sow discord between religious and sectarian groups.[43] While America and Israel are usually singled out as the main conspirators behind the Lebanese civil war,[44] other Western nations are not exempted from any responsibility for the conflict. According to one party exponent, all the problems, unrest and bloodshed that characterise most Islamic and Arab states were orchestrated by Western 'spies' disguised as members of non-governmental humanitarian and social organisations, such as the Red Cross.[45]

By fomenting civil strife throughout the Middle East, the West seeks to 'control the area's economic infrastructure'[46] by subordinating it to 'the Western economic wheel and industrial machine'[47] and by 'stealing/usurping' its 'wealth and resources'.[48] But that is not to say that the West's, or at least the US', Middle East policy is governed purely by self-interest.

According to Fadlu'llah and Hizbu'llah, the US' regional policy is not based on real US interests but on Israeli interests. Therefore, the US does not have an American policy in the Middle East, but an 'Israeli policy',[49] which stems from the US' ideological commitment to Israel.[50] So closely intertwined are Israel's and the US' interests that the two states are deemed identical and are alternately cast as being the other's instrument.[51] On the one hand, Israel is depicted as the US' 'spearhead' in the region,[52] while on the other, the US is portrayed as Israel's 'tool'.[53]

Although the rest of the Western world's Middle East policy differs from the US' Israeli policy, insofar as it is not based on Israeli interests but on its own 'strategic' interests,[54] it is also held responsible for Israel's continued existence. Europe's overall support for Israel and the US' ardent pursuit of Israel's 'strategic superiority' in the region[55] therefore emerge as another element in the Western conspiracy against Islam.

The roots of this conspiracy lie in the Balfour Declaration of 1917, in which the British government pledged to do its utmost to ensure the establishment of a Jewish homeland in Palestine. Although the

British were unable to fulfil their promise, and despite the fact that they 'rejected US intervention in the Palestine issue',[56] they are maligned for pursuing the creation of a Jewish state so as to fulfil their expansionist aims.[57]

Not only is the West, or Europe, implicated in the establishment of the Israeli state, but it is found culpable of sustaining the existence of this illegitimate state. By extension, the West is held ultimately responsible for the continued displacement of the Palestinian diaspora[58] and is accused of conspiring, over the past half century, 'to erase the identity' and 'to annihilate the existence' of the Palestinian people.[59]

But it is the US' unparalleled support, protection and defence of Israel,[60] which issues from its 'instinctively Zionist background'[61] that renders it directly accountable for the fate of the Palestinians, and for Israel's crimes generally. The US' complete sponsorship of a state which 'practices the worst kind of terrorism',[62] places responsibility for 'all the massacres committed by Israel' squarely on its shoulders.[63] This is especially the case when Israel wages its 'genocide campaign' on southern villages with the help of American weapons.[64]

The US is even accused of masterminding some of Israel's atrocities. As believed by Hizbu'llah, Israel's 'Grapes of Wrath' invasion was not 'an Israeli operation with an American green light', but was directly orchestrated by the US.[65] Accordingly, the Qana massacre which occurred within the context of the invasion was attributable to the US not only for the above reason, but also because of the US' harsh denunciation of the United Nations' condemnation of the incident, which confirmed to Hizbu'llah that the US truly was 'the Great Satan'.[66]

While other Western states are not subject to such rebukes, they are still castigated for remaining silent about Israel's many crimes.[67] All that international and humanitarian organisations do in the face of Israeli aggression is 'watch and listen without even blinking'.[68] When Israel and the Phalangists committed the notorious Sabra and Chatila massacres for example, Hizbu'llah protested that not a single international organisation denounced the act.[69] By 'international' Hizbu'llah clearly does not imply the non-Western world (though it did also imply the 'arrogant East' before the break-up of the Soviet Union), but the West which is perceived to control these organisations, first among which is the United Nations.

Rather than being a podium for oppressed people, the United Nations is perceived as an instrument of the arrogant West, especially the US and, by connection, a tool of Israel.[70] For Hizbu'llah, the UN's accusation that the Resistance shelled Israeli targets only 250 metres away from the UN headquarters at Qana was clearly the product of US pressure on the organisation 'to hold the victims responsible for their fate'.[71] Furthermore, the UNIFIL (United Nations Interim Force in Lebanon), whose role is to keep the peace in southern Lebanon, is viewed as an obstruction to resistance activity and a 'treacherous and conniving' force that protects the security of Israel.[72]

The Double Standards of the West

It becomes apparent that the major criticism levelled at Western civilisation centres on its employment of double standards which are tailored to suit its interests and Israel's.[73] According to the party, the world has come to be bereft of any democratic or humanitarian values, and is governed instead by the 'law of the jungle'[74] where there are no uniform standards by which to judge actions, but rather different criteria for the same actions.[75]

When Israel blasphemes against Islam and Christianity, as when the Prophet Muhammad, the Qur'an and the Virgin Mary are desecrated, the West does not react in a manner commensurate with the gravity of the offence. If that same desecration is directed at Jewish religious symbols, the international media would launch a campaign against the perpetrators of such a sacrilege, and 'the voices of the followers of other faiths would be raised even before the Jews'.[76]

In a similar vein, the entire world rushed to defend writer Salman Rushdie's right to curse and insult the Prophet of Islam by withdrawing its ambassadors from Iran in protest at Khumayni's *fatwa* against 'the apostate'.[77] But when French scholar Roger Garaudy stated that the number of Jews killed in World War Two was far less than the conventional six million estimate, he was condemned worldwide and prosecuted by the French authorities.[78]

Furthermore, although Israel possesses the same chemical and biological weapons that Saddam Husayn has, it is not the target of Western aggression as Iraq is.[79] What particularly irks Hizbu'llah is that the West is punishing Iraq for using weapons that it supplied it with in the first place.[80] After all, it was the West – the US, Britain and France specifically – which once supported the 'despicable' Saddam Husayn regime.[81] In fact, the West furnishes all oppressive

Arab regimes with its unbridled support. This, despite the fact that the ruling elites in Iraq, Morocco, Tunisia, Algeria, Kuwait, Bahrain, Saudi Arabia and Egypt do not know the meaning of Western-touted values such as human rights or democracy.[82]

It follows that the West is not genuinely committed to the Universal Declaration of Human rights or to the United Nations Charter, which enshrine these values. The Western portrayal of Hizbu'llah as 'terrorist'[83] further corroborates this point, insofar as these covenants stipulate the right of all nations to liberate their land from foreign occupation.[84]

The flagrant disregard of this universal right is ascribed in particular to the US because of its persistent attempts to delegitimise Hizbu'llah's right to resist the Israeli occupation. By classifying the party as a terrorist organisation in its 'Patterns of Global Terrorism Report', which is formulated annually by the State Department, the US seeks to 'mislead public opinion'.[85] This attempt to distort Hizbu'llah's image is also evident in the US government's habitual practice of pointing the finger at the party when any act of terrorism occurs in the world. One such example was the Oklahoma City bombing of 1995, which was initially blamed on Hizbu'llah, but which was actually the work of American citizens.[86]

Based on these practices, Hizbu'llah concludes that the US' criteria for terrorism are the rejection of its domination and the refusal to succumb to Israel. This accounts for its refusal to categorise undemocratic and repressive Arab regimes, which happen to be pro-Western and lenient towards Israel, as terrorist states. Servility to America therefore emerges as the sole criterion by which states and organisations are judged.[87] In this way, 'the brute is made to appear innocent and the victim is made to appear brutal',[88] a perversion of the truth which constitutes an act of 'political and intellectual terrorism' for Hizbu'llah.[89] Coupled with its responsibility for 'the largest quantity of international crises and problems',[90] the US is thereby designated as the 'greatest terrorist state in the world', whose practice and sponsorship of terrorism even surpasses that of Israel.[91]

In effect, the West is reviled not only for employing double standards, but also for not having any standards or values at all. Not even the Pope escapes Hizbu'llah's vituperation in this regard, for he too is perceived as a 'tool of American imperialism' who acts more like 'an intelligence element' than 'someone who serves the Church'.[92] This conceptualisation of the Vatican closely mirrors the opprobrium Khumayni heaps on the Pope for being indifferent to the 'state of the oppressed'.[93] Implicit in both Hizbu'llah's and Khumayni's characterisations of the Pope is the notion of sancti-moniousness. While Khumayni refrains from directly accusing the Pope of hypocrisy, it is implied in his assertion that 'the Pope should show some concern for the honour of Christendom'.[94] Hizbu'llah spells out this notion more explicitly when it affirms that it would have 'liked to see the Pope following the path of Jesus and the ancient monks who were far removed from politics and serving the tyrants of the earth'.[95]

This observation is significant in that it shows that Hizbu'llah does not censure the West for being Christian, but for professing to be Christian. Accordingly, the confrontation with Western civilisation is not a confrontation with Christianity as a religion, but with the West as a cultural collectivity which has chosen to renounce Christianity.

Views on Political Violence as a Means of Confronting the West

In addition to Hizbu'llah's discernment of the Western conspiracy against Islam and the perceived Western-Israeli nexus, both the nature and extent of Hizbu'llah's anti-Westernism can be gauged by examining its views on the practice of terrorism and political violence as a means of confronting the West. The following analysis will focus on the party's views on the Western hostage crisis in Lebanon, the suicide attack on the US Marines' compound in October 1983, which took the lives of 241 servicemen, and other instances of political violence directed against Western targets both inside and outside Lebanon.

Although no concrete evidence has yet transpired which directly incriminates Hizbu'llah in the taking of hostages, this has not prevented many observers of contemporary Islamic movements from finding the party culpable for the abduction of over 87, mainly Western, foreigners.[96] In arriving at this conclusion, they have deemed it sufficient to declare Islamic Jihad, one of the groups that claimed responsibility for some of the kidnappings, an affiliate organisation of Hizbu'llah, based on pure speculation. The sole exception to this conventional wisdom has been journalist Hala Jaber who contends that Islamic Jihad was more of a 'phantom' who took credit for the kidnappings than a real organisation.[97]

While Hizbu'llah does not depict Islamic Jihad as a phantom, it does deny any organisational link to it.[98] Fayyad believes that the reason the West considers the two organisations to be one lies in the single social milieu they share and the similar slogans and principles they espouse, especially those that relate to the US.[99] Hizbu'llah has consistently denied any responsibility for the kidnappings,[100] though it does admit that other Islamic groups such as Islamic Jihad, the Revolutionary Justice Organisation and the Oppressed of the Earth were behind them.[101] The party even claims to have intervened on behalf of the hostages so as to secure their release.[102] As articulated by Husayn al-Mussawi: 'We would encourage someone [who held the hostages] through a speech, or other means of exhortation, that it was in our interest for this hostage to be released.'[103]

Jaber sees much truth in these repeated denials of involvement. Like Fayyad, she refers to the 'common ideology' shared by Hizbu'llah and the kidnappers, and even affirms that the party permitted them to operate in areas under its control. However, she does not believe that these factors alone implicate Hizbu'llah in the hostage crisis.[104] According to Jaber, most of the kidnappings were actually masterminded by Iran and executed by individuals such as 'Imad Mughniyeh,[105] whose agenda coincided with the Islamic Republic's, but who were organisationally distinct from Hizbu'llah. These individuals were afforded military training by the Islamic Revolutionary Guards and were accorded a number of privileges that were not granted to Hizbu'llah,[106] which upon closer inspection was but one of the Guards' proteges in Lebanon.[107]

Jaber's exclusive reliance upon primary sources of information, including former kidnappers and Western hostages, Lebanese security officials and Hizbu'llah specialists, makes it very difficult to simply discount her theory. It also makes it even harder to accept the conclusions of others, such as Magnus Ranstorp, whose entire work is based on interviews with Israeli government, security and intelligence sources. Needless to say, Israeli sources are not the most objective of observers, nor are they likely to depict Hizbu'llah as anything other than a terrorist organisation.

But since Hizbu'llah's involvement in the hostage crisis is beyond the scope of this book, no attempt will be made to refute the torrent of accusations that directly implicate the party in the series of kidnappings. As topically relevant as the investigation into Hizbu'llah's involvement in the hostage taking, is the analysis of the party's deliberation of violence as a means of confronting the West. Accordingly, the following discussion will scrutinise the many statements made by party officials regarding hostage-taking, irrespective of Hizbu'llah's actual culpability for the affair.

As maintained by Ra'id, although the party was not responsible for the kidnappings, it was engaged in a lengthy debate over whether or not it should legitimise and justify such activities.[108] But despite Ra'id's claim that this debate was never resolved, the views of several party officials that were expressed after the early stages of the hostage crisis appear to be fairly consistent in their ambivalence towards the issue.

In principle, Hizbu'llah is unequivocally opposed to hostage-taking on both moral and religious grounds. From the Islamic viewpoint, hostage taking is proscribed insofar as it is deemed unlawful 'to encroach upon the freedom of an individual who has not harmed you in any way'.[109] Moreover, Islam teaches that 'the honour of the aim lies in the honour of the means' and so, even if the ultimate end of kidnapping is a noble one, the act cannot be granted full legitimacy.[110] Thus, even though the party sympathised with the objectives of the kidnappers, it could not lend its approval to kidnapping as a means of realising those objectives, especially since its support for such means would have meant that it was sanctioning an act that it was not willing to engage in.[111]

Not only does the party disavow the concept of kidnapping, it upholds the principle that hostage-taking is an indictable offense. In the opinion of Fnaysh, individuals who seize other civilians for political purposes ought to be punished by the relevant states.[112] Thus, Hizbu'llah claims that it has 'no objection' to the Lebanese parliament's ratification of the US-sponsored Hostage Convention, whose signatories pledge to fight hostage-taking.[113]

But Hizbu'llah's views on hostage-taking are not so clear-cut. While the party does not approve of kidnapping in principle, it is not willing to condemn the practice either. As expounded by Fnaysh: 'We do not condemn the kidnappings because we have a problem with the West, and especially with the Americans who do not condemn Israel's acts against our people. So why should we serve them politically by condemning the kidnappings?'[114] This view is echoed by Qasim who asserts that the party's non-committal position stems from its belief that a condemnation of the kidnappings would only serve the interests of 'the arrogant' (the US and Israel).[115]

It also stems from the fact that Hizbu'llah considers the kidnapping of Westerners to be justifiable. For Hizbu'llah, kidnapping may not have been an honourable means, but it certainly was vindicable. Thus, although the practice of hostage-taking could not be accorded legitimacy or support, it could be justified in relative moral terms. In the case of suspected spies, such as Lieutenant-Colonel William Higgins, a US Marine Corps officer and deputy commander of the United Nations Truce Supervision Organisation (UNTSO) in the South, providing a justification for their seizure posed no moral dilemma for Hizbu'llah. Both Husayn al-Mussawi and Subhi al-Tufayli not only justified, but fully supported the capture of such individuals.[116]

What was more morally problematic, however, was the construction of a justification for the kidnapping of Westerners who were not directly accused of espionage. While the party does not state this explicitly, part of its rationale for the capture of such individuals lies in the assumption that any Westerner in Lebanon could be a spy, even in the absence of any concrete evidence to prove such a supposition.

In his analysis of one American film which deals with the kidnapping of a doctor, the commentator of the *Poison and Honey* television programme repeatedly warns of the duplicitous nature of Westerners who are affiliated with non-governmental social and humanitarian organisations operating in the Arab and Islamic world. Based on the presumption that most of them are actually spies, he insinuates in one of his remonstrations against the film that kidnapping them is a justifiable offence. For him, the main fault in the film lay not in its depiction of the Arabs as kidnappers, but in its portrayal of them as 'human traders'. Had the film shown that the doctor was kidnapped 'so that they could interrogate her to ascertain that she was on a political and intelligence mission, we would have said that this film was on the sound path'.[117]

But it is not this unproven assumption which the party publicly cites as a justification for the hostage-taking. The party's customary vindication of the kidnappings is founded on the premise that the hostages were innocent. Had this not been the central assumption, it would not have felt compelled to create 'moral logics' in order to justify the kidnappings.[118] It also would not have compared the taking of hostages to the consumption of alcohol, as Husayn al-Mussawi does when he states that 'alcohol is forbidden under Islam, but when it is a medicine you are allowed to take as much as you need for recovery'.[119]

Hostage-taking was therefore perceived as something 'forbidden', which nonetheless had to be resorted to under certain 'extenuating circumstances'.[120] Accordingly, Hizbu'llah does not believe that the kidnappings should be viewed in abstraction but in their proper context, with an eye towards the 'causes' which provoked them rather than the 'consequences' they generated.[121]

First of these causes was the 'oppressive environment' created by the West, and especially the US.[122] According to Qasim's moral construction, the West's support for Israel and its general regional policy were conducive to the hostage crisis insofar as people felt they had no other means available to them with which to fight.[123] Specifically, the US Marines' shelling of the Shuf, the French bombing of Ba'albakk, and the West's support for the despised Amin Gemayel regime, are cited by Husayn al-Mussawi as factors which contributed to the 'resort' to kidnapping by Shi'ite Islamist groups.[124]

That the Western military presence was highly conducive to such measures, is further evidenced by Ra'id's claim that the Algerian Islamists had no excuse for kidnapping French civilians as the Lebanese Islamists did, since France no longer had a military presence in Algeria. The French were 'fighting the Algerians politically' – insofar as they were partly responsible for the cancellation of the elections that the FIS were poised to win – but this did not warrant kidnapping them.[125] The Lebanese, by contrast, were being fought both politically and militarily by both the French and the Americans which thereby rendered the kidnapping of French and American citizens justifiable.

Another factor that was conducive to the kidnappings was the disappearance of hundreds of Lebanese Islamists between 1982 and 1983, including Qasim, who were believed to have been kidnapped and tortured by Maronite militias as well as Israeli forces. Since the West supported the Gemayel regime and Israel, the natural targets for retaliation were Western civilians.[126] The kidnappings were thus seen as instrumental in the release of Shi'ite hostages, as well as Shi'ite prisoners in Israeli jails.

From this relative moral perspective, hostage-taking was perceived as a form of 'self-defence' which was fully 'understood' by Hizbu'llah.[127] So understandable was the resort to hostage-taking, that 'Abbas al-Mussawi urged the kidnappers to sever any dialogue they may have had with concerned Western states so as to deprive the US and Israel of an excuse for 'unlawfully detaining innocent Lebanese clerics and Muslims generally'.[128]

Thus, to the extent that the US, Israel and the Gemayel regime were viewed as one 'side', the use of violence against any one was considered a blow to the other. By harming the West, the kidnappers were contributing to the eviction of Israel, and in turn, to the downfall of the Gemayel regime.[129] To all intents and purposes, the ends did seem to somewhat justify the means.

In the case of the bombing of the Marines' barracks, the ends are not merely seen as justifying the means, but the means itself are vociferously applauded, even though the party has always denied any responsibility for the attack. [130]According to Hizbu'llah's moral logic, the killing of American soldiers was far easier to justify and support than the capture of innocent civilians. Moreover, while the Western hostages were not the direct targets of Hizbu'llah's or the kidnappers' wrath, the American soldiers were. In Hizbu'llah's view, the very presence of the Marines in Lebanon warranted such an act of violence, in that 'it was not an innocent presence' but 'a military expedition'.[131] Although the purported aim of the Marines, and the Multi-National Forces (MNF) of which they were a part, was to supervise the departure of the PLO in August 1982, they overstepped the boundaries of this supposedly neutral role. By shelling Druze and Syrian targets in defence of the Maronites, the Marines reduced their status to that of 'the international militia of Lebanon'.[132]

Moreover, the US' sponsorship of the much detested 17 May Agreement, which was clearly to Israel's benefit, further made the Marines the subject of Shi'ite execration.[133] Hizbu'llah therefore perceived the Marines as a force that came to bolster the pro-Israeli Gemayel government and 'to consolidate Israel's hegemony over Lebanon', thereby rendering them indistinguishable from the Israeli forces.[134] By shelling the Marines' base, the perpetrators were contributing not only to the US' withdrawal from Lebanon, but also to the 'weakening' and eventual withdrawal of Israel.[135] Accordingly, Nasru'llah 'blesses' the operation and 'congratulates' those who executed it,[136] while Husayn al-Mussawi extols the attack to such an extent that he regards it as 'immoral' to unjustly take credit[137] for such a 'glorious' act.[138]

Although the killing of 63 people in the American embassy bomb blast, a few months before the Marines' attack, is not described in such terms, it is designated as the 'first punishment' for the US in Hizbu'llah's Open Letter. Apart from this public statement, there is very little else on the issue. Still, one could speculate that justifying such an act would not be morally problematic for Hizbu'llah, considering that the targets of the attack were local and American CIA agents who were in the building at the time of the blast. Since the majority of those killed were considered to be American spies, who are abhorred even more than American politicians, the attack would be morally equivalent to the bombing of the Marines. This is substantiated to some extent by the designation of the attack on the Marines as the 'second punishment' in the party's Open Letter.[139]

However, Hizbu'llah draws the line at the killing of Western civilians, which it strongly condemns. In the aftermath of the massacre, committed by the Islamic Group, of 58 mainly Western tourists at the Temple of Hatshepsut in Luxor, Egypt, in November 1997, Hizbu'llah described the assault as 'bloody and terrible'.[140] So appalled was Hizbu'llah with the Islamic Group that it accused it of being 'an instrument which is utilised by the *umma*'s real enemies [i.e. Israel]'.[141] In a similar vein, the party 'expressed regret' for the killing of 18 Greek tourists in Cairo in April 1996, at the hands of the Islamic Group.[142] Furthermore, the party described the killing of seven Trappist French monks in Algeria in the same month of that year, by the GIA (Armed Islamic Group), as 'deplorable and horrible'.[143]

Hizbu'llah therefore makes three clear distinctions. First is the distinction between ordinary civilians who are considered innocent of any crime such as espionage – though there is always the tacit suspicion that they may not be – and military and intelligence personnel who are guilty of abetting Israel and of generally oppressing the Muslims.

Second is the distinction between the kidnapping and the killing of civilians. Although the provision of a rationale for hostage-taking does not pose an acute moral dilemma for Hizbu'llah, the killing of Western civilians clearly does. With kidnapping, there is a strong possibility of the hostage's release, especially since hostage-taking is a purposive act that requires that the hostage be kept alive in order to use him as a pawn with which concessions from a particular state can be obtained. Killing, on the other hand, is an irrevocable crime with no purposive end except to threaten and terrorise the inhabitants of offending states.

The innocence of the victims of arbitrary killings further distinguishes the act from kidnapping. While the innocence of the hostages remains in question simply because their decision to work and reside in Lebanon is considered suspect, the underlying motives of tourists are not usually questioned.

A third distinction the party makes is between the use of violence to fight Western military targets within Lebanon and its use on

Western soil. Though this distinction is not clearly expressed, it reveals itself in Husayn al-Mussawi's statement on the attack on the Marines: 'It was not they who went to New York or Washington. New York and Washington came to them, and the act occurred in Beirut not in the US.'[144] What can be inferred from this assertion is that, while the killing of American soldiers in Lebanon is considered a commendable act on account of their unwanted presence and intervention in Lebanon, the killing of American soldiers on their own turf is not.

In light of the party's disapproval of the use of violence on Western territory and the abhorrence it displays towards the killing of Western civilians, the accusation that Hizbu'llah masterminded a series of terrorist bombings in Paris in 1986 becomes difficult to swallow.[145] Aside from the lack of any concrete evidence to substantiate such an accusation, it would be ideologically inconsistent for Hizbu'llah to denounce the killing of Western tourists in Egypt and French monks in Algeria, if only a few years earlier it had engaged in a lengthy terrorist campaign that cost several French lives and injured over 300 French civilians.

Moral considerations apart, Hizbu'llah views the killing of Western civilians as inimical to Islamic interests. Not only do such acts tarnish the reputation of Islam,[146] but they further complicate issues, and most importantly, 'distract international and Arab public opinion from the large-scale aggression and terrorist massacres committed by Israel'.[147] Instead of targeting Westerners, Islamic groups should use their arms to liberate Jerusalem and confront the *umma*'s 'main enemy', Israel.[148] In effect, Hizbu'llah's liberation priority would not have been served by the party's involvement in the killing of innocent French civilians.

The Rejection of Western Culture

Thus far, the exposition of Hizbu'llah's antagonistic stand towards the West has revolved around political issues. But if Western foreign policy were the sole determinant of the party's anti-Westernism, then the struggle against the West would be a purely ideological one, which is clearly not the case. Not only does this assertion stem from the declarations of Hizbu'llah officials cited previously, but from the party's extensive critique of Western culture and its staunch resistance to its infiltration of Arab and Islamic society – a rejection of Western cultural norms and values, which necessarily translates itself into a civilisational confrontation.

The cornerstone of Hizbu'llah's repudiation of Western culture is its abomination of the materialist doctrine,[149] which underlies the West's 'brutal capitalism'.[150] As an 'intellectual and philosophical distortion',[151] Western capitalism cannot ensure the right balance between 'human nature and the public interest', and by extension, cannot achieve social justice.[152] Moreover, its inherent defectiveness as a socio-political system is evinced by its responsibility for all the world's 'crises, hunger, poverty, pollution, corruption and wars'.[153] Modern materialism is therefore perceived as the 'new Pharaoh', which seeks to 'enslave man and especially the poor and oppressed'.[154] As such, it is the root cause of the Western drive to subjugate the oppressed world, which in turn, has fallen prey to its corrupting influence, thereby rendering it a slave to consumerism.

The identification of modern materialism with the West leads to the ineluctable conclusion that Hizbu'llah rejects Western culture. Further intensifying this rejection is the West's desire to spread its civilisation throughout the entire world,[155] and more specifically, its attempt to impose its way of life and thinking on the region's people by means of its educational institutions and media.[156] In Hizbu'llah's lexicon, it is a 'cultural invasion'[157] which seeks to disseminate Western values and norms in the Muslim world, based on the premise that its culture is superior to all others.

As noted by one Hizbu'llah commentator, the West 'holds all other nations in contempt', even the ex-Soviet Union which was its scientific and technological peer. If this is how such a powerful nation is perceived, then 'where does that leave us?' who clearly are no scientific and technological match for the West.[158] Another media specialist, affiliated to Hizbu'llah, observes that the Western media's portrayal of the West as the epitome of order, and its co-extensive depiction of Third World nations as the epitome of disorder, is indicative of its sense of *noblesse oblige* towards the Third World peoples.[159]

More menacing than the West's perception of the Arabs and Muslims is the latter's self-deprecation as a civilisation, which is evident from their emulation of Western culture, or to borrow the term coined by Jalal al-e Ahmad, their 'Westoxification' (*Gharbzadagi*).[160] The Arabs and Muslims have come to identify themselves with 'Western living patterns, which are quite remote from our Islamic and Eastern values and culture'[161] and which consequently 'damage our people's thoughts and capabilities'.[162] So firmly implanted in the Arabs' and Muslims' psyche has their inferiority complex vis-à-vis the West become, that the Western cultural invasion has succeeded in impacting on 'all aspects of our lives'.[163]

But rather than progress, the Muslims have only become more 'backward' as a result of this cultural assault.[164] By aping the West, the once 'pure society'[165] that typified the region's people has become afflicted with the same social ills as Western society. Amongst these is the 'moral dissolution', 'familial disintegration'[166] and 'exploitation of women', insofar as they are treated as 'commodities',[167] that is characteristic of Western society.

Not only has the Western 'academic assault' been conducive to this general state of Muslim 'weakness',[168] but the Western media have also greatly contributed to it through the promotion of Western culture and Israeli interests, as well as the defamation of Islam. For these reasons, the Western media 'invasion' is considered a 'cultural and moral danger' from which 'people should protect themselves'.[169]

In particular, it is the Zionists' domination of the American film industry, and to a lesser extent the British media, which underlies the great threat posed by the Western media to Arab and Islamic culture. As discerned by Hizbu'llah's media specialist, the Zionists' control of major US film production companies, such as MGM, Paramount, Columbia, Warner Brothers and United Artists, serves to promote the advancement of Jews.[170] Furthermore, the vast media empires owned by Britons perceived to be Zionists such as Rupert Murdoch (of Australian origin) and Robert Maxwell, are also cited by this Hizbu'llah media expert as evidence of the Zionist infiltration of the British media.[171]

Hizbu'llah conceives of the Western media as a 'powerful and oppressive weapon in the hands of the enemy', through which the Israeli depicts himself as an innocent and oppressed survivor of the Nazi era.[172] It is precisely this 'exploitation' of the Holocaust, which the party views with contempt. The Jews use the Holocaust as 'a means of troubling the West's, especially Europe's, conscience because when the Holocaust occurred, the West did nothing to help the Jews'.[173] The West is thereby impelled to garner sympathy for the Jewish people through its media, which in turn, constantly dwell on the theme of the Holocaust. Presumably, Hizbu'llah fears the cumulative effect this perceived overemphasis on the Holocaust might have on the Arab and Muslim psyche.

However, Hizbu'llah's excoriation of the Western media does not only stem from its domination by Zionists or Jews. The party also views the media as an instrument used by the West to propagate its culture throughout the world, and as a propaganda tool which denigrates other cultures while accentuating the superiority of its own. While this view applies to the Western media generally, it relates to the American media specifically.

The US' self-characterisation as a 'paradise for all the inhabitants of the world', where all Third World cultures aspire to emigrate to,[174] particularly infuriates Hizbu'llah which views American culture and society in completely antithetical terms. American films invariably portray the US as the 'mother of freedom', who emancipates the poor and oppressed,[175] the 'dove of peace' and the archetype of racial harmony where equal opportunities abound.[176] Through a process of subliminal indoctrination, these notions have become deeply ingrained in the minds of viewers, to the extent that the entire world has come to believe them.

Thus, through a process of overlooking, and at times fabricating, American history, the American media distort reality which is passed off as the truth. So effective is this propaganda, that everyone applauds the American 'hero' for killing the Native American, although it is the latter who is the true victim.[177] Moreover, the prestigious occupations and public posts accorded to black actors in American films give people the mistaken impression that racial discrimination is non-existent in the US, when in actuality, 'American history is replete with instances of racial discrimination.'[178] Aside from the racial segregation which characterised American society until the mid-twentieth century,[179] the enslavement and inhumane treatment of black people who were brought into America by means of the slave trade attests to the essentially racist nature of American society.[180]

Parallel to the distortion of American reality is the media's distortion of Islam. As maintained by Hizbu'llah, the 'great falsification'[181] and 'fabrication of lies'[182] practised by the Western media endeavour to 'distort our society and religion'.[183] By putting 'our religion, history, heritage and customs' under the microscope[184] and 'emphasising and exaggerating our mistakes',[185] the West attempts to tarnish the image of Islam. So staunchly does the party uphold this conviction that it has produced a television series, titled *Poison and Honey*, which devotes itself to analysing the propaganda content of Western films in order to uncover and underline to viewers the insidious Western attempt to distort Islam.

In fact, the party perceives the Western misrepresentation of Islam as the central preoccupation of the West.[186] Presumably, it is also perceived as the latest in a series of preoccupations with other cultures. Just as the plethora of 'Western' films reflected the US' fixation with the Native Americans,[187] and the numerous anti-Soviet films were symptomatic of the US' 'Cold War' with the Soviet Union,[188] the many films which portray the Arabs and Muslims in a negative light today are also manifestations of the West's current preoccupation with Islam. What is more, just as these films played a cardinal role in the 'elimination' and 'defeat' of the Native Americans[189] and the disintegration of the Soviet Union,[190] their purpose now is to 'erase us'.[191]

In effect, the West is conceived as a counter-civilisation, which not only 'confronts Islamic civilisation',[192] but seeks to efface or 'melt' Islamic culture and identity.[193] Therefore, the party's struggle with the West is justified as a defence of 'our religion, existence and dignity'.[194] The addition of this existential element further exhibits the civilisational dimension of the struggle between Hizbu'llah and the West, and more generally, the confrontation between Islamic and Western civilisations.

The Struggle with the West as a Civilisational Dispute

However, Hizbu'llah does not call for the eradication of Western society, nor does it deny the legitimacy of Western states as it does that of Israel. To the extent that the party accuses the West of seeking to uproot the Islamic identity, there can be no denying that there is an existential element in Hizbu'llah's struggle with the Western world. But for a civilisational struggle to be truly existential, both civilisations must aspire to annihilate the existence of the other. Although the customary burning of the American flag by Hizbu'llah adherents could be construed as an act that symbolises the party's aspiration to annihilate American state and society, the party contends that it is not an existential expression of hostility directed at the American people, but 'an expression of condemnation of the American administration's policies'.[195]

The party therefore confines its hostility to the US government's perceived bias towards Israel, and does not extend it to the American people,[196] who are presumably neither held responsible for their government's 'oppressive' policies, nor for the 'cultural invasion' launched by their media and educational institutions. Therefore, the existential nature of the West's struggle against Islam on the cultural and political levels does not translate itself into an existential confrontation between the Western and Islamic civilisations. For that reason, it is not comparable to the existential conflict with Israel in any way.

Moreover, insofar as the liberation of Jerusalem and the eradication of Israel remain strategic (albeit unrealistic) goals for Hizbu'llah, the existential struggle with Israel necessarily entails the use of violence. On the other hand, violence is perceived as a last resort in the party's resistance to the West's political hegemony, and consequently cannot be classified as an existential struggle.

As a non-existential struggle, dialogue and reconciliation with the West are very real possibilities for Hizbu'llah. Thus, although the Rushdie affair is cited as an instance of the West's refusal to hold a dialogue with others,[197] the very fact that the West is rebuked by the party for not wanting a dialogue with Islam implies that dialogue between cultures is a valued goal for Hizbu'llah. This inference is corroborated by Qasim's approval of Iranian President Khatami's desire to hold a dialogue with the American people. In Qasim's opinion, dialogue should occur among all the world's nations, since 'interaction with different cultures is good'.[198] The high value placed on dialogue is more clearly expressed by another Hizbu'llah official who discloses the party's desire to hold a direct dialogue with the American people.[199]

Another indication of the party's desire to reconcile with the American people, and Western society generally, lies in its repeated intention to project a better image of itself to the American people and to the West[200] by 'waging a campaign to show them that the Resistance is not terrorist'.[201] Hizbu'llah's endeavour to erase the damage inflicted upon it by 'American intelligence and media exaggeration',[202] confirms the above stated assumption that the party's non-adversarial position towards the American people stems from its perception of them as completely detached from the policies of their government and the malevolent intent of their national media.

Although this desire to reconcile with the West as a whole, and the American people specifically, does not extend to the American state, Hizbu'llah does not invalidate its existence as it does in the case of Israel. Furthermore, the party does not invalidate the existence of Western-inspired, international organisations such as the United Nations. While such organisations are subject to Hizbu'llah's condemnation – on account of their submission to Israeli and American interests – their declared purposes and values are endorsed by the party, as demonstrated by Hizbu'llah's frequent references to international laws, conventions and charters in justifying its right to resist the Israeli occupation.[203]

From these observations, it emerges that the struggle between Hizbu'llah (or Islam) and the West is not an existential one. It should also be stressed that the struggle between the two should not be characterised as a civilisational 'conflict' or '*khilaf*', as Samuel Huntington has chosen to do,[204] but as a civilisational 'dispute' or '*ikhtilaf*'.[205] For Fayyad, the distinction between the two terms is a crucial one insofar as the former term denotes civilisational irreconcilability whereas the latter term implies the possibility of civilisational co-existence and harmony.[206]

The fact that this struggle is a dispute rather than a conflict is evident in the party's improved relations with the West, with particular reference to Europe. Hizbu'llah's rapprochement with Europe is epitomised by the radical change in its stand towards France. In contrast to Hizbu'llah's animosity towards the François Mitterrand government, which ordered French troops into Lebanon in support of the detested Gemayel regime, the government presided by Jacques Chirac is viewed favourably by the party.[207] This perspective is due to the new administration's 'understanding of the Lebanese people's suffering in the face of the Israeli occupation',[208] and its generally 'balanced' role which serves to countervail the US' hegemony over the region.[209]

As conceived by Meri', the party's rapprochement with France is demonstrative of its willingness to reconcile with any Western state that changes its regional policy. Viewed from this angle, the party could even reconcile with the execrated US administration if the latter chose to adopt a more impartial stand towards the Arabs and Muslims.[210] Thus, although Hizbu'llah's struggle with the US, and the West in general, is not confined to the political realm but is essentially civilisational, stripped of its political content, the struggle between the two could be reduced from a civilisational dispute to a civilisational disagreement.

In addition, Fayyad's categorisation of Hizbu'llah's confrontation with the West as a dispute is not only confirmed by the party's willingness to conduct civilisational dialogue and improve political relations with the West, but also by the fact that it does not reject all Western cultural values and norms. As expounded in a detailed critique of Western culture published by Hizbu'llah's Student Mobilisation Unit, 'Western proposals must be studied in depth' by the Muslim student so that he will be able to extract the 'truths' they contain while 'refuting their subjective assumptions'.[211] Since there is an acknowledgement of the existence of 'truths', it follows that there are certain aspects of Western culture that Hizbu'llah deems worthy of emulation.

Qasim drives this point home when he asserts that no culture or civilisation can be completely accepted or rejected, not even American culture which has 'positive, as well as negative, elements'.[212] One such element is the high value Americans place on the freedom of expression, notwithstanding the fact that they do not apply this value to other nations.[213] Another value worthy of emulation is the social equality that characterises Western society,[214] which according to Hizbu'llah parliamentarian 'Ammar al-Mussawi, was the product of the French Revolution which championed the values of 'justice and liberty' and 'opposed oppression'.[215]

As well as selectively accepting certain Western values, the party admires Western science and knowledge and appreciates Western educational institutions. Even though the West is accused of using its schools and universities as mediums through which Arab and Muslim culture can be infiltrated and Western values and norms propagated, the party views the Western educational system as superior to all other educational systems in the contemporary Arab and Muslim world.[216] Thus, although the overwhelming majority of party members have been educated in non-Western secular educational institutions, a small minority have attended Western universities in Lebanon, such as the American University of Beirut (AUB).

But this small proportion only accounts for Hizbu'llah's organisational members. A much larger number of party sympathisers affiliated with Hizbu'llah's Student Mobilisation Unit, many of whom are recipients of Hizbu'llah's educational grants, attend the AUB and the Lebanese American University. So pervasive is their presence on the university campus that they even have their own party representatives on the student councils.

In addition, several party officials have pursued their postgraduate studies at universities in the UK, France and Italy.[217] Rima Fakhri (herself an AUB graduate), a leading official in Hizbu'llah's Women's Association, even considers the US one possible venue for her children's higher education.[218]

For some, these disclosures might appear to contradict Hizbu'llah's belief in the surreptitious purpose and somewhat conspiratorial nature of Western educational institutions. However, one could quite confidently postulate that, although the party does fear the ulterior motives of Western schools and universities, it is not averse to using them to counter the Western monopoly on science and knowledge.[219] On the basis of the above-cited admonition to the Muslim student to discern between the false and true assumptions of Western knowledge, one could further speculate that Hizbu'llah believes in the ability of the Muslim student to remain impervious to the Western endeavour to impose its way of life and values on the entire world.

The underlying theme of both assumptions is that erudition and modernity are as valued by Hizbu'llah as they are by the West, to the extent that the party is willing to utilise the very institutions it denounces in order to develop the academic potential and scientific and technological know-how of Islamic society.[220] This goal is clearly articulated in an *al-'Ahd* article, in which the party decries the dearth of Muslim scholars, doctors, scientific researchers and economic experts.

The party's new policy of encouraging (and presumably, financing) its rank-and-file members with high-school degrees to pursue a higher education, is a reflection of this concern for academic and scientific advancement, as is the high number of university-educated high-ranking party officials. Out of the nine party officials interviewed by this author, all nine had received a secular university education, including the two clerics. Although both Shaykhs Na'im Qasim and Husayn al-Mussawi had attended religious seminaries, they had degrees in chemistry and mathematics, respectively.[221] In fact, the conjunction of secular and religious higher education is not an exclusive feature of Hizbu'llah, but is common to other Islamic movements, as Emile Sahliyeh astutely observes.[222]

By extension, the embrace of modernity in general is not unique to Hizbu'llah but is shared by many Islamic movements. In his study of the Islamic Salvation Front (FIS) in Algeria, John P. Entelis observes that 'political Islam is fundamentally modern' in that it employs 'modern ways' – i.e. modern education, modern technology, modern science, modern management and modern government – to rectify the social, political and economic problems that plague society.[223] Similarly, William E. Shepard classifies Islamic movements which adopt modern material technology, accept modern institutions such as parliaments and political parties, and believe in 'progress', as being essentially 'modern'.[224]

Bearing these criteria of modernity in mind, it becomes apparent that Hizbu'llah typifies the Islamic party that espouses modernity. In addition to its pursuit of academic and scientific development by means of modern, and even Western, educational institutions, and its acceptance of modern political institutions (to be discussed in greater detail in the following chapter), the party's self-description as the bearer of the 'banner of change',[225] or in other words a 'progressive' party, renders it favourably disposed towards modern technology. This can be deduced from its utilisation of modern weaponry and communications, and its embrace of high technology.

Like many other Islamic movements, Hizbu'llah has its own Internet website, as well as one for the Islamic Resistance and one for its television station, al-Manar. What is more, the party is a strong advocate of satellite television, as evinced by its criticism of the Hariri government's decision to ban political broadcasts on satellite television.[226] This is also demonstrated by its call for the creation of a Lebanese satellite television station that would broadcast programmes in Hebrew as part of its psychological warfare against Israel.[227]

6   The Resistance to the Israeli Occupation of South Lebanon

As Hizbu'llah's initial *raison d'être*, its resistance to the Israeli occupation of South Lebanon and the West Biqa' constitutes the very backbone of its intellectual structure. It is the one pillar of Hizbu'llah's political thought that is not amenable to any form of temporisation or accommodation to reality, not only on account of the party's inbred abomination of Zionism, but also by virtue of the pure logic of armed resistance, as opposed to non-violent means of confrontation. The invariable nature of Hizbu'llah's resistance is also a function of the party's commitment to fulfil its religious legal obligation (*wajib shari'*) to wage a defensive *jihad*, in the cause of God.

The Resistance Priority

Hizbu'llah defines itself first and foremost as a '*jihadi* movement'[1] or a 'party of the resistance'[2] whose paramount function is the liberation of Lebanese territory from Israeli occupation by means of armed resistance. It is a role which represents 'the core of Hizbu'llah's political and organisational concerns', and which therefore constitutes its 'fixed and invariable dossier' (*al-malaf al-thabit*).[3] Accordingly, the party depicts its resistance to Israel as 'the priority of all priorities',[4] and the 'red line which cannot be crossed'.[5]

The clearest indication of the party's prioritisation of the resistance lies in its dealings with Lebanese state and society. From its very inception, Hizbu'llah has continuously striven to show that the attainment of political power is secondary to its goal of liberating the occupied zone. At the height of the civil war, Nasru'llah announced that Hizbu'llah was 'ready to leave the domestic scene', if it could be 'left' to confront Israel.[6] The implication was that the perceived onslaught by leftist groups against the party in 1985 was responsible for obstructing its resistance course, as opposed to any political designs Hizbu'llah was actually harbouring.

By extension, the party maintained in 1984 and 1985 that, although it was opposed to the sectarian distribution of the Lebanese political system, it had no interest in securing a larger slice of the sectarian pie[7] (as Amal was) 'at a time when the Israeli presence governs Lebanon'.[8] This, despite the fact that the abolition of political sectarianism is cited by the party in its 1992 electoral programme, as one of its two '*thawabit*' (fixed principles) – the other being the liberation of South Lebanon from the Israeli occupation.[9]

But this does not imply that the abolition of political sectarianism is now deemed as imperative as the party's resistance priority, nor does it indicate that the abolition of political sectarianism never was a real concern for the party. Hizbu'llah has consistently upheld the conviction that Israel represents the ultimate oppressor, and therefore perceives its resistance to Israel's occupation of Lebanese territory as a far more exigent need than the overthrow of an unjust political system. Thus, even if Hizbu'llah's electoral programme did state that the party's struggle against political sectarianism was one of its two fixed and invariable principles, this does not mean that it placed this struggle on an equal rank with its resistance priority.

Furthermore, even though the party claimed to have no interest in pursuing sectarian rights in the early 1980s, this had more to do with the circumstances than anything else. Prior to 1985, the Israeli occupation extended to all areas south of the Awali River in Sidon, in addition to other parts of Lebanon. So pervasive was Israel's presence in Lebanon until its gradual retreat to the 'security zone' in 1985, that its removal from Lebanese territory was Hizbu'llah's sole preoccupation. The pursuit of sectarian rights was not even contemplated against such a hostile milieu.

But this was not the only factor behind Hizbu'llah's initial negligence of the Shi'ite community's political rights and, by implication, the demoted status it accorded to the goal of overthrowing the oppressive political system. As a regime identified with Israeli interests, the Gemayel government was viewed as a lesser threat than the Israeli occupation. In fact, the very existence of the Gemayel regime was attributed to the Israeli occupation and therefore regarded as dependent upon it for its perpetuation. Compared to the 'serpent's head', which was represented by Israel, and its 'back' which was analogised with the US, the Lebanese government was viewed as the mere 'tail', which would be incapacitated once the head and back were truncated.[10]

In effect, the struggle against the Gemayel government and the sectarian political system which underpinned it was not just considered as secondary to the resistance to Israel's occupation, but as tertiary to it, for the 'serpent's back', the US, was judged to be a greater threat than its 'tail'.

This analogy with the serpent is also invoked in the party's Open Letter, though the 'tail' is equated with the Islamicisation of society rather than the government and political system. With reference to the US' attempt to distort Hizbu'llah's image by portraying it as a party whose sole concern is to enforce the censorship of morals in Lebanese society, the party belittles such acts as the 'blowing up [of] drinking, gambling and entertainment spots and other such activities,' as 'peripheral' ones that only serve to derail their perpe-trators from 'the tail and make them forget the head'.[11]

Fnaysh's admission that the resistance priority has overshadowed the campaign to 'restrict the moral dissolution of society',[12] is also demonstrative of this ordering of priorities. Thus, not only is the quest for sectarian equity and the subversion of the oppressive political system viewed as subordinate to the goal of liberating Lebanon from Israeli influence, the Islamicisation of society is viewed in the same way.

This prioritisation stands in sharp contrast to the Sunni Islamist perspective, which considers the struggle against Israel to be secondary to the deposition of indigenous secular governments and the institution of Islamic governments in their place. Seyyid Qutb is one proponent of this view insofar as the primary focus of his activities in the 1960s was Egyptian President Naser's purported 'paganism', rather than Israeli threat.[13] Even after Israel annexed the Sinai in 1967, Qutb's movement, the Egyptian Ikhwan al-Muslimin (Muslim Brotherhood), did not actively resist Israel's occupation of Egyptian territory.

According to the logic of 'Abd al-Salam Faraj, leader of the militant offshoot of the Muslim Brotherhood, the Egyptian Jihad Organisa-tion: 'To fight an enemy who is near is more important than to fight an enemy who is far ... We have to establish the rule of God's religion in our own country first, and to make the word of God supreme.'[14] The title of Faraj's work, 'The Neglected Duty', therefore refers to the misplaced focus by some Islamists on Israel, which Faraj believes, should have been directed instead towards the various 'apostate' regimes governing the Arab-Islamic world.[15] Only once society is sufficiently Islamicised and Islamic rule instituted, can the external enemy be confronted.[16]

Conversely, the logic behind the primacy Hizbu'llah placed on the resistance to Israel over confrontation with the Gemayel regime and the overthrow of the political system lay in the party's conviction that, 'if we want to give a people the right to choose [the political system it wants], it must first be free [from occupation] and only then can it choose'.[17] The external enemy must first be confronted, and only then can society choose Islamic, or any other, rule.

Together, these statements undermine the credibility of Magnus Ranstorp's and Chibli Mallat's accusations that Hizbu'llah's resistance to Israel is a 'tool' or 'instrument' for the party's legitimisation and popular expansion, and is therefore 'secondary' to the party's goal of establishing an Islamic state in Lebanon.[18] One of the basic flaws of this allegation lies in its presumption that the concept of the Islamic state is a concrete political goal for Hizbu'llah, when in fact, the notion of instituting Islamic rule in Lebanon has become too much of a Utopia to merit serious political deliberation or to be considered a realisable political goal by the party. It is highly unlikely that Hizbu'llah would subordinate its resistance activity to an ultimately unattainable goal.

But realisability is not the only consideration that renders resistance activity Hizbu'llah's priority. In addition to the party's aforementioned declarations on the supremacy of its resistance over the subversion of the political system and the Islamicisation of society, the precedence it accords to resistance activity is also evidenced by the fact that its principal dispute with Amal revolves around the primacy the latter places on the attainment of political power. As elaborated by Nasru'llah, 'Amal is more concerned with affairs related to power and the domestic agenda than it is with the resistance priority', which Hizbu'llah regards as a clear instance of misplaced priorities.[19]

The authenticity of Hizbu'llah's commitment to its resistance priority is also demonstrated by the party's political behaviour. As stated in Chapter 2, both in the parliamentary elections of 1992 and 1996, Hizbu'llah was pressured by Syria into an electoral alliance with Amal for the southern constituency, although in both cases it could have secured a greater number of parliamentary seats had it run on its own.

The rationale behind the party's decision to acquiesce to Syria's demands was that its resistance priority would have been seriously jeopardised had it disregarded Syria's wishes. It would still have been able to contest the elections – as it did in the Mount Lebanon constituency of Ba'bda where it refused to comply with Syria's desire for it to forge an alliance with the Maronite rightist leader, Eli Hubayka – but the Resistance would have been threatened in two ways.

In the first place, Syria would have directly obstructed resistance activities in the South. In the second place, had the electoral results not been in Amal's favour, there was the very real possibility that Amal would have dragged Hizbu'llah into a civil war in the South, which would have deflected its attention from its resistance priority, and reduced the party to a militia. Although the party does not state this rationale explicitly, it can be inferred from Fnaysh's admission that, had the party insisted on running on its own electoral list, 'the contest would have surpassed the political realm and threatened the security of the South'.[20]

In effect, Hizbu'llah sacrificed its political independence and integrity, and perhaps even its political size, for the sake of preserving its resistance to the Israeli occupation. Thus, there is much truth in Nasru'llah's claim that, rather than subordinate its resistance to its political activity, Hizbu'llah's political activity serves its resistance.[21]

So integral to Hizbu'llah's political thought is the resistance priority, that both the military and political wings of the party are identified with each other, as Husayn al-Mussawi's statement demonstrates: 'The Resistance is Hizbu'llah and Hizbu'llah is the Resistance.'[22] Nasru'llah echoes this view when he avers that, although the resistance is composed of groups other than Hizbu'llah – with reference to the occasional operations staged by Amal and various leftists groups – 'all of Hizbu'llah is a Resistance'.[23] It is in light of this conceptual symbiosis that Hizbu'llah fervidly denies that the Islamic Resistance can be disjointed from Hizbu'llah, the party.[24] Just as all members of Hizbu'llah's political and social institutions are considered a part of the Resistance, all Resistance fighters are considered 'part of the Hizbu'llah body'.[25]

As euphuistic as these statements sound, there is actually much truth in them. A close inspection of the party's internal dynamics reveals that it is virtually impossible to extricate the military from the political or vice versa. According to one party observer, Hizbu'llah truly is 'a resistance party' whose 'main body' is its army.[26]

The observer hints at the latent power wielded by Hizbu'llah's military wing, on account of the large number of Resistance martyrs (now numbering around 1300) who have inadvertently furnished the living *mujahidin* with an invaluable means of political leverage. Their desire to see a particular official elected or appointed to or removed from the *Majlis al-Shura* (Decision-Making Council) and the *Shura al-Tanfiz* (Executive Council) has come to resemble 'a password' which cannot simply be ignored by the political leadership.[27] Over and above this, high-ranking commanders in the Resistance are entitled to vote in party elections.[28]

In the final analysis, it is the Resistance which necessitated the creation of the political and social institutions that now constitute Hizbu'llah, and not the other way around. The Resistance cannot therefore be reduced to an appendage of the party. It is in this respect that Hizbu'llah departs significantly from other political parties in the world that are divided into political and military wings. At least for now, Hizbu'llah is more akin to an army with administrative and combative departments, than a party with two mutually exclusive wings. This analogy stems from the fact that each and every male affiliated with Hizbu'llah's social and political institutions is considered a potential Resistance fighter. For this reason, all male adherents are subject to military training upon subscribing to the party, and are thereby expected to partake in the Resistance if and when the need arises.[29]

However, this is not tantamount to saying that Hizbu'llah's military mind has come to dominate its political mind. Although the political leadership does not interfere in the day-to-day activities of the Resistance, it is ultimately responsible for determining the overall military strategy of the Resistance, such as whether or not to employ Katyusha rockets. Moreover, insofar as the rank-and-file *mujahidin* do not directly participate in party elections, a fair degree of institutional autonomy does appear to characterise the party's political wing, with the implication that the party's political institutions are not overly constrained by military considerations.

Thus, although it was asserted earlier that the Resistance could not be demoted to the status of military appendage to the party, the converse is also true. Hizbu'llah cannot be reduced to a socio-political adjunct of the Resistance, for if this truly were the case, then the party would be willing to withdraw from the political arena, or to simply disband, once the occupied zone is liberated from Israeli occupation. But as Hizbu'llah has now become an active participant in the newly reconstructed political system, and a politically mature one at that, the prospect of this eventuality appears highly improbable. For the time being, the party is synonymous with the Resistance, but once Israel withdraws from the occupied zone, Hizbu'llah will become synonymous with other political goals and priorities.

The Logic of Resistance

Hizbu'llah's resistance priority is partly a function of its commitment to fulfil its religious obligation to fight oppression, and partly attributable to its reasoning that armed resistance is the only means of ensuring an Israeli withdrawal from Lebanese territory. On the surface, the party's adherence to the dictates of Islam appears to be a far more compelling reason for its resistance to the Israeli occupation, and hence a more firmly entrenched part of its intellectual foundations, than its logic that armed confrontation is the only means of liberating national territory. However, for Hizbu'llah, the logic of its resistance has continuously validated itself over time, to the extent that it has become an indissoluble part of the party's intellectual structure.

Based on the premise that 'there are no occupations which last', Hizbu'llah has always believed that Israel's occupation of South Lebanon would eventually end as have other occupations in history by armies much larger than Israel's.[30] Of course, it was only with the active resistance of the occupied peoples that these occupying forces were defeated. One such example that is frequently invoked by the party is the US' enforced withdrawal from Vietnam in 1975 at the hands of the Vietcong. By killing tens of thousands of American soldiers, the Vietcong generated huge controversy in American society, whereby a large section of the American electorate came to staunchly oppose the war.[31]

According to Hizbu'llah's logic, 'the more body bags that are sent to Israel' the greater the heated debate that will be ignited within Israeli society. In turn, the growing domestic opposition to the continuation of Israel's occupation will pressure the Israeli government to unilaterally withdraw from Lebanon.[32] After killing over 640 Israeli troops,[33] this is precisely what Hizbu'llah was able to achieve in 1985 when it forced Israel to retreat from the West and Central Biqa', Mount Lebanon, East and West Beirut and the southern suburbs of Beirut, to the 'security zone'.[34]

As perceived by Hizbu'llah, Israel's enforced withdrawal only confirmed and accentuated the logic of its resistance. It also served as a valid argument against those who contended that Hizbu'llah's resistance activity only incurred Israel's wrath, and that therefore the party should cease enraging it. Tufayli remonstrated that, had the party adopted this line of reasoning, 'we would have become Israel's soldiers and it would have made us reach the point whereby we constituted another security zone for it, just so it would not get angry!'[35]

Thus, in addition to the aim of inducing an Israeli withdrawal from the occupied zone, the prevention of further Israeli expansion into Lebanon is another aim of the Islamic Resistance. Nasru'llah's reasoning that the threat the Resistance poses to 'settlements in North Palestine' has the effect of 'preventing the building of settlements in South Lebanon',[36] illustrates this logic.

So effective was this strategy of deterrence, that Israel not only failed to expand its occupation beyond the security zone after 1985, but announced in 1999 its intention to unilaterally withdraw from the occupied zone by July 2000. Hizbu'llah therefore prides its 'war of attrition' against Israel for creating a 'great dilemma' for its government, Knesset, military, and society in general, who were all divided over whether a withdrawal should be unilateral or accompanied by security guarantees, or within the context of a peace agreement.[37] In any event, it was the Israeli government's admission of 'defeat' that has proven to Hizbu'llah that its resistance logic is a sound one.[38]

It has also proven to the party that violence is the only means that could ensure an Israeli withdrawal, as Israel only understands 'the logic of force'.[39] Concomitantly, it has lent credence to Hizbu'llah's belief that land-for-peace negotiations with Israel are unnecessary and ultimately futile. This conclusion is further bolstered by the fact that Israel's unconditional withdrawal to the security zone in 1985 was directly attributable to 'the pressure of the *mujahidin*'s attacks' rather than any negotiations or international agreements.[40]

Accordingly, Hizbu'llah sees no point in 'begging for peace or security' from Israel when it can attain both, unconditionally, through armed confrontation: 'We want to make peace for our *umma* with our blood, rifles, and severed limbs … This is the peace we believe in.'[41] Assuming then, that both armed confrontation and negotiations are equally conducive to a hasty Israeli withdrawal, faced with a choice between the two, Hizbu'llah would opt for the former.

This choice stems not only from the party's non-recognition of Israel, but also from its insistence on an unconditional Israeli withdrawal based on the principle that oppression cannot be rewarded. Fayyad's assertion that the party would only agree to Israel's 'unilateral withdrawal' from Lebanon[42] is therefore predicated on the principle that 'the occupier must not acquire any gains'.[43] As stipulated by 'international and divine law, the occupier is punished for the crimes he committed during his occupation'. Accordingly, Hizbu'llah 'opposes the bestowal of gains or rewards on the Israeli, on account of his occupation and all the massacres he committed'[44] – a stance which has come to constitute a part of the party's intellectual 'identity'.[45]

Not only does Hizbu'llah view negotiations as unnecessary, it also perceives them as futile. The following assertion by 'Abbas al-Mussawi attests to this point: 'Any rational person who thinks objectively will reach one conclusion: that force is the only option when political activity and negotiations are of no avail. We announce that resistance is our only choice and that our talk is based on logic.'[46] In effect, even though Hizbu'llah's rejection of the concept of negotiations is grounded in its non-recognition of the Israeli entity and its refusal to reward oppression, it firmly believes that, even if it did grant Israel recognition and was therefore willing to negotiate with it, Israel would not relinquish any Lebanese territory.

Hizbu'llah attempts to validate this reasoning by pointing to the Zionists' violation of UN Resolution 182 – which partitioned Palestine into Jewish and Muslim halves – by 'swallowing all of Palestine'. By extension, it is naive to think that, in the absence of military pressure, Israel would implement Resolution 425, which calls for Israel's unconditional withdrawal from Lebanon,[47] when Israel aspires to 'evict' the inhabitants of South Lebanon and to plunder the region's land, water and resources.[48] The party also cites the failure of Arab diplomats, 'even in the heyday of Arab unity, to liberate one inch of Palestinian land' by means of negotiations,[49] as further proof of the futility of any course of action other than resistance.

The logic behind Hizbu'llah's resistance option is therefore not only grounded in the principles of non-recognition and the refusal to reward oppression, but also in the accumulation of historical experiences which attest to Israel's intransigence.

Although this logic was confirmed by Israeli Premier Ehud Barak's pledge to withdraw all Israeli forces from Lebanon by July 2000, with or without a peace agreement with Syria, prior to this development, the party had reached the conclusion that the chances of a unilateral Israeli withdrawal were extremely slim. Hizbu'llah based this analysis on the fact that a unilateral withdrawal would be tantamount to an acknowledgement of Israel's defeat vis-à-vis the Resistance and would set a precedent for the Palestinian people who would come to appreciate the logic of resistance.[50] Consequently, the party reached the ineluctable conclusion that an Israeli withdrawal would only occur within the context of a comprehensive peace agreement between Israel, on the one hand, and Syria and Lebanon, on the other.

Although such an admission appears to conflict with the party's principled rejection of the negotiations and its belief in their ultimate futility, it does not undermine the logic of Hizbu'llah's resistance. Even if Hizbu'llah did acknowledge that Israel's withdrawal from the occupied zone would not be unilateral, but would have to come about through peace negotiations, the party did not construe this as an indication of the fruitlessness of its armed resistance.

If anything, Hizbu'llah views the war of attrition waged by its resistance as having been conducive to Israel's search for a way out of its quagmire in Lebanon. Thus, although negotiations are regarded as futile in light of Israel's customary obduracy, Hizbu'llah believes that the Islamic Resistance has compelled it to pursue negotiations with Syria as a means of extricating itself from its increasingly hazardous occupation of Lebanese territory. Negotiations with Syria and Lebanon are therefore perceived as an invaluable face-saving device for Israel, which would not otherwise have contemplated relinquishing the occupied zone, or even the Golan Heights.

But although this vindicates the logic behind Hizbu'llah's resistance, it implies a grudging acceptance of the negotiations by the party, as will be seen in the following chapter. Nonetheless, Hizbu'llah's resignation to the concept of negotiations with Israel is offset by the party's continuation, and occasional escalation, of its resistance activity against the Israeli occupation, thereby rendering the party's recognition of the negotiations a de facto as opposed to a de jure one. Accordingly, the party is able to maintain its non-recognition of the state of Israel and its refusal to reward Israel's occupation with security guarantees, despite its tacit acceptance of the peace negotiations.

The Resistance to Israel as a Defensive *Jihad* and as the Fulfilment of the Religious Legal Obligation

Hizbu'llah's resistance to the Israeli occupation is not only grounded in logic, but is also rooted in the party's commitment to fulfil its religious legal obligation to wage a defensive *jihad* against oppressors such as Israel.

Derived from the Arabic verb *jahada* (to endeavour, strive, struggle or exert), the Qur'anic concept of *jihad* denotes any activity which strives in the cause of God and Islam, on either a personal or communal basis.[51] According to Hizbu'llah's definition of the concept, 'any act which exerts effort in God's cause is *jihad*'.[52] By God's cause, Hizbu'llah does not imply God's personal cause, since God does not need the individual's *jihad*, but the cause of mankind.[53] God's cause is 'the cause of the people, the cause of the oppressed, the cause of pride, honour and glory, the cause of the defense of the land, the cause of the defense of the sacred, of religion and of the values of humanity'.[54] *Jihad* is therefore an essentially defensive, as opposed to an offensive, activity in Hizbu'llah's conception.[55]

Any effort that is exerted in defence of one of the above-cited causes can be called a *jihad*. By the same token, any death that results from the individual's conviction in one of these causes can be depicted as an instance of martyrdom.[56] The subtext here is that an individual can be designated a martyr even if he has not engaged in a military *jihad*. For example, Hizbu'llah's former secretary-general, Sayyid 'Abbas al-Mussawi, who was assassinated by Israel, is hailed as a martyr even though he was not killed in battle. By extension, *jihad* need not be confined to military activity. As expounded by one Islamic scholar, in the Qur'an and *hadith's* usage of the term, *jihad* is 'an injunction for believers to strive with their possessions and selves in the path or cause of God'.[57]

In fact, the inner struggle with the self is considered by Hizbu'llah to be an even greater battle than the military struggle with the enemy, in light of the perceived difficulty of overcoming one's desires. Furthermore, Hizbu'llah maintains that success in the latter is contingent upon success in the former. Only after man has triumphed in the *jihad* with his desires is he capable of confronting the enemy. Accordingly, the party designates the struggle with the self as the *Jihad al-Akbar* (the Greater *Jihad*), while the struggle with the enemy is deemed the *Jihad al-Asghar* (the Lesser *Jihad*).[58]

However, Hizbu'llah's conception of *jihad* is not as simplistic as signified by this distinction. In the speech where this distinction was made, Nasru'llah deliberates other aspects of *jihad* that render this distinction somewhat meaningless. In the first place, although Nasru'llah defines the *Jihad al-Akbar* as the internal battle with the self, he also subsumes the political and cultural resistance to the enemy under this category.[59] In the second place, despite the elevated rank accorded to the *Jihad al-Akbar*, Nasru'llah asserts that political and cultural *jihad* is actually a lesser *jihad* than the military *jihad* with the enemy, or what he calls the *Jihad al-Asghar*.[60] So the Lesser *Jihad* appears to be greater than the Greater *Jihad*.

As equivocal as Nasru'llah's discussion on *jihad* appears, there is an underlying theme in his many ambivalent statements. Thus, when Nasru'llah categorises political and cultural *jihad* as a Greater *Jihad*, he does so in the context of the Qur'anic verse in which God counsels the Prophet Mohammed not to surrender to the Quraysh tribe but to fight it with non- military means. The intended meaning of '*jahidihum bihi jihadan kabira*' ('strive against them with utmost strenuousness, with the [Qur'an]') (25:52), was that the Prophet should avail himself of the Qur'an in his Greater *Jihad* with the polytheistic Quraysh. It was in this sense that non-military forms of *jihad* are deemed by Nasru'llah to be equivalent to the battle with the self. By arming themselves with the Qur'an and thereby invigorating their faith in God, the Prophet's companions would be able to wage a political and cultural *jihad* against the Quraysh and to resist the temptation of surrendering to them.[61]

Furthermore, the apotheosis of military *jihad,* or the *Jihad al-Asghar*, over and above all other forms of *jihad*, presupposes the fulfilment of the *Jihad al-Akbar*. In other words, military *jihad* is not considered superior to the *jihad* with the self, but conditional upon it – only he who has defeated his self, and his fear of death specifically, can confront, and perhaps even defeat, his enemy. Drawing from Imam 'Ali's dictum that one's worst enemy is oneself, Nasru'llah concludes, 'you are a worse enemy to yourself than Israel is'.[62]

Not only is the Smaller *Jihad* contingent upon the Greater *Jihad*, but the latter is also dependent upon the former. This interdependence is evident in the following example proffered by Nasru'llah: A man who actively seeks to avoid the Lesser *Jihad*, i.e. military combat, but claims to pursue the Greater *Jihad*, has necessarily failed the Greater *Jihad* 'test'. Even if a man prays, fasts and performs other commendable acts, his Greater *Jihad* is reduced to meaningless ritual when his 'baser self that incites him to evil' has prevented him from fulfilling his Lesser *Jihad*. Accordingly, the *raison d'être* of the Greater *Jihad* is the Lesser *Jihad*, for the performance of the former necessarily entails a willingness to fulfil the latter. In effect, the *jihad* with the self is only greater than the military *jihad* in the sense that it is its precondition, but not in an abstract or absolute sense.

The upshot of all this is that both a Greater and a Lesser *Jihad* are required of each and every Muslim. Although this does not apply to offensive *jihad*, since only the Twelfth Imam is entitled to wage such a war, it does apply to defensive *jihad*, which is one of the five articles of the Islamic faith,[63] and one of the eight '*Ibadat* (ritual practices) of Shi'ite Islam.[64] This religious observance is grounded not only in the logic of self-preservation, but is also a function of the Shi'ites' historical preoccupation with the rejection of injustice and humiliation.

Although defensive *jihad* is an integral part of Sunni Islamic doctrine, the Shi'ite history of suffering and oppression, coupled with the exemplary defensive *jihad* waged by Imam Husayn, have served to place a certain primacy on this religious tenet in Shi'ite Islam that is unmatched in Sunni doctrine. As will be recalled from the first section of this chapter, both Khumayni and Hizbu'llah regard the protection of the *umma* from external danger, or defensive *jihad*, as a far more pressing concern than other religious rituals such as praying or fasting. This paramountcy granted to defensive *jihad* in the religious political thought of Hizbu'llah, and in Shi'ite Islam generally, is not mirrored in Sunni Islam, which tends to accord equal importance to all Islamic observances.

The difference in emphasis is reflected in the fact that, as of 1985, Hizbu'llah's military wing, the Islamic Resistance, has almost single-handedly confronted Israel's occupation of South Lebanon. Although some individuals affiliated with Sunni Islamist groups have on rare occasions participated in resistance attacks against Israeli forces, there has been a notable absence of Sunni Islamists in the defensive *jihad* against Israel.

It could be argued that Hizbu'llah's monopolisation of resistance activity is partly due to the Shi'ite predominance in the territories occupied by Israel. Nasru'llah, however, discounts this explanation by pointing out that, had this been the sole factor behind the Resistance, then only youths from the occupied zone would have filled the Resistance's ranks. However, as a large proportion of Resistance fighters originate neither from the occupied zone nor even the South, but from the Hirmil region in the Biqa', it could not be claimed that the Resistance was motivated by personal and territorial considerations.[65]

While the territorial explanation cannot be rejected wholesale, as Nasru'llah appears to think, it does not provide an adequate explanation for the almost exclusively Shi'ite Islamic character of the resistance to Israel, and accordingly, due credit should be given to Nasru'llah's reasoning. What was implied by Nasru'llah's contention was that an alternative explanation for the appropriation of the resistance by Shi'ite Islamists was their affiliation to the 'Husayni school'.[66]

This explanation is not only attested to by the significant number of Resistance fighters who do not originate from the occupied zone or the South of Lebanon, but also by the pan-Islamic focus of Hizbu'llah's discourse on defensive *jihad*. Had territoriality really been the pre-eminent factor governing Hizbu'llah's resistance to Israel, then the liberation of the pan-Islamic symbol of Jerusalem would not have figured so prominently in the party's political thought to an extent only matched by Palestinian Islamic organisations.

Thus, the discrepancy between the status accorded to defensive *jihad* by Sunni and Shi'ite Islamists is mainly attributable to the Shi'ites' canonisation of Imam Husayn as the personification of *jihad* and resistance. So firmly ingrained in the Shi'ite psyche has the epitomisation of the Karbala episode become, that Hizbu'llah acknowledges that the Islamic Resistance in Lebanon could not possibly have emerged without it.[67]

As construed by the party, the primary message conveyed by the Karbala drama was that the submission to oppression, and the 'life of humiliation' such a submission entailed, was tantamount to death.[68] The *umma* which did not embark on a *jihad* would not only be a humiliated and dead *umma* in this life, but would be marred by 'disgrace, shame and degradation' in the afterlife as well.[69] According to this logic, 'an honourable death' is considered 'preferable to a humiliating life',[70] which leads to the ineluctable conclusion that the true meaning of life lies in resistance and martyrdom, as exemplified by Karbala.[71]

It is against this backdrop that Hizbu'llah insists that, as a re-enactment of Husayn's defensive *jihad* against oppression and his rejection of humiliation, its resistance to Israel's occupation of South Lebanon is not merely a 'sacred right' which can be relinquished, but a 'religious legal obligation' (*wajib shari'*), which cannot.[72] This obligation remains incumbent upon all believers, even if Israel does not fire a single bullet, because its very occupation is an act of aggression and a form of subjugation, which necessitates a defensive *jihad*.[73]

Hizbu'llah qualifies this belief with the provision that not all Muslims are obliged to engage in this duty if its assumption by a portion of the community will suffice, in which case it becomes a 'wajib kifaya' (a collective rather than an individual obligation).[74] Thus, although in theory defensive *jihad* is a 'wajib 'ayn' (personal obligation) upon every Muslim,[75] in practice it can be 'tied to the battle front's need'[76] and thereby made volitional.

However, it would be erroneous to conclude that Hizbu'llah does not view other forms of resistance to Israel as a personal duty incumbent upon every individual. Even if the party is willing to consider its military *jihad* against Israel as a *wajib kifaya*, by no means does it view the cultural, political and economic *jihad* or resistance to Israel's occupation as a voluntary activity. On the contrary, the party maintains that 'it is the right and duty of all people [whose land is occupied] to resist occupation'.[77] They may not be 'required to do what the Islamic Resistance does', but they must make the resistance their 'priority'[78] in the political, cultural, and educational fields.[79]

Viewed from this angle, resistance becomes a 'humanitarian' and 'moral' duty which all members of society, whether Muslim or otherwise, are obliged to undertake.[80] The party acknowledges the existence of this moral element in its *jihad* with Israel, when it claims that 'the Resistance is spurred by humanitarianism and the defense of the land'.[81] Nonetheless, 'our religious ideology is the first of its [the Resistance's] conditions'[82] – an affirmation which underlines the religious underpinnings and essentially Islamic character of Hizbu'llah's resistance.

As though the title 'the Islamic Resistance' were not a sufficient indication of the doctrinal basis of Hizbu'llah's *jihad* against Israel, the party repeatedly emphasises the religious origins and motivations behind its resistance. It does this by constantly portraying the Resistance as the enactment of its *wajib shari'*, and by stressing the role of the mosque and *Husayniyya* (a religious and social place of gathering for Shi'ites) in its launch.[83]

The party's attribution of the emergence of the Resistance to Islamic ideology, in contradistinction to other ideologies such as nationalism, is another recurrent theme in the party's discourse on *jihad*.[84] Supposing that the Islamic Resistance adhered to any other ideology but Islam, the most probable outcome would have been its termination and its eventual acquiescence to Israel's conditions.[85] Thus, the continuation of the Resistance as well as its emergence are contingent upon adherence to Islamic ideology.[86]

Only conviction in Islam can sustain the Resistance's determination and steadfastness in the face of Israel's occupation. In fact, the greater the difficulties and obstacles to be overcome, the more determined and steadfast the resistor becomes, for all trials and tribulations are interpreted as God's way of 'testing' him.[87] On the other side of the coin, all the calamities that befall the Israeli enemy are also considered God's doing. When, for example, two helicopters carrying elite Israeli forces collided in February 1997 killing all 73 passengers on board, Nasru'llah hailed the incident as 'a great holy victory' which served as a confirmation of 'God's promise to defend the *mujahidin*'.[88]

This 'divine intervention' is also believed to have enabled the Resistance to score its many successes.[89] Nasru'llah admits as much when he claims that all of the Resistance's victories are the work of God and not 'the products of our own hands'.[90] Thus, when Nasru'llah claims that the victories achieved by the Resistance are proof of the supremacy of faith over modern military technology,[91] the implication is that *jihad* is not merely conceived as a religious duty in the abstract, but as a divinely guided and thereby an axiomatically rewarding, course of action.

It is in this context that the Qur'anic concept of '*Hizbu'llah*' acquires even more meaning: 'As to those who turn [for friendship] to God, His Messenger and the believers, it is the party of God that must certainly triumph' (5:56). Perceived through this scriptural lens, all of the sacrifices made by the Resistance and the martyrs lost to it are rationalised as not having been fruitless, but as ultimately worthwhile.[92] As prophesised by Nasru'llah on more than one occasion, the prospective liberation of the occupied zone from Israeli occupation is 'a certainty'.[93]

The Centrality of the Notion of Martyrdom

An integral part of Hizbu'llah's conceptualisation of *jihad* is the notion of martyrdom. From the party's standpoint, the *wajib shari'* to launch a defensive *jihad* not only entails a willingness to fight for God's cause, but also a willingness to die for this cause – both of which are exemplified by the Karbala episode. Thus, Imam Husayn's martyrdom both serves as an exemplar of defensive *jihad* and a model of self-sacrifice.

As the 'greatest confirmation in history – from [the time of] Adam until the Day of Judgement – of martyrdom',[94] Karbala is considered the benchmark with which all acts of martyrdom are analogised. At 'Abbas al-Mussawi's funeral, for example, all the orators drew parallels between his assassination and Imam Husayn's martyrdom.[95] Hizbu'llah's definition of martyrdom therefore covers both premeditated deaths that result from suicide missions, as well as unpremeditated deaths, which are those that occur on the battlefield as well as outside of it. The implication here is that martyrdom is associated with all forms of defensive *jihad* that involve the impending possibility of death, which can thereby be classified as instances of self-sacrifice. Accordingly, the title of 'martyr' was conferred upon Mussawi by virtue of the self-imperilling and self-sacrificial nature of his political *jihad* against Israel.

The willingness to die for God's cause by means of a political or military *jihad* is designated by Hizbu'llah as the '*irada istishhadiyya*' ('martyrological will'),[96] which the party believes sets it apart from the Israeli enemy. The Israeli soldier may have advanced weaponry at his disposal, but he does not possess this 'will' since he 'proceeds to fight but does not want to die', which renders him inferior to the Resistance fighter. As explicated by Nasru'llah: 'The fighter's strength and superiority does not stem from the type of weapon he carries inasmuch as it stems from his will … and his advance towards death.'[97]

In effect, the Israelis' 'point of departure is the preservation of life', while 'our point of departure is the preservation of principle and sacrifice',[98] which in turn generates the martyrological will. The martyrological will therefore presupposes the principled rejection of humiliation, which as stated earlier, is one definition of God's cause. Nasru'llah corroborates this causality when he asserts that, faced with the choice between 'preserving their purity of character and preserving their existence', Hizbu'llah's adherents would rather lose their existence.[99]

What greatly facilitates this choice is the party's belief that those who die for God's cause will be rewarded in the hereafter, based on the tenet that 'the most preferable death is to be killed for God's cause'.[100] However, Hizbu'llah admits that most people are too shortsighted to conceptualise death in such terms. People's over-attachment and 'enslavement' to this world causes them to fear death, which in the final analysis is nothing more than a 'short bridge' to the afterlife.[101] Hizbu'llah attaches an unparalleled value to the hereafter, or 'true and eternal life', which renders this life on earth meaningless in comparison.[102]

It is in this context that Nasru'llah invokes the following saying by Imam 'Ali: 'One thousand strikes of the sword are easier than one death on the mattress.'[103] Since man is doomed to die anyway, it is far more morally and rationally logical that he make his death a purposive one that serves the cause of God and ensures him a place in paradise. All that is required of him is to hasten the prospect of his death by engaging in a military or political *jihad* against the oppressor, which today is represented by Israel.

Based on this line of reasoning, Hizbu'llah 'sanctifies' its resistance to Israel insofar as it serves as 'a path to God, paradise and the afterlife'.[104] But that is not to detract from its value in this life, for it is exalted by the party precisely because it has two different values: one in this life, and one in the afterlife. Its this-worldly value lies in its military triumphs over the enemy, whilst its other-worldly value lies in its securement of a place in paradise for its *mujahidin*. By considering both military and spiritual victory equal, it follows that Hizbu'llah considers both the Resistance fighter's martyrdom and survival as 'victories' for the Resistance.[105]

Despite the equation of these two values, a preference for martyrdom over survival can be detected in other party statements, and even in the same text where this equation was made. This preference reveals itself most explicitly in the party's proclaimed 'desire',[106] 'passion',[107] 'yearning'[108] and 'love'[109] for martyrdom and death. It can also be inferred from Nasru'llah's depiction of his son's death in September 1997 at the hands of Israeli troops as an act of martyrdom which brought 'the greatest feeling of joy that a father can know' to him.[110] Another indication of the party's apotheosis of martyrdom can be found in a speech Nasru'llah made a few months before his son's death, where he praised parents who beseeched God to 'bless' their children with 'the honour of martyrdom'.[111]

Viewed collectively, these declarations leave the indelible impression that martyrdom is not merely valued as a means to an end, but as an end in itself. To a certain extent, this impression and the declarations which generate it can be construed as mobilisational rhetoric aimed at Hizbu'llah's support base, or as a sample of the terminology that is employed in the party's psychological warfare against Israel. Nevertheless, there is also a non-purposive and ideological dimension to these statements, which can be detected in other contexts.

One such example is provided by Nasru'llah's belief that 'the martyr begins a new, much more beautiful life in paradise',[112] which explains his joy, and that of other parents, at losing a son. This conviction is rooted in a central article of the Islamic faith which posits that all the sins committed by a martyr throughout his life will be absolved by God upon his martyrdom. As enunciated in the Qur'an: 'If you are slain or die in God's way, forgiveness and mercy from God are a better thing than that you amass' (3:151–2). So when the party loses martyrs, it is 'happy for them' for 'passing the test' and for departing from this ephemeral world to the true and eternal world.[113]

It could be postulated that such beliefs imply that the *mujahidin* who survive armed confrontations with Israeli forces will not be considered martyrs if they are to die off the battlefield. However, the very fact that they fulfilled their *wajib shari'* to resist Israel earns them a place in paradise, even if they were not martyred in battle. The presumption that Hizbu'llah maintains such a belief is authenticated by the following Qur'anic verse:

> Count not those who are slain in God's way as dead but rather living with their Lord, by Him provided, rejoicing in the bounty that God has given them, and joyful in those who remain behind and have not joined them, because no fear shall be on them, neither shall they sorrow, joyful in blessing and bounty from God, and that God leaves not to waste the wage of the believers (3:164–5).

In theory at least, the likelihood of this eventuality diminishes with the passage of time, since the number of sins one commits would naturally increase over time. As maintained by Nasru'llah, the longer man lives, the more 'trials and tribulations' he will be subjected to which may imperil his status in the afterlife, which is why death must be actively sought by the believer.[114] The corollary of such mobilisational rhetoric is that the believer who has fulfilled his *wajib shari'* to partake in the *jihad* against Israel should continue seeking martyrdom so as to limit the number of 'tests' to which he will be exposed.

The upshot of all this is that resistance and martyrdom have come to be perceived as ends in themselves. In effect, 'it is not important who kills today or who gets killed today. What is important is the result', which is that the final destiny of Hizbu'llah's *mujahidin* is paradise, while that of Israeli soldiers is hell.[115] So although survival and martyrdom are both considered victories for the Resistance's *mujahidin*, they are not deemed equal victories. Although defeating

Israel on the battlefield is a great victory, defeating it in the afterlife is deemed an even greater victory. The ultimate end of resistance and martyrdom therefore emerges as personal salvation rather than liberation, a conclusion that is borne out by Nasru'llah's affirmation that martyrdom is 'the greatest thing about our resistance, greater than victory and liberation'.[116]

It must also be stressed that resistance and martyrdom are not only perceived as ends in themselves and sanctified insofar as they represent paths to the afterlife, and to paradise specifically. Their apotheosis is equally attributable to the fact that they are also viewed as indicators of the fulfilment of the *wajib shari'* to partake in a defensive *jihad* against Israel's occupation of South Lebanon.

Not only is personal salvation valued more than liberation, but so is the completion of the *wajib shari'*. Even if Lebanese territory is not liberated, the realisation of the religious duty to engage in a *jihad* is considered an even greater victory for Islam and humanity, and a greater victory for the martyr whose fulfilment of this duty has rewarded him with God's eternal blessing. Both the *mujahid* who is martyred whilst engaging in this religious obligation and the *mujahid* who is not will have served both Islam and themselves.

Ultimately, however, it is the *mujahid* who has embarked on a suicide mission, referred to euphemistically as a 'martyrdom operation' by the party, who is deemed to have served Islam and himself to the furthest possible extent. The designation of Ahmad Qasir, the first of Hizbu'llah's suicide bombers, whose martyrdom operation took the lives of over 90 Israeli soldiers and military personnel in November 1982, as '*Amir al-Shuhada*' (the Prince of all Martyrs) testifies to this point.

It is also attested to by Hizbu'llah's annual commemoration of '*Yawm al-Shuhada*' (Martyrs' Day). According to Fayyad, this event, along with 'Jerusalem Day', is the oldest and by far the most significant of the commemorations devised by Hizbu'llah.[117] Although the deaths of all party martyrs are commemorated on this day, the fact that is made to coincide with the day on which Qasir was martyred, 10 November, is symptomatic of the paramountcy of the martyrdom mission over and above all other forms of martyrdom.

Another indication of this paramountcy can be found in party speeches. On more than one occasion, Nasru'llah has referred to the differentiation of martyrs – and by extension, *mujahidin* – by rank in the afterlife. Just as the living are differentiated along a religious and moral continuum, martyrs are distinguished from one another in terms of the level of 'loyalty [to God's cause], worship, piety and asceticism' they exhibited in their lifetimes. In addition, they are ranked according to the way in which they were killed, with regard to 'the level of deprivation' they had to endure.[118]

Thus, although the *mujahid* who dies on the battlefield and the *mujahid* who outlives all his battles are considered equal in God's eyes, the *mujahid* whose death is not premeditated is actually inferior in rank to the *mujahid* whose death is premeditated.[119] The implication here is that the *mujahid* who dies as a result of a martyrdom mission exhibits the highest possible level of self-sacrifice, which explains his elevated status. Although this is not explicitly stated, it can be deduced from Nasru'llah's claim that 'even the Karbala martyrs do not all belong to the same rank; not all martyrs at Karbala were like Husayn'.[120] As construed by Hizbu'llah, Imam Husayn's martyrdom was not an unpremeditated death on the battlefield, but 'a clearly voluntary act of martyrdom'.[121] It can therefore be surmised that Husayn's martyrdom was superior to the other martyrdoms at Karbala on account of its calculated nature. Furthermore, the fact that Husayn suffered more than any other martyr at Karbala also served to elevate the status of his martyrdom.

Regardless of his infallibility and extreme piety, the volitional character of Husayn's martyrdom was deemed proof of his deep loyalty to God's cause, while the psychological and physical torment he experienced rendered the circumstances which immediately preceded his death as manifestations of extreme deprivation – both of which correspond to Nasru'llah's criteria for differentiation.

As the epitome of martyrdom, Imam Husayn's voluntary death is employed as a legitimisation of the suicide mission, which Hizbu'llah has continuously attempted to justify to those who claim that all forms of suicide are prohibited in Islam. One such instance is Amal al-Islami's declaration that 'our suicide squads are as precious to Allah as are the martyrs of Karbala'.[122] Moreover, the martyrdom operation is also legitimised on purely rational grounds: 'Martyrdom is not suicide. Like a fighter who is surrounded by the enemy, it is required of him to fight until death. Martyrdom [as suicide] is the same concept.'[123] Despite the fact that Fadlu'llah never did issue a *fatwa* in support of the martyrdom operation, he adopted the exact same rationalisation as the party's.[124]

Another justification for the suicide mission, which is cited by both Fadlu'llah and the party, is the fact that the Resistance does not have the same advanced weaponry that Israel possesses, which thereby necessitates the resort to suicide by some of its cadres.[125] By treating the martyrdom operation as an act one resorts to out of desperation and abandons once other means are found, as opposed to an act which is valued in its own right, the party implies that the preservation of life is a highly valued goal for it. This is evinced by the fact that as of the mid-1980s, the martyrdom operation has been virtually abandoned by the Resistance and replaced by more conventional forms of warfare, such as attacking Israeli and SLA positions and launching cross-border raids into Northern Israel.

It is also substantiated by Nasru'llah's assertion that the party does not send someone on a martyrdom mission without taking due account of the likelihood of its success.[126] Tufayli echoes this view when he claims that the operation 'must have a political impact which changes the enemy from one state to another and makes him think of altering his positions', otherwise it cannot be religiously sanctioned.[127] The logical conclusion to this line of reasoning is that Hizbu'llah 'does not pursue martyrdom as an end in itself', but as a means of achieving victory.[128]

Prima facie, this conclusion clashes with the above-cited predication that, as an indicator of the fulfilment of the *wajib shari'* and a path to paradise, martyrdom is valued as an end in itself. But it is only valued as such, within the context of oppression. That is, without the imperative need for a defensive *jihad,* martyrdom becomes suicide, which is clearly proscribed in Islam and thereby not rewarded with an everlasting life in paradise, as is true martyrdom. The following contention by Nasru'llah confirms this theory: 'Maybe some people think we crave martyrdom because we like to die in any way. No, we like to die if our blood is valued and has a great impact [on Israel].'[129]

Accordingly, it is not intellectually inconsistent for Hizbu'llah to pursue martyrdom as a means of successfully confronting oppression on the one hand, and to pursue the preservation of life in cases where martyrdom is ineffectual or unnecessary, or when there is no oppression to confront, on the other. The apotheosis of the martyrdom operation, and the sanctification of martyrdom in general, is therefore contingent upon the political and military instrumentality of both.

7   Anti-Zionism and Israel

The Excoriation of Israeli State and Society

Notwithstanding the fact that Israel's occupation of Lebanese territory was the main impetus for the formation of Hizbu'llah, the occupation is not the sole basis of the party's conflict with Israel or its execration of it, as Anoushiravan Ehteshami and Raymond A. Hinnebusch would have us believe. As propounded by these scholars: 'Much of the energy behind Hizbollah's resistance to the Israelis in the south derived from the occupation of Lebanese territory, not some ideological crusade against Israel itself' or 'some permanent cultural characteristic'.[1]

Not only does this statement ignore the existential, as well as civilisational, nature of Hizbu'llah's conflict with Israel, it overlooks the party's inveterate antipathy towards Israel which stems from its occupation of Palestine. As explicated by Ibrahim al-Amin al-Sayyid, the state of hostility with Israel and the party's depictions of it as '*al shar al-mutlaq*' (an absolute evil) are not due to 'the circumstances of the occupation', but to the very existence of the Israeli state.[2] Qasim concurs with this assertion when he claims that 'this occupation is not an occupation because it was present in the South. It is an occupation because it is present in the South, In Palestine and in Jerusalem.'[3] Thus, even if Israel withdraws from South Lebanon, Hizbu'llah's abomination of Israel will remain unchanged and it will continue to withhold legitimacy from the Israeli state.[4]

Hizbu'llah's reluctance to grant Israel recognition is rooted in its rendition of the origins of the Israeli state, which it unequivocally portrays as a 'rape'[5] or 'usurpation' of Palestinian land, thereby rendering it a state which 'is originally based on aggression'.[6] By extension, the continued existence of the Israeli state constitutes 'an act of aggression',[7] insofar as it represents a perpetuation of the original act of aggression. Therefore, Hizbu'llah 'does not know of anything called Israel'. It only knows a land called 'occupied Palestine'.[8] In fact, the party never refers to the state of Israel as such, but to 'occupied Palestine' or 'the Zionist entity'.

Such a designation not only reflects the party's non-recognition of the Israeli state, but also serves as a constant reminder that Israel cannot be legitimised with the passage of time. Fifty years may have passed since the inception of the Israeli state, but Hizbu'llah contends that this should not detract from the illegitimacy of the Israeli entity. The Israeli scholar Yehoshafat Harkabi, for example, postulates that, the longer Israel continues to exist, the more irrelevant its establishment in the past becomes to its present existence.[9] Hizbu'llah argues the exact opposite: 'Even if hundreds of years pass by, Israel's existence will continue to be an illegal existence',[10] because both divine and human justice repudiate the notion that '*al-batil*' (falsehood) can become '*al-haq*' (righteousness) over time.[11]

In effect, the origins of the Israeli state have impinged upon its present existence so that it is forever tainted with the stigma of usurpation and aggression. On that account, it is destined to remain a representation of falsehood, irrespective of its current behaviour. This is one reason why the conflict with Israel is portrayed as 'an existential struggle' as opposed to 'a conflict over land'.[12] Thus, unlike the struggle with the West, which is essentially civilisational and therefore amenable to reconciliation, there can be no prospect of reconciliation with Israel whose very existence is called into question and whose eradication is pursued.

There can be no denying that Israel's dealings with the Arab-Islamic world have reinforced the existential nature of the struggle between it and Hizbu'llah. Hizbu'llah does not just anathematise Israel on account of the circumstances of its establishment, but also because of its contemporary political and military activity. The depiction of Israel as 'the greatest evil in the world'[13] and the 'greatest abomination of our era'[14] stems not only from the historical origins of the Israeli state, but also from its continuous aggression thereafter. Accordingly, it is Israel's essential 'nature',[15] which reveals itself in Israel's past and present, that deems it 'the central enemy of the *umma's* civilisation'.[16]

Cultural stereotyping is therefore a chief ingredient of Hizbu'llah's diatribe against Israel. An 'unparalleled' level of 'arrogance, superiority and depravity'[17] is believed to inhere in the Israeli's unique 'psychological make-up'.[18] By arrogance and superiority, Hizbu'llah means Israel's racism, which the party believes is a universally recognised trait insofar as the UN issued a Resolution in 1975 (later repealed in 1991) equating Zionism with racism.[19]

As a racist state and society, Israel attempts to 'enslave' the Arabs and Muslims, whom it regards as culturally inferior, by perpetrating the 'worst kind of terrorism and massacres' against them.[20] Accordingly, the party likens Israel's racist crimes to Nazism, and even claims they are 'worse' than Hitler's persecution of the Jews.[21]

But for Hizbu'llah, the depiction of Israel's racist and criminal practices in the most scurrilous terms does not convey the true extent of Israel's iniquity. In order to present Israeli state and society as evil incarnate, the party clearly feels that it must specify the atrocities committed by Israel in its public discourse. It frequently avails itself of the depiction of the Israeli as one who commits such heinous crimes as 'slaughtering children' and, even more morally repugnant, as one who 'rips open pregnant women's stomachs' and 'bets on the sex of the embryos'.[22]

This is actually a reference to a gruesome practice that was enacted in the Sabra and Chatila massacres, according to the accounts of several eyewitnesses who saw fetuses placed on stakes at the site of the massacre. Although Lebanese Maronite militias such as the SLA and the Phalangists perpetrated the actual slaying, and were therefore directly responsible for these monstrous acts, they are ultimately attributed to Israel since Israeli Shin Beth officers oversaw the entire massacres.[23]

According to one Hizbu'llah official, the party's frequent invocation of this practice also alludes to the Dar Yasin massacre of 1948, whereby commandos affiliated with the Zionist Irgun and Stern Gang slaughtered over 100 inhabitants of the Palestinian village. There too, the Israelis are claimed to have committed this particular atrocity.[24]

Hizbu'llah's repeated reference to this atrocity reflects its attempt to demonise the Israeli in two ways. Insofar as the removal of the fetus symbolises the Israeli attempt to curb Arab population growth in the party's conception, the accentuation of this act underscores the Israeli objective of depopulating the region of its Arab inhabitants.[25] Furthermore, the frequent recourse to this act as an instance of the Israeli's unparalleled depravity and malevolent intentions dehumanises him to such an extent that the mere notion of reconciliation or normalisation of relations with the Israeli state appears absurd.

These attempts at demonisation can also be discerned from the party's emphasis on the deceitful aspect of the Israeli's fundamentally nefarious nature. 'Abbas al-Mussawi's citation of the Torah as an example of the inbred nature of the Israelis' deceitfulness illustrates this point:

You should advance thirty miles and then prepare for civil strife and plant it and then retreat twenty-eight miles. Remain in the twenty-eight mile distance and watch until the fire of civil war burns the people. Then return, intensify [the war] and occupy.[26]

By analogy, the Israeli withdrawals from the Shuf Mountain in 1983 and from East Sidon in 1985 were successful ploys to ignite civil war in both regions. Therefore, Israel's contemplation of a withdrawal from the South is nothing but a plot 'to incite a civil war and then return and destroy us'.[27] The corollary of this is that the Israeli's motives cannot be trusted, no matter how benign they may appear outwardly, because he will abuse that trust to commit even greater evil.

The virtual impossibility of a durable peace or normalised relations with the Israeli becomes even more apparent when one considers the magnitude of his duplicity. As believed by Nasru'llah, the Israeli Mossad orchestrated the March 1992 bombing of the Israeli embassy in Buenos Aires, which resulted in 30 fatalities and over 250 wounded, in order to lay the blame for the incident on Hizbu'llah and other Islamic groups. In fact, Nasru'llah maintains that striking at Jewish civilian targets is a customary practice of the Israelis, who have attacked such targets in the past in order to incriminate the Arabs.[28]

The Israelis are also perceived as spineless cowards. The Israeli soldier 'only fights behind fortresses and walls',[29] which is a clear indication of his unwillingness to die, and hence of his essential cowardice.[30] His cowardice induces him to shell civilian areas, as he is 'incapable of face-to-face combat'.[31] Consequently, both his cowardice and his iniquity are closely interwoven to produce the most despicable of enemies – the enemy whose cowardice prompts him to exploit the weaknesses of others.

Despite the Israeli's 'racist, immoral and uncivilised' character, Hizbu'llah claims to 'respect' this enemy for the concern he displays towards his civilians, prisoners (i.e. the missing pilot Ron Arad) and casualties of war.[32] When bombs land on 'settlements' in Galilee, leading Israeli officials, from the prime minister down, rush to the scene, in stark contrast to the Lebanese government.[33] The Israeli government's willingness to trade 40 bodies of Resistance martyrs and tens of prisoners in return for the severed limbs of a dead Israeli soldier is also cited by the party as a quality that the Lebanese authorities should emulate.[34]

To some extent, such an admission clashes with the above mentioned attribution of the Buenos Aires attack, as well as other attacks on Israeli civilian targets, to the Mossad. On the one hand, the party claims that the Israeli government is willing to expend the lives of its civilians in order to discredit Islamic groups, but on the other hand it claims to respect the value the Israeli government places on the lives of its civilians. One Hizbu'llah official explains away this incongruity by pointing to several interrelated factors.

In the first place, Hizbu'llah does not view the Mossad's involvement in the Buenos Aires attack as an indication of the Israeli state's disregard for the lives of its civilians. Rather, it views the Israeli government's resort to such acts as an attempt to serve the general Israeli interest, insofar as acts of terrorism against Israeli targets generate mass sympathy for the Israeli cause and distort the image of Islamic groups such as Hizbu'llah to whom such acts are always attributed.[35]

In the second place, Hizbu'llah perceives the Israeli government's close attentiveness to the lives and wellbeing of its civilians and soldiers as being a function of its differentiation between internally sanctioned attacks, which are under the state's control, and attacks by external enemies, which imperil state security. Accordingly, it does not value its people's lives in an absolute sense, but only in relation to those who endanger them.[36]

Third, while Hizbu'llah admires the Israeli government's persistence in regaining the body parts of its dead soldiers and in discovering the whereabouts of its long lost pilot Ron Arad, it acknowledges that this is not a reflection of the Israeli state's profound respect for its soldiers' lives or corpses. Notwithstanding the religious significance of Jewish burial rites, Hizbu'llah believes that the preponderant element in the Israeli state's persistence in reclaiming its missing soldiers is the propaganda value of such a show of concern. In other words, the party believes that much of the Israeli state's commotion over its killed or missing servicemen is designed to publicise the Israeli cause to the world and to portray the Israelis as a united and humane society.[37] The fact that the Israeli government's show of concern is contrived does not detract from Hizbu'llah's respect for its display of it, for it is also viewed as an act that serves the general good of Israeli society.

The Zionist Essence of Israeli State and Society

Inherent in Hizbu'llah's cultural stereotyping of Israeli state and society is the notion of ideological homogeneity. The party's excoriation of Israel as a racist, iniquitous, and deceitful state stems from Israel's adherence to the Zionist doctrine that gave birth to it. Hizbu'llah's equation of Israel with Zionism and the attribution of the former to the latter are most clearly evident in its portrayal of Israel as 'the ulcerous growth of world Zionism'.[38] It is also evinced by the party's almost invariable juxtaposition of the term 'Zionist' with any mention of Israel, as well as in the interchangeability of the two terms in the statements and speeches of party officials.

The state of Israel is therefore viewed by the party as a socio-political monolith, characterised by a Zionist ethos that is impervious to ideological fragmentation. Accordingly, it is naive to assume that there are any substantial differences between the Likud and Labour parties or the candidates nominated by them for the general elections, for they are all essentially 'Zionists',[39] and by extension 'murderers, terrorists and savage racists'.[40] It is therefore sheer 'stupidity' on the part of the Arabs to claim a preference for Ehud Barak or the supposedly moderate Labour party which nominated him for the premiership. After all, it was the Labour Party that staged Operation Accountability in July 1993 and Operation Grapes of Wrath in April 1996,[41] as well as most of the wars against the Arabs.[42] It is also this very party which 'crushed the Palestinians' bones' during the *Intifada*.[43]

The only significant difference between the two parties is the 'means' they endorse for implementing the same Zionist ends. The principal distinction between the two revolves around their ability to 'adapt to the American need'. The Likud is less pliant to American pressures and is more inclined to 'blackmail the Americans' in order to obtain concessions, while the Labour Party is better able to 'read international changes' and accommodate itself to the American need.[44]

But the Labour Party's realism does not make it any less committed to Zionist ideology than the Likud, for both parties formulate their policies based on 'a vision of Israel's interests'.[45] The Labour Party merely masks its realism as doveishness, making it a greater liar than the Likud,[46] which makes no pretence of its hawkishness. Thus, although Likud is acknowledged to be the more radical and hard-line of the two parties, it is actually perceived as a lesser threat to the Arab world than the Labour Party, because of its 'clarity' which better enables 'the Arabs to determine their options'.[47]

In the final analysis, both parties are equally loyal to the Zionist cause and are committed to the same ideological '*thawabit*' (fixed principles),[48] at the core of which is the belief that the land extending from the Nile to the Euphrates is the Jews' inalienable right.[49] Furthermore, both parties are equally devoted to the notion of Jerusalem as the eternal capital of Israel, to 'degrading the Arabs and Muslims' and to 'dominating the region's resources'.[50]

These '*thawabit*' are not only adhered to by all political forces, but by Israeli society in its entirety.[51] To the extent that the Israeli people are, by and large, Jewish immigrants from all parts of the world, their inhabitancy of Israel betokens their commitment to the Zionist project. Israeli society is therefore a 'Zionist society' with a fundamentally ideological outlook and a deeply entrenched 'ideological enmity' towards the Arabs and Muslims.[52] Hizbu'llah also maintains that the Israeli people harbour expansionist designs on the region insofar as they are reputed to 'dream of the establishment of a Greater Israel', along with their government.[53]

The characterisation of Israeli society in this manner further underlines the existential nature of Hizbu'llah's conflict with Israel. The party's struggle with the West may be a civilisational one, but Western society is not considered synonymous with Western states in the same way that Israeli society is identified with the Israeli state. In point of fact, even if Western society were identified with Western states, the struggle between Hizbu'llah and the West would still not be considered an existential one, for the simple reason that the party does not withhold legitimacy from Western states or seek their eradication as it does in the case of Israel. There is no possibility of dialogue or reconciliation with Israeli society as there is with Western society.

The inconceivability of a rapprochement with Israeli society is not only a function of the identification of Israeli society with the delegitimised Israeli state, but is also a function of the existential threat posed by both. For Hizbu'llah, Zionism constitutes a threat to 'our very existence and aims to uproot us from our land, values and civilisation',[54] which necessarily renders the party's struggle with Israeli state and society as an irrevocably existential as well as a civilisational one.

As discerned by Hizbu'llah, the underlying aim of the Zionist project is to eradicate the Arab and Islamic identity by 'Judaising' all of Palestine at the expense of its Muslim inhabitants, which is most clearly evinced by Israel's policy of amassing Jewish immigrants from all over the world. It is also evident in the acts of sacrilege committed by Israelis, which are not construed as isolated instances of religious fanaticism, but as part of a concerted effort to remove all traces of Islam, and even Christianity, from Palestine. Accordingly, the desecration of mosques by Israeli soldiers in the West Bank and Hebron, the digging of the tunnel beneath the al-Aqsa mosque, and the drawings which profaned the Prophet Mohammed and the Virgin Mary, are all considered to be rooted in a single 'ideology, vision … and project'.[55]

However, the Judaisation of Palestine is not the final end of the Zionist project, but is merely the first step towards the establishment of '*Eretz Israel*' (the Land of Israel),[56] or the Judaisation of the entire region. As mentioned above, the ultimate Zionist objective is to realise the Jewish biblical dream of expanding from the Nile to the Euphrates, which is symbolised by the two blue lines on either side of the Star of David on the Israeli flag.[57] The Greater Israeli state would therefore encompass parts of Egypt, Syria and Iraq, as well as Palestine, Jordan and Lebanon in their entirety, which would become Judaised in the process.

From Hizbu'llah's perspective, Israel's occupation of southern Lebanon is a living testimony of the Zionist scheme to expand the borders of its present state. Israel's original justification for its 1978 and 1982 invasions of Lebanon was to extirpate the PLO presence in South Lebanon, from where Palestinian groups were launching cross-border raids into northern Israel. The fact that the Israeli forces remained after accomplishing this goal, when the PLO was forcibly evacuated in the summer of 1982, is adduced by the party as proof of Israel's 'undeclared aim to dominate South Lebanon and its water resources'.[58] In particular, Israel is believed to covet the Litani River, which the founder of national Zionism and the World Zionist Organisation, Theodore Herzl, is reported to have openly admitted to during the First Zionist Congress in 1897.[59]

In line with their aspiration to incorporate Lebanon into their Greater Israeli state, the Israeli Zionists also seek to undermine Lebanese interests abroad. The political instability in Africa, for example, is directly ascribed to the Zionists, who are accused of inciting civil strife in African countries where large groups of Lebanese expatriates reside.[60] But it is not only the Lebanese who are the subjects of Zionist machinations. As the central enemy of Islamic civilisation, Zionism confronts the entire *umma* 'from every location in the world'.[61]

Not only does Zionism aim to dominate the Islamic *umma*, it aspires to control the entire world,[62] even though the party concedes that it is ultimately incapable of effecting this.[63] However, the party still appears to assume that world Zionism has the power to affect the destinies of other states insofar as it asserts that the world's social, political, military and moral problems are all attributable to world Zionism. In effect, Zionism is 'the most dangerous and malicious enemy of humanity',[64] and not just the archenemy of the Arab-Islamic world.

Existential Dimensions of the Struggle with Israel

Based on the party's delegitimisation of the Israeli state, its excoriation of Israeli state and society and its emphasis on the Zionist essence of both, certain existential elements of Hizbu'llah's conflict with Israel can be readily discerned. Upon closer examination of these elements, the following three existential themes emerge: the party's legitimisation of the use of violence against an essentially Zionist society; its rejection of the notion of a negotiated peace settlement with the Israeli state; and its pursuit of the liberation of Palestine.

As existential as the struggle with Israel is, however, Hizbu'llah has been compelled to accommodate these themes (with particular reference to the latter two) to the dictates of reality, while preserving them as intellectual pillars. Thus, although the struggle has theoretically remained an existential one, its translation into operation has been postponed indefinitely.

The Legitimisation of the Use of Violence Against Israeli Society

As noted earlier, Hizbu'llah's reluctance to resort to the use of violence against Western civilians betokens the non-existential nature of its struggle with Western civilisation. Conversely, although Hizbu'llah claims that it confines its struggle against Israel to fighting Israeli troops on Lebanese soil,[65] its willingness to justify and even enjoin the use of violence against Israeli civilians – either as part of its conventional warfare against the Israeli occupation or in the form of suicide attacks carried out by Palestinians against civilian targets in Israel – signals the existential foundations of its conflict with the Israeli state.

However, it must also be emphasised that, despite Hizbu'llah's legitimisation of the use of violence against Israeli civilians, it neither pursues their killing as an end in itself,[66] nor does it view it with a sense of moral impunity. In principle, the party maintains that it 'prefers to deem Israeli civilians neutral' in its struggle against Israel's occupation of South Lebanon, because of its 'humanitarian Islamic consideration'.[67] As explicated by former Hizbu'llah spokesman 'Abdu'llah Murtada, 'in our religion it is not something desirable to kill an enemy who is not about to kill you'.[68]

Thus, even though Hizbu'llah occasionally launches Katyusha rockets onto northern Israel, it claims that it only resorts to such measures in order to deter Israel from shelling civilian targets in Lebanon. Nasru'llah recalls the fact that, prior to 1992, when Israel attempted to invade the Lebanese villages of Kafra and Yater, Hizbu'llah had refrained from launching cross-border attacks.[69] Only after this incident did the party embark on its Katyusha policy.

The upshot of all this is that the party would content itself with fighting Israeli soldiers if Israel did not compel it to shell civilian targets in Israel. But when Hizbu'llah is faced with no other option but to attack Israeli civilians, it does not view the resort to such action in morally problematic terms for three central reasons. In the first place, such action is viewed as a totally legitimate form of defensive warfare, which is employed by practically the entire world. From Hizbu'llah's perspective, 'if one is defending one's cause and self, and Israelis are killed in the process, then this is something legitimate'.[70]

In the second place, although Hizbu'llah insists that it does not pursue the killing of Israeli civilians as an end in itself, it would be unlikely to deny that it views such action as a means to an end. Thus, despite the party's professed commitment to the Islamic and humanitarian principle which dictates that civilians should be 'neutral', Qasim admits that this is virtually impossible to implement in reality. This is especially the case when the threat posed to Israeli civilians by Hizbu'llah's Katyushas represents an invaluable 'element of force' for the party in its relentless endeavour to liberate Lebanese territory from the Israeli occupation.[71]

In the third place, Hizbu'llah rationalises that it is not killing innocent Israeli civilians, but hostile, militant Zionists. As stated in the previous section, Hizbu'llah perceives Israeli society as an essentially Zionist and ideological monolith, characterised by an inveterate animosity towards the Arabs and Muslims. In accordance with the party's moral relativism, such a depiction of the Israeli people countervails Islamic and humanitarian considerations, which call for the exclusion of civilians from the line of fire. This moral logic can be detected in several party statements.

One such instance is Nasru'llah's reference to dead and wounded Israelis as 'Zionist casualties'.[72] One might argue that this statement cannot be used to demonstrate the moral relativism displayed by Hizbu'llah towards Israeli civilians, since Nasru'llah's designation of these casualties of war as Zionists applies only to Israeli soldiers. To some extent, this contention is supported by the fact that, to date, very few Israeli civilians have been killed or wounded by the Resistance's Katyushas.

However, it must be pointed out that, even if Nasru'llah's depiction of the Israelis as Zionists was confined to Israeli soldiers, it can still be taken as an indication of the party's rationalisation for the killing of Israeli civilians. Insofar as Israeli soldiers are conscripted into the army, their presence in Lebanon is an involuntary one, which renders them ideologically indistinguishable from Israeli civilians. Consequently, their occupation of Lebanese territory does not make them any more Zionist than other segments of Israeli society. Nasru'llah's reference to dead and wounded Israelis as Zionists implies that Hizbu'llah does not perceive Israeli civilians as detached from the Zionist project, and therefore 'innocent', but as co-conspirators in this malevolent scheme, and thereby somewhat deserving of death.

This moral relativism is more clearly enunciated by other Hizbu'llah officials who also refer to the ideological convictions of Israeli society as a warrant for the party's attacks on civilian targets, in retaliation for Israeli raids on civilian targets in Lebanon. As affirmed by Muhsin, Hizbu'llah considers both the Israeli state and Israeli society 'a danger to the Muslim world', in light of their shared ideology.[73] This point is expounded further by Qasim, who maintains that the 'cohesion' of Israeli state and society is a product of the 'nourishment' the latter provides to the former, in terms of 'popular choice', 'popular defence' and system 'continuity'.[74]

In this manner, Israeli society is held accountable for the iniquity practised by its government, which necessarily includes its occupation of South Lebanon. In fact, all Israelis are deemed links in the 'chain' of occupation and, as such, are considered members of a 'war society' vis-à-vis the 'resistance society' in Lebanon.[75] Husayn al-Mussawi's characterisation of Israeli society conforms to this line of reasoning: 'The Israeli soldier in Lebanon has a mission to expand occupation; the Israeli civilian in Israel is a confirmation of that occupation. They both serve one aim and are both considered enemies.'[76] To all intents and purposes, the distinction between Israeli state and society is merely a 'theoretical' distinction and not a 'technical' one for Hizbu'llah.[77]

But the clouding of this distinction, and the consequent perception of Israeli society as an extension of the Israeli state, is not only attributable to the Israeli occupation of South Lebanon. It is also attributable to the bellicosity of Israeli society that issues from its Zionist beliefs, at the core of which is the belief that the occupation of Palestine is the Jews' inalienable right. To the extent that the party views Zionism as an intrinsically belligerent ideology on account of this belief, the Zionist essence of Israeli society *ipso facto* renders it a society that is not only ideologically predisposed to animosity, but is inherently militant.

Despite the fact that it is Israeli soldiers and not Israeli civilians who are occupying South Lebanon, the fact that Israeli civilians occupy Palestinian homes means that they too are aggressors.[78] Thus, even if Israel did not occupy Lebanese territory, Israeli civilians would still be considered legitimate targets for attack, in light of their Zionist ideology, which instructs them to occupy Palestinian homes.

Yet neither this hypothetical reasoning nor the party's perception of Israeli society as an extension of the Israeli state should be taken to imply that Hizbu'llah would launch such attacks in Israel proper, only that it would justify them if they were staged by Palestinian groups such as Hamas and Islamic Jihad. This attitude is clearly reflected in Fnaysh's assertion that, 'while Hizbu'llah understands Hamas' circumstances [when it stages suicide attacks], it does not engage in such activity'.[79] The occupation of Palestinian homes by Israeli civilians may provide the party with another reason to conceptualise Israeli society as synonymous with the Israeli state – and therefore to mitigate the moral implications of its strikes on Israeli civilians – but it does not provide the party with a justification to kill Israeli civilians solely on that account.

Fnaysh affirms that, if the Israeli state was founded on Lebanese land, Hizbu'llah would have resorted to the same violent means as Hamas.[80] The significance of this assertion lies in the party's flagrant disregard for the universal distinction between conventional warfare and terrorism. While the international community generally does not consider Hizbu'llah's cross-border strikes on northern Israel as instances of terrorism, but as guerrilla and hence, normal warfare,[81] it does consider the suicide attacks launched by Hamas and Islamic Jihad as terrorist acts.

Insofar as any premeditated act of violence against innocent civilians that seeks to create an atmosphere of fear in order to influence a specific audience can be defined as terrorism, then Hizbu'llah clearly advocates the resort to terrorism by armed Palestinian groups. For Hizbu'llah, however, whether civilians are killed as a result of conventional warfare or as a result of so-called 'terrorist' attacks, the moral equation remains the same. Since both means of violence produce the same end result, neither means can be considered any more moral than the other.

Therefore, the party upholds the conviction that the principal determinant of the terrorism of an act lies in the circumstances that surround it, and not in its conformity to conceptual definitions. In line with this situational ethics is the belief that violence cannot be viewed in absolute terms, but must perceived in a relative sense. Hizbu'llah's conception of terrorism hinges on the essential goodness or badness of a cause, irrespective of whether the means of violence employed were conventional or unconventional ('terrorist') ones.

According to this moral dictum, Israel's successive invasions, its occupation of Lebanese territory, its indiscriminate, and often surgical, bombardment of civilian areas, in addition to its unlawful detention or 'kidnapping' of Lebanese civilians, render it a terrorist state in the eyes of Hizbu'llah. But from Israel's standpoint, and that of much of the Western world, such acts are considered part of Israel's conventional warfare against Hizbu'llah and the Lebanese state.

On the other side of the coin, Hizbu'llah does not view Palestinian suicide attacks against Israeli civilians as terrorist acts, on account of their situational context, which consists of two principal extenuating circumstances. First is the party's perception of Palestinian violence as legitimate self-defence in the face of Israeli oppression. Not only do Israel's current oppressive policies vindicate the acts of violence against Israeli civilians perpetrated by Hamas and Islamic Jihad, but Israel's very existence also warrants such violence.

Because the Israeli state was founded on the displacement of an entire people, Israel is ultimately responsible for the Palestinians' attempt to retrieve their land through violent means.[82] The perpetuation of the Israeli occupation of Palestine, coupled with the Israeli state's 'practice of the worst kind of aggression and violence against the Palestinians, necessitate all kinds of self-defense',[83] which are the 'natural right'[84] of the subjugated Palestinian people.

Viewed through this relative moral lens, suicide missions that are universally deemed terrorist become 'great' 'martyrdom operations',[85] and their perpetrators exalted as 'great *mujahidin*'[86] and 'heroes'.[87] So glorified are these attacks, that in Hizbu'llah's disclaimer of one of these suicide missions, the party finds it necessary to add, 'this is not something we have to exonerate ourselves from. We said before that we did not do it because we did not have the honour to execute these operations',[88] in order to establish the religious legitimacy of operations that the party did not partake in.

Over and above this, the party unabashedly and regularly enjoins the Palestinians to kill Israeli civilians, though always with reference to the instrumentality of such violence in defending Palestinian rights. More than anything, suicide attacks are perceived as the 'solution' to the Palestinian predicament in that they are the only 'way' of 'reminding' the world of the Palestinians' grievances.[89] For Hizbu'llah, the exigency of such acts of violence is even more pronounced when the futility of diplomacy in effecting the required level of international awareness is taken into account. As reasoned by Nasru'llah: 'We live in a world where talk [negotiations] means nothing, a world, which only understands the logic of blood.'[90]

By implication, another objective of Hizbu'llah's exhortation to the Palestinians to stage more suicide attacks is to underline Palestinian discontent with the overall peace process, and with specific bilateral agreements such as the Wye Plantation accords.[91] The use of violence to voice this discontent serves the dual purpose of conveying the Palestinians' rejection of the accords to the outside world, and of providing the discontented with an effective means of 'abolishing' such 'treacherous' agreements and of obstructing the peace process generally.[92]

As crucial as these concrete goals are to Hizbu'llah, the party is equally concerned with the symbolic impact of such acts of violence. In one of Nasru'llah's fierier speeches, the Palestinians are incited to violence so as to confront the 'Judaisation of Jerusalem'.[93] Although the Arabisation of Jerusalem is a highly unfeasible goal, Nasru'llah exhorts the Palestinians to 'transform it into a cemetery for every Jewish invader who wants to change the characteristics of this holy city',[94] because of its religious symbolism.

As critical as the religious symbolism of this incitement is its usage of the term 'Jewish invader' in depicting the Israeli inhabitant of Jerusalem. Significantly, the terms 'Zionist settlers', 'Israeli settlers',[95] 'invading occupier Jews'[96] and 'coloniser, usurper Jews'[97] are inserted in other speeches that glorify and encourage Palestinian suicide attacks. Herein lies the second extenuating circumstance, which warrants Palestinian violence against Israeli civilians: by referring to Israelis as settlers, invaders, colonisers, usurpers and occupiers, Hizbu'llah attempts to militarise Israeli society, in order to afford religious and moral sanction to the utilisation of violence against it by Palestinian Islamists.

This attempt is epitomised by Nasru'llah's assertion that, 'in occupied Palestine there is no difference between a soldier and a civilian, for they are all invaders, occupiers and usurpers of the land'.[98] It is also visible in Ra'id's claim that there is no such thing as a 'civil society' in Israel, but only a 'military society' which comprising 'occupiers and usurpers'.[99] As stated earlier, the Israeli civilian's inhabitancy of Palestine *ipso facto* renders him an occupier of Palestinian territory, and hence an aggressor.

Yet it is not this factor alone which imbues him with the same militancy that characterises the Israeli soldier, and consequently blurs the distinction between them both. Israeli civilians willingly migrated from various parts of the world to settle in Palestine, and in so doing 'gave their consent to the [wholesale] occupation of Palestine'[100] and the displacement of an entire people.[101] Therefore, each and every immigrant Jew who now resides in Palestine actively partook in the usurpation of Palestinian land and in the eviction of the Palestinians. It is against this background that Husayn al-Mussawi affirms that 'there is not a single innocent Jew in Palestine now'.[102]

Implicit in Mussawi's remark is the consideration of the post-1948 generation of Israelis who did not willingly immigrate to Israel, but who were born there, as militant Zionists. Thus, although the voluntary migration of Jews to Palestine accounts for the militancy of the Israeli people, the continuation of their occupation of Palestinian homes also contributes to this status. The corollary of this reasoning is that Israeli-born Jews are as militant as immigrant Jews, in that they have not only accepted the usurpation of Palestinian land as a fait accompli, but have wholeheartedly embraced it by continuing to live on land that is not rightfully theirs.

In effect, the post-1948 generation of Israelis (recent immigrants included) are just as culpable as the original Jewish settlers of Palestine for the displacement and oppression of the Palestinian people, and are thereby also designated by Hizbu'llah as settlers and occupiers. It follows that 'Israel is nothing but a military residence. Anyone who lives inside this residence is under the military umbrella', and accordingly cannot claim to be an ordinary civilian.[103]

This begs the question of whether Israeli children who live under this 'military umbrella' are also deemed militant occupiers. Judging by the statements of Hizbu'llah parliamentarian Sayyid 'Ammar al-Mussawi and *Shura* Council member Shaykh Muhammad Yazbek, it would appear that the party does view Israeli children in the same manner that it views the rest of Israeli society.

In their commentary on the killing of seven Israeli schoolgirls by a Jordanian soldier in the Jordan River island of Naharayim, in March 1997, both Mussawi and Yazbek referred to the Israeli teenagers as 'Jewish settlers'.[104] Yazbek even goes so far as to lambaste King Husayn of Jordan for 'shamefully' 'offering his condolences to the families of the killed Jews, while the images of the victims of the Zionist massacres in the South and Palestine did not affect him'.[105] The invocation of Israel's habitual killing of Lebanese children (most notably in the Qana massacre) and Palestinian youths is clearly employed by Yazbek as a justification for the killing of Israeli children.

In a similar vein, Mussawi justifies the incident as 'an expression of great distress among the sons of the *umma* in the face of the enemy's provocative policies' and as a manifestation of their 'rejection of the approach of some regimes in handling this issue'.[106] As with the party's rationalisation of the use of violence by Palestinians against Israeli society as a whole, the theme of legitimate self-defence against Israeli oppression re-emerges as the moral vindication for such acts. Moreover, the same sub-theme of the perceived futility of non-violent means of action, such as negotiations, is also revisited.

Thus, even though Israeli children are depicted as 'settlers' in both of these justifications, which would lead one to presume that their occupation of Palestinian territory warrants their death, it is not cited as a mitigating factor for their slaying. However, it is implied in Ra'id's response to a question on his view of the incident:

Every incident has its circumstances. We know that the emotions and sympathy that are associated with [the killing of] children differ from those associated with adults. But in the end they are all serving one project. This child may have been wronged, but it is the project that brought him [to Israel] that is responsible for his oppression, not the person who killed him.[107]

Insofar as the Zionist project is executed by Israeli state and society, both are held accountable for the death of Israeli children. By emigrating to Palestine or simply residing there, the parents of these unsuspecting children have implicated them in the Zionist project, and are therefore ultimately responsible for their deaths. By the same token, the aggressive climate the Israeli government has fostered, coupled with its promotion of the emigration of Jews to Palestine, also incriminate it in the deaths of these children. The Israeli state is fully cognizant of the channels of expression which discontented Palestinians and Arabs frequently resort to, yet it continues to expose the lives of its citizens to violence, and even encourages Jewish families, far removed from the scene of violence, to settle in a politically volatile country.

In all this, the Israeli child emerges as the unwitting accomplice to an iniquitous project. Yet although the Israeli child is not aware of the moral implications of his residence in Palestine, both the depiction of Israeli children as 'settlers' and the rationale propounded by Ra'id suggest that the party is more concerned with the end result of this inhabitancy than with its unwittingness.

In fact, it is supposed that this inhabitancy will not remain an unwitting one, but will eventually become a willed and deliberate occupation, once the child comes of age and his indoctrination in Zionist ideology has been completed. This undeclared assumption is implied by Ra'id's postulation that 'one day this child will become Prime Minister [of Israel]'.[108] As posited by this moral logic, the circumstances of the child's death are mitigated by the predetermination of his militancy – an assumption that issues from the party's view of Israeli society as a Zionist monolith, and its associated cultural stereotyping of the 'Israeli personality'.

However, one must not overlook the fact that, despite these moral justifications, the party's perception of the use of violence against Israeli children is not identical to its view of the killing of Israeli civilians generally. Although the same mitigating factors are adduced, one crucial distinction remains: while Hizbu'llah does not shy away from enjoining the use of violence against Israeli civilians, it does not incite the Palestinians, or anyone else, to kill Israeli children. The vindication of the killing of Israeli civilians is a permanent feature of the party's intellectual discourse, but the rationale it invokes for the killing of Israeli children is presented only after the fact (and only one incident at that).

Thus, despite the party's justifications for the Naharayim massacre, the absence of any inflammatory speeches by Hizbu'llah officials relating to the killing of children is indicative of the moral constraints that govern the party's views on the use of violence against Israeli society. Even when Israeli Foreign Minister David Levy made a highly incendiary speech to the Israeli Knesset on 23 February 2000, in which he threatened to kill Lebanese children if settlements in northern Israel came under fire,[109] Hizbu'llah's reaction was relatively muted. The party refrained from making a similarly phrased retort[110] and contented itself with declaring that Levy had stepped on ground 'where no Zionist terrorist has gone before'.[111]

The Rejection of a Negotiated Settlement with Israel

Another indication of the existential nature of Hizbu'llah's struggle with Israel is its principled rejection of the Arab-Israeli peace negotiations. As it is a delegitimised and abominated state, the very notion of negotiating with Israel is perceived by the party as 'something impure'[112] and 'a blasphemy'.[113] In congruence with this conceptualisation, Hizbu'llah characterises those states and organisations that pursue such impure and blasphemous agreements, and who generally 'agree to barter land for peace', as 'deviant'.[114]

The rationale behind this representation of the peace process and those who partake in it is founded on two central premises. First is the argument that Arab participation in the negotiations necessarily entails a tacit recognition of the 'Zionist entity'.[115] As construed by Hizbu'llah, a recognition of the existence of the Israeli state is tantamount to a legitimisation of Israel's occupation of Palestine and an approval of the resettlement of the Palestinian diaspora. By extension, the peace process is designated as 'a capitulatory path, which recognises the legitimacy of the Israeli presence on Palestinian land and the permanent departure of the Palestinians from their land'.[116]

It follows that Hizbu'llah is particularly vituperative about the Palestinian-Israeli negotiations, in that they not only represent a recognition, and hence legitimisation, of the Israeli state, but also an official relinquishment of the great bulk of Palestine to Israel. This view is reflected in Nasru'llah's castigation of the PLO for 'transforming the battle of liberating all of Palestine into the battle of liberating part of Palestine'.[117] It is also evident in Qasim's denunciation of the Israeli-Palestinian negotiations for only taking account of the land occupied by Israel since 1967 [the West Bank and Gaza] at the exclusion of the remaining 'eighty percent of Palestinian land', occupied since 1948.[118]

Hizbu'llah therefore condemns the PLO, and Yasser 'Arafat specifically, for conceding Palestine and reconciling itself to the notion of an emaciated Palestine state, which the party portrays as a 'betrayal' of the Palestinian cause.[119] What is more, in forsaking Palestine, 'Arafat has not only betrayed the Palestinian cause, but also the pan-Islamic cause of Jerusalem. As stated in Chapter 4, Hizbu'llah considers Jerusalem the sacred religious symbol and cause of the Islamic *umma*. The party maintains that 'no one has the right to sell or relinquish or betray'[120] a land that belongs to present and future generations of Muslims.

But the refusal to accord Israel legitimacy, and the perception of the PLO's participation in the negotiations as a national and Islamic betrayal, are not the only considerations behind the vitriol displayed by Hizbu'llah towards the Arab-Israeli peace negotiations. The second premise on which the party's rationale for rejecting the peace process is founded relates to specific Israeli policies which render the prospect of an Arab-Israeli peace an 'illusory' one.[121] Especially indicative of this view is the fact that Hizbu'llah rarely refers to the negotiations as 'the peace process', as they are commonly referred to, but chooses instead to call them 'the settlement process' ("*amaliyyat al-taswiyya*'). Such an appellation signifies that the ultimate end of the negotiations is a settlement rather then peace, and an essentially 'unjust'[122] one at that.

This perception of the negotiations stems from Hizbu'llah's conviction that any agreement that emerges from them will not be in the interests of the 'oppressed' Arab side, but will be skewed in Israel's favour.[123] Hizbu'llah frequently adduces the Palestinian experience to corroborate this view: Despite the fact that Hizbu'llah rejects the entire 'peace process', it censures Israel for 'Judaising' Jerusalem,[124] and for building settlements in the West Bank and Gaza,[125] even though it has pledged to halt the construction of all Jewish settlements. Coupled with Israel's insistence on retaining more than 60 per cent of West Bank territory,[126] Israel has effectively reduced the independent Palestinian state to 'a disfigured entity'[127] whose security and sovereignty will continue to be in Israel's hands.[128]

Yet even this politically impotent state remains 'an inapplicable slogan' by dint of Israel's 'control over the course and development of events',[129] which do not appear to be conducive to its establishment. The upshot of all this is that Israel does not consider itself bound by its agreements with the Palestinians, but merely uses them to end its political and economic isolation from the Arabs.[130] Any peace agreement between Israel and any other Arab state will ensure that relations with Israel are normalised and will thereby serve to entrench Israel's dominance over the region.[131]

But one cannot overlook the room for ideological manoeuvre, which the party has left itself with. The fact that Hizbu'llah inveighs against Israel for failing to abide by the spirit of its agreements with the Palestinians, rather than confine its diatribes against the peace process to the very principle of negotiating with the illegitimate Israeli state, leaves one with the distinct impression that the party is not completely detached from reality, and would therefore not be averse to the notion of an independent Palestinian state.

This inference is greatly substantiated by Fnaysh's assertion that the stand towards the Palestinian-Israeli negotiations 'need not be a case of everything or nothing', when 'there are political and security conditions which compel one to deal with reality'.[132] The liberation of part of Palestine cannot be rejected outright simply because the liberation of all of Palestinian territory is currently unfeasible and potentially self-destructive. What is important is that this 'interaction with reality', as Fnaysh calls it, should not negate 'historical truths' which call for the liberation of all of Palestine, as 'Arafat erroneously believes they do.[133] In this manner, Fnaysh is able to maintain a delicate balance between ideological *thawabit* and political realities. The liberation of all of Palestine will remain an ultimate objective, but in the meantime the liberation of part of Palestine can be considered the penultimate goal, provided it does not metamorphose into a blind pursuit which loses sight of the original goal of retrieving Palestine in its entirety.

This logic is echoed by Fadlu'llah, whose views may not always be typical of the party's, but nonetheless often reflect its general tone. Asked if he would object to the establishment of an independent Palestinian state, Fadlu'llah replied: 'If the establishment of such a state entails the recognition of Israel, then we reject it. However, if the Palestinians were to gain control over any piece of land on which to establish a state without having to recognise Israeli sovereignty over the rest of Palestine, then we do not object.'[134]

Like Fnaysh's formulation, Fadlu'llah's middle-ground solution is not so much an ideological compromise, which necessarily results in ideological concessions, as it is a balance between 'truth' and reality. Such a balance merely involves the indefinite postponement of certain '*thawabit*', which can thereby be retained as intellectual pillars that betoken the existential dimension of Hizbu'llah's struggle with Israel.

In a similar fashion, Hizbu'llah has adroitly reconciled the principle of refusing to grant Israel legitimacy and the aim of liberating Jerusalem with a tacit acceptance of the potentiality of a Lebanese-Israeli peace agreement. This balance can be discerned from Hizbu'llah's views on United Nations Resolution 425, which entails a Lebanese-Israeli agreement of some sort, the April 1996 Agreement, and the party's political discourse on the multilateral negotiations between Syria and Lebanon on the one hand, and Israel on the other.

In theory, Hizbu'llah categorically rejects the US-sponsored UN Resolution 425, which calls for an 'immediate' Israeli withdrawal from Lebanese territory, on several grounds. To the extent that the Resolution 'contains a recognition of the Israeli entity' and affirms the 'necessity of safeguarding its security as stipulated by an article [number three] of the Resolution', Hizbu'llah denounces it.[135] Furthermore, it is rejected on the basis of its sponsor, the US, whom Hizbu'llah accuses of being incapable of issuing a resolution 'which benefits us as a Muslim nation'.[136] That the Resolution was adopted in the midst of Israel's invasion of Lebanon in 1978, under Israeli 'military pressure', only confirms these suspicions for Hizbu'llah.[137]

However, Hizbu'llah's prognosis that 'the day will come when Israel will have no choice but to unilaterally withdraw or implement Resolution 425'[138] seems to militate against the entrenchment of this stand, as does its denunciation of Israel for 'refusing to implement Resolution 425, in flagrant violation of international resolutions'.[139] Thus, although Hizbu'llah rejects the Resolution in principle, its expressed hope of seeing it implemented, coupled with its condemnation of Israel for failing to implement it, signals its grudging acceptance of it.

This tacit acceptance of the Resolution is facilitated by its inherent ambivalence. While the Resolution may bestow legitimacy on the Israeli state and furnish it with security guarantees, as would a peace accord, these clauses are counterbalanced by its call for an 'immediate', and hence unconditional, Israeli withdrawal. Thus, despite the Resolution's bid to 'immediately' establish a UN interim force for South Lebanon, the task of which would be to ensure 'international peace and security', an Israeli withdrawal is not made contingent upon the creation of such a force. Accordingly, the party rejects the third clause, which offers Israel security guarantees, but accepts the second, which relates to Israel's immediate withdrawal from Lebanon. This explains why Hizbu'llah can neither accept nor reject the Resolution outright.

Another consideration at play here, which has also been conducive to the party's undeclared endorsement of the Resolution, is the fact that Hizbu'llah does not explicitly call for its implementation, but merely rebukes Israel for not conforming to the requirements of international law. In so doing, the party benefits from the second article, which calls for an unconditional Israeli withdrawal, without having to recognise the Israeli 'entity' or commit itself to the third article, which guarantees Israel's security after a withdrawal.

A similar logic can be discerned in the party's adherence to the April Agreement, to which both Lebanon and Israel are theoretically bound. Brokered in the aftermath of Israel's 'Grapes of Wrath' in April 1996, the accord contains provisions for limiting military activity on both sides to the 'security zone', thereby prohibiting both sides from launching attacks on or from civilian areas. Despite the fact that the accord entails a recognition of the Israeli state and contains provisions for the peace negotiations, Hizbu'llah has adhered to the general terms of the agreement.[140]

As reasoned by the party, its abidance by the agreement does not constitute a compromise of principle, since it is the Lebanese state, rather than Hizbu'llah, which is signatory to it. This means that, although Hizbu'llah is technically bound to the understanding, it is not theoretically. The party therefore sees itself as being committed to the 'spirit' or 'content' of the understanding, which serves to protect the lives of Lebanese civilians, and not to its 'text' or 'wording', which refers to the legitimacy of the Israeli state and encourages a return to the negotiating table.[141] As in the case of Resolution 425, such an ambivalent position permits the party to reap the benefits of the understanding without having to make any ideological concessions related to the legitimacy of Israel or the peace process.

But even this latter point is amenable to accommodation, as evinced by the party's views on the independent Palestinian state. The same holds true for the Lebanese-Israeli negotiations. As discussed previously, Hizbu'llah's rationale for rejecting the peace process is founded on two premises: its refusal to legitimise Israel's occupation of Palestine and the essentially unjust and illusory nature of an Arab-Israeli peace. For these reasons, the party's Open Letter declares that Hizbu'llah will withhold recognition from any 'separate or non-separate peace treaty' with Israel, should one be formulated.[142] These premises also account for Nasru'llah's affirmation 15 years later that 'Hizbu'llah refuses any reconciliation with Israel in principle.'[143]

In accordance with this firmly ingrained stand, Nasru'llah has repeatedly declared that 'our ink and the Israelis' ink will never meet on the same paper'.[144] Of course the Lebanese government is free to conclude an agreement with Israel, but if it does decide to do so, then Hizbu'llah will surely reject it.[145] The channels it would adopt to express this rejection, however, would be non-violent ones. As avowed by Nasru'llah, Hizbu'llah would most certainly 'disagree' with the Lebanese government about its peace agreement with Israel, but it would not 'make turmoil out of it'.[146] The most that Hizbu'llah would do is vote against any Lebanese-Israeli agreement that required parliamentary ratification.[147]

The corollary of these assertions is that, since the party would not resort to military means to voice its rejection of a Lebanese-Israeli peace, it would not stage cross-border attacks onto northern Israel once the Israeli army and the SLA withdrew their forces from the occupied zone. Nasru'llah admits as much when he avers, 'let it be understood, that once the region is freed, Hizbu'llah will not exercise any security measures there. That is indisputable, because the region will be under the sovereignty of the Lebanese government.'[148]

Implicit in these statements is a willingness on Hizbu'llah's part to reconcile a principal component of its intellectual structure with the dictates of reality. While the party is highly antagonistic to the notion of a Lebanese-Israeli agreement, it accepts the prospect of its realisation. This form of accommodation can also be observed in the party's frequently declared support for the 'shared/single fate' between Lebanon and Syria, and the 'inseparability' of the Lebanese and Syrian tracks in the peace negotiations with Israel.[149] Thus, despite the fact that Hizbu'llah 'is not concerned with the negotiations or the fate of the negotiations, it is concerned with Lebanon and Syria's single fate [in the negotiations]'.[150]

As a result, the party stood resolutely opposed to the 'Lebanon First' policy proposed by Israel in 1997, which aimed at reviving peace talks with Lebanon before resuming negotiations with Syria. Hizbu'llah read further into the proposal an attempt to 'drag' Lebanon to the negotiating table without Syria so as to weaken Lebanon's bargaining position.[151] So abhorrent was this notion to Hizbu'llah, that the party claimed that its 'daily *jihad*' against Israel was but one means of expressing its rejection of the proposal: 'With the rifle we say: we are for the single fate as a guarantee for Lebanon's future.'[152]

Taken in the abstract, such vocal support for the unity of the Lebanese and Syrian stands in the negotiations, and the lengths the party is willing to go in order to preserve it, could be construed as a relatively overt endorsement of a Lebanese-Israeli accord, and of the peace process generally. But viewed in their proper context, such declarations are more likely to be comprehended as reluctant acknowledgements of the peace process, governed by rational considerations of strength and weakness.

The following explication by Husayn al-Mussawi exemplifies this rationale:

Now that the negotiations have begun and we could not do anything to stop them, our judgement tells us to support the side who will minimise our losses. If losses occur they will be reduced. If the Lebanese participate in the negotiations alone, they will be defeated and they will have to retreat [from their original positions] because they are weak. They will not be able to confront the Americans, Israelis and the group of Arabs who will pressure them on behalf of America and Israel, as they intend to do at the Doha summit. So we oppose the negotiations but we approve of the joint Lebanese-Syrian track because Syria will be able to realise Lebanon's interests.[153]

This logic is echoed by Fayyad who argues that, although the party rejects any form of negotiations with the Israelis, it 'refuses to accept the isolation of Lebanon' in the negotiations, in light of its inability to single-handedly confront Israel.[154]

One could quite conceivably argue that such rationales are adopted in order to appease Syria, who stands as much to gain as Lebanon, if not more, from a united negotiating position. Doubtless, there is much truth in such a contention. As Syria is the overseer of the Lebanese political system, no local political force stands a chance of political inclusion or longevity if it is inimical to Syrian interests. This may well explain why Hizbu'llah, as well as all Lebanese politicians, find it necessary to curry favour with Syria by advocating a single negotiating stand.[155]

Nevertheless, one cannot dismiss Hizbu'llah's justifications for supporting the united Syrian-Lebanese stand as pure sycophancy. Hizbu'llah may well be promulgating its view on the issue for Syrian consumption, but that does not imply that it is not genuinely convinced of it. The above-cited justification proffered by Husayn al-Mussawi may not prove Hizbu'llah's sincere belief in it, but it is a very plausible argument that could easily be espoused by the party or anyone else. Unlike Lebanon, Syria is a powerful regional actor and a force to be reckoned with, as exemplified by its decades-long domination over Lebanon. Its strong relations with the Arab world could greatly benefit Lebanon in thwarting Israeli and American attempts at forcing concessions out of it.

Another point worth considering is that Hizbu'llah does not deny that Syria would benefit from a joint negotiating stand with Lebanon, nor does it deny that it is Hizbu'llah's Islamic Resistance, rather than the Lebanese state, which has strengthened Syria's bargaining position. This admission is evident in the party's affirmation that the 'inseparability' of the Lebanese and Syrian positions 'makes Lebanon's and Syria's balance in the confrontation greater and their ability to confront stronger'.[156] It is also manifest in Hizbu'llah's insistence that Syria will 'still' have a need for Hizbu'llah in the event of a peace agreement with Israel,[157] intimating that it is currently in need of Hizbu'llah's Resistance.

The very fact that the party openly admits to this Syrian need and its willingness to fulfill it, indicates that its call for a united Lebanese-Syrian stand also stems from ideological considerations related to Arab territorial rights and to Syria's unyieldingness vis-à-vis Israel. As the only 'impregnable stronghold in the Arab world',[158] Syria's intent to 'safeguard Arab rights',[159] coupled with its unqualified support for the Islamic Resistance,[160] earns it Lebanon's full co-operation in the negotiations. That Syria is party to the 'blasphemous' peace process in the first place, is vindicated by 'circumstances which compelled Syria to participate' in it, and by Syria's unparalleled 'brave and callous' negotiating stand, which sets it apart from its capitulatory Arab brethren.[161]

In effect, Hizbu'llah's rejection of a Lebanese-Israeli peace is tempered by rational and ideological considerations that demand its adaptation to the requirements of reality. Faced with a choice between a completely unjust peace and a less unjust peace, Hizbu'llah is more inclined to opt for the lesser of 'the two evils', to borrow Meri''s term.[162]

That Hizbu'llah has settled for an 'evil' could lead one to the conclusion that the party is undergoing a process of ideological dilution. As tempting as this surmise may be, one must bear in mind that an accommodation of reality, and even an evil one at that, is not synonymous with an ideological watering down. While this maxim may not apply to all political movements or parties that accommodate many of their central beliefs to the circumstances at hand, Hizbu'llah's tactful balance between its rejectionist principles and an objectionable reality has enabled it to avoid the charge of intellectual inconsistency.

Hizbu'llah has been able to achieve this balance by retaining its intellectual pillars as fixed and invariable principles and concomitantly accepting political developments that appear to contradict them. Rather than simply phase out such elements of its intellectual discourse and thereby expose itself to the accusation of ideological adulteration, Hizbu'llah juxtaposes the intellectual with the political so as to underline the preservation of the former, notwithstanding the adoption of the latter.

But what has really facilitated this seeming casuistry is the fact that, as the signatory of any future peace agreement with Israel, it is the Lebanese state's ink, as opposed to Hizbu'llah's, which would have met Israel's. Therefore, the party would neither have granted Israel legitimacy, nor pledged to safeguard Israel's security or to normalise relations with it, as demanded of the Lebanese state. In this manner, the party would be able to reap the rewards of a Lebanese-Israeli accord, as in the case of the April Agreement, without having to recognise or abide by its text. Accordingly, it would 'consider the liberation of the territories [by means of a peace agreement] a victory, while confronting the normalisation of relations with Israel'.[163]

In effect, Hizbu'llah's rejection of the prospect of normalised relations with Israel is one intellectual construct that is not amenable to an accommodation with political reality. While the party can be forgiven for accepting the reality of the peace negotiations, which it is powerless to change, it cannot be exonerated from its responsibility for confronting normalisation, which it is fully capable of obstructing since normalisation is carried out by people as well as states.

That is not to say, however, that Hizbu'llah is not committed to this essentially existential principle. Hizbu'llah may be willing to temporarily countenance an Arab-Israeli peace (*salam*), which it most probably conceives of as a transient lull, but it is definitely not willing to condone a full-scale reconciliation (*sulh*) with Israeli state and society, at any phase in time. Viewed from the perspective of the party, the normalisation of economic, social, cultural and political relations with Israel would extirpate the existential foundations of the conflict with it, and would be tantamount to an approval of Israel's continued occupation of Palestine. As propounded by Qasim: 'Even if Israel withdraws from our land, this does not give it the right to keep Palestine. We therefore reject the normalisation of relations with Israel.'[164]

What has greatly helped Hizbu'llah in maintaining this stand is its iron-clad conviction that the *umma*, and the Palestinian people in particular, will 'categorically reject' the Palestinian-Israeli accords,[165] and all other agreements forged between Israel and other Arab states. If peace agreements are rejected on the mass level, it follows that the Arab people will repudiate the demand for the normalisation of relations with Israel, which inheres in the agreements.

This certainty that peace agreements will be repudiated on the popular Arab level stems from the supposition that any Arab-Israeli agreement would be 'contradictory' to the Arab peoples' 'history, beliefs, heritage and present', and would thereby have been forcibly 'imposed' on them,[166] as evinced by the Jordanian people's boycott of the Israeli trade exhibition in Amman.[167]

Another factor that has been conducive to Hizbu'llah's ability to indemnify its position on normalisation from political acclimatisation is the supposition that its plan to confront normalisation will not be hindered by Syria. This assumption is based on the premise that the conflict with Israel will remain an existential one, not only in the collective consciousness of the Arab people, but even on the official state level. Thus, despite the potential conclusion of Lebanese and Syrian peace agreements with Israel, 'the conflict between Israel and the Arab world would not have ended but would assume a different character'.[168] As the most likely candidate for an anti-nor-malisation drive that would effectively counter Israeli efforts to dominate the region politically and infiltrate it economically and culturally, Hizbu'llah would be 'needed' by Syria as much as, if not more, than it is now.[169]

Hizbu'llah therefore envisages a new confrontational role for itself in the aftermath of an Israeli withdrawal from the occupied zone. Although the Arab people's aversion to the notion of normalisation is virtually taken for granted by the party, the imperativeness it places on educating people about 'the dangers of normalisation'[170] betrays an uncertainty about the exact magnitude of this aversion.

The party believes that the Arab people must be fully 'immunised' from Israel's insidious and conspicuous attempts at normalisation by means of a grass-roots anti-normalisation campaign, which would presumably be spearheaded by Hizbu'llah.[171] Such a campaign would involve political elites, '*ulama* and intellectuals[172] and would necessitate manifold cultural, social and political means such as religious education, the mass media, mobilisational rallies and demonstrations, and various political institutions[173] to engender the required level of 'political awareness'.[174]

Thus, although the party can attune itself to the concept of a Lebanese-Israeli peace, it believes that the existential foundations of its struggle with Israel can still be preserved so long as it refuses to accommodate its principles to the concept of reconciliation with the Israeli state. The party's anti-normalisation plan has therefore acted as an ideological safety net for Hizbu'llah, in that it has cushioned its self-imposed accommodation to the notion of *salam* with a steadfast rejection of *sulh*.

The Liberation of Jerusalem

As the direct corollary of Hizbu'llah's delegitimisation of the Israeli state, the party's long cherished aim of liberating Jerusalem – and by extension, Palestine – from Israeli occupation, constitutes the most rudimentary existential foundation of its struggle with Israel and the underlying theme of the aforementioned existential dimensions.

According to the party, this aspiration to return 'every grain of Palestinian soil' to its rightful owners[175] necessitates Israel's 'oblit-eration from existence'.[176] Put simply, the reconstitution of one state is contingent upon the annihilation of another. The only way that the Palestinians can return to Jerusalem, and the 'original Palestine of 1948' generally,[177] is for all Jews, with the exception of those native to Palestine,[178] to 'leave this region and return to the countries from whence they came'.[179]

It follows that Hizbu'llah's conflict with Israel is a question of existence rather than borders (*ma'rakit wujud wa laysa hudud*), which leads to the ineluctable conclusion that Israel's withdrawal from South Lebanon will neither render Israel any less of an occupier for Hizbu'llah, nor invalidate this reasoning. The following assertion by Qasim substantiates this inference: 'Even if Israel withdraws from South Lebanon, it will remain an occupier in our eyes and the duty to liberate Palestine will remain incumbent upon us.'[180]

In congruity with this perceived duty is the consideration of Israel's full withdrawal from Lebanon as a mere 'prelude to its final obliteration from existence and the liberation of venerable Jerusalem'.[181] The state of war with Israel 'cannot possibly end when Israel withdraws' from South Lebanon, but will continue indefinitely until Palestine is liberated in its entirety.[182]

But it is not only the retrieval of Palestinian land that necessitates that the *jihad* against Israel be a perpetual one. As an 'absolute evil' and an inherently expansionist state, Israel will not allow the Lebanese or Arabs 'to live in peace'.[183] So long as Israel continues to exist, it will remain a 'threat' to the 'existence' of the current and future *umma*.[184] Viewed from this existential angle, an Israeli withdrawal from the South will not ensure the security of Lebanon's national borders, but will almost indubitably result in its 'continuing aggression' against the people of South Lebanon.[185]

The only way that the security of 'the Muslims' can be safeguarded is by making the 'obliteration of the existence of the usurper Zionist entity', a *'wajib shari'*.[186] The 'logic of existence'[187] therefore dictates that the eradication of Israel and the resulting retrieval of Palestine become the responsibility of the entire *umma*.[188] Every Muslim 'must bear arms' as long as Israel remains in existence, and should not so much as 'consider laying them down' before this existence is terminated.[189] In light of this religious imperative, Hizbu'llah will view the liberation of Palestine as religious a duty as prayer is.[190]

Yet as religiously imperative as the eradication of Israel and the liberation of Jerusalem are to Hizbu'llah, other statements by the party detract from the Islamic nature of this obligation and imbue it with a nationalistic character. This tendency can be inferred from Fnaysh's declaration that Hizbu'llah would have resorted to the same violent means as Hamas had the Israeli state been founded on Lebanese territory.[191]

Although the original purpose of this statement was to vindicate the use of violence against Israeli civilians by Palestinian Islamists, a distinctive subtext can be detected in it. Fnaysh's assertion that Hizbu'llah 'would have' resorted to violence as a liberation strategy had Lebanon been fully usurped by Israel, indicates that it neither has the right nor the obligation to adopt this strategy to liberate another land. Hamas' adoption of this violent liberation strategy therefore emerges as a national right and duty that is exclusive to the Palestinians.

This inference is borne out by other, more explicit utterances by party officials. One such example is Qasim's declaration that 'we will not be substitutes for others in liberation. In liberation, only the owners of a land can constitute its basis.'[192] This assertion echoes Nasru'llah's affirmation that Hizbu'llah 'cannot be an alternative to another people's [liberation] movement. We can be an element of support or assistance but it must carry the banner, I cannot carry it in its place.'[193]

Thus, although the liberation of the pan-Islamic symbol of Jerusalem remains a religious duty incumbent upon the entire Islamic *umma*, whose existence is also imperilled by Israel, it is first and foremost a national duty, which must be assumed by a section of the *umma*. Jerusalem therefore emerges as a Palestinian city in the first place, and an Islamic one in the second place.

Yet despite this implication, in neither Nasru'llah's nor Qasim's declarations is there an intimation that Hizbu'llah would not play a military role in the liberation of Palestine, only that the party cannot be expected to lead this role. By the same token, although Fnaysh's statement contains an undeclared admission of the party's unwillingness to deliberately kill Israeli civilians as a means of liberating Palestine, it does not bar the use of other military means. Other forms of military assistance would still be open to Hizbu'llah, such as providing the Palestinians with military training and logistical support, or even fighting alongside them as an auxiliary force.

In any case, the question of the kind of military support that Hizbu'llah would furnish the Palestinians with in the event of an Israeli withdrawal becomes purely academic when the actual feasibility of such support is taken into account. In effect, the question becomes one that centres on whether the party will provide the Palestinians with military or non-military assistance, given a particular political-military context. That Hizbu'llah's pursuit of the liberation of Palestine through military means is not the inevitable outcome of an Israeli withdrawal from Lebanon is evinced by the party's virtual unanimity in asserting that the exact means it will adopt to liberate Jerusalem will depend entirely on 'future circumstances'.[194]

As expounded by Ra'id, Israel's withdrawal from Lebanon will occur within the context of specific circumstances, which will determine whether Hizbu'llah will resort to political and cultural or military means to liberate Palestine.

> If Israel withdraws under Hizbu'llah pressure is one thing, and if it withdraws as a result of a peace agreement with the Lebanese state is another. If it withdraws from the South only, in order to separate the Lebanese and Syrian tracks, is one thing, and if it withdraws from the South and the Golan Heights, is another. If it withdraws while the US is meddling in the region is one thing, and if it withdraws while the US is preoccupied with another crisis is another. If it withdraws when there is an Arab atmosphere which will accept nothing less than the liberation of Jerusalem is one thing, and if it withdraws at a time when the Arabs are fragmented is another.[195]

In accordance with this political analysis, Hizbu'llah would not be able to pursue the liberation of Palestine through military means, if either the second, fourth, sixth or eighth scenario materialises. Conversely, the occurrence of the first, third, fifth and seventh scenarios would permit Hizbu'llah to provide the Palestinians with military support.

With regard to the first possibility, a unilateral Israeli withdrawal from the South not tied to a comprehensive peace agreement, would not signal a definitive end to the Lebanese-Israeli conflict for Hizbu'llah, as such a withdrawal would not necessarily be a complete one. The Israeli army's recent 'Morning Twilight' proposal, which calls for the retention of up to 500 metres of Lebanese territory (the so-called 'Purple-Line') in the event of a unilateral Israeli withdrawal, attests to this point. Even if it were a complete withdrawal, in conformity with UN Resolution 425, the South would still remain exposed to Israeli cross-border attacks, which would leave the southern battlefront effectively open.

On the other side of the coin, if Israel withdraws from Lebanon within the framework of a Lebanese-Israeli peace agreement, the security of the South would fall into the hands of the Lebanese state. This would make it virtually impossible for Hizbu'llah to launch cross-border attacks on Israel. Moreover, since the conclusion of a Lebanese-Israeli agreement necessarily implies that a Syrian-Israeli agreement would also have been concluded – in light of the 'inseparability' of the Lebanese and Syrian negotiating tracks – Hizbu'llah would not be able to transfer its troops from the South to Palestine, in the teeth of Syrian opposition.

Not only would Syria actively thwart Hizbu'llah's attempts to extend the armed struggle to Palestine, but it would also indirectly hinder this possibility by either expelling the sundry armed Palestinian factions bent on liberating Palestine in its entirety, who currently take sanctuary in Syria, or by prohibiting them from engaging in military activity against Israel. Without the help of these radical groups, Hizbu'llah's militant attempts at liberating Palestine would be futile.

Another factor which would determine the means Hizbu'llah would adopt to liberate Palestine is the nature of the US' role in the region at the time of an Israeli withdrawal. If the US was still 'meddling' in the region, or in other words, impeding the progress of the peace negotiations by continuing to back Israeli demands, and thereby hampering the likelihood of an Israeli withdrawal from the South and the Golan, this would also serve to escalate the military situation.

Yet assuming the occurrence of any of the above conditions, which are conducive to the possibility of a military endeavour to liberate Palestine, no single one would directly result in such an endeavour in the absence of a concerted Arab decision to retrieve Palestine. Without sufficient Arab backing, any military assault on Israeli territory would be not only futile, but also counter-productive in the face of the Israeli army's superior military technology and conceivable Western opposition to a scheme that seeks to eradicate Israel's existence.

Bearing these contingencies and Hizbu'llah's realism in mind, it would be very hard to envisage the party embarking on an ultimately losable war against Israel. After all, Hizbu'llah's resistance to Israel's occupation of South Lebanon would not have been as successful, or even possible, had it not been for Iran's military and financial support, and Syria's political endorsement of the Resistance – an observation which cannot possibly be lost on Hizbu'llah. Therefore, it would be highly unlikely for the party to wage a military offensive against Israel on the sole grounds of principle.

That Hizbu'llah would not be disposed to take such drastic action in the absence of a united Arab stand to liberate Palestine is clearly demonstrated by Meri''s admission that the party was compelled to rethink its plan to liberate Jerusalem after the Gulf war (between Iran and Iraq) in 1988.[196] Up until that time, the party had made the liberation of Palestine contingent upon Iran's victory in the war, which would have signalled the deposition of Saddam Husayn and the institution of a (possibly Shi'ite Islamic) regime that would have been favourably disposed to the concept of a liberated Palestine.

In the words of Meri':

> When Hizbu'llah spoke of liberating Palestine, it was based on something other than ideology. If Saddam fell [from power], and there was unity or at least cooperation between Iraq and Iran, the face of the entire region would have changed. However, after Iran's implementation of UN Resolution 598, which called for a permanent cease-fire, the party had to re-evaluate its strategy and modify its discourse, in such a manner that it began to raise the slogan of liberating Lebanese soil, whilst devoting less discourse to the liberation of Palestinian soil.[197]

In effect, the party's consistent refusal to reveal its intentions for the post-withdrawal phase, or what it refers to as its 'hidden card',[198] does not appear to be so hidden after all. While the declared aim of concealing its true intentions is to provide Syria and Lebanon with a 'source of strength', or a useful bargaining tool, in the negotiations[199] – insofar as giving Israel free 'reassurances' would preclude the possibility of an Israeli withdrawal – the aforementioned factors effectively diminish the value of this trump card.

Not only is this card unmasked by Ra'id's exposition of the circumstances required for a military assault on Israel, and Meri''s admission of the current unfeasibility of such a scheme, but it is also revealed by Nasru'llah's previously-cited claim that Hizbu'llah would not 'exercise security measures' in the South once Israel withdraws its forces from the region. Another statement that points to this conclusion is Fnaysh's assurance that, in the event of an Israeli withdrawal from Lebanon, Hizbu'llah would not 'take any action or confront the Zionist threat [in a manner] that would harm the interests of the Lebanese people'.[200] All these assertions go hand in hand with the party's tacit acceptance of an independent Palestinian state and the peace process in general, which itself is incongruous with an armed offensive against the Israeli state.

But it must also be stressed that, although the party has accommodated its principled rejection of an Arab-Israeli peace to the circumstances at hand, it has not relinquished its goal of liberating Jerusalem, but merely postponed its implementation in light of these circumstances. Admittedly, 'with the present balance of power, there is no capability to liberate Palestine'.[201] But, as rationalised by Fnaysh, 'this does not mean that we have forsaken Palestine, or that we have settled for Palestinian self-rule in parts of Palestine, as Yasserr 'Arafat has'.[202]

Thus, as 'unrealistic' as the aspiration to liberate Palestine may now appear, it will remain a 'strategic', and hence long-term, goal for Hizbu'llah.[203] Just as the establishment of an Israeli state was an unrealistic goal for the Jews one hundred years ago, the reconstitution of a Palestinian state could quite conceivably be realised one hundred years from now.[204] Even if Palestine remains occupied one hundred years from now, its eventual liberation is expected, in accordance with the party's millenarian beliefs, which posit that the Hidden Imam will lead the Prophet Jesus in prayer at Jerusalem's al-Aqsa mosque, 'where there will be no Jews, or Star of David, or a usurper entity'.[205]

The upshot of all this is that the party acknowledges that the liberation of Palestine will not be accomplished in 'a day or two, a month or two, or a year or two', but in 'eras'.[206] Presumably, the party envisages it will take this long for the Islamic *umma* to amass the necessary resources and capabilities required for establishing 'the Jerusalem army' to liberate Palestine.[207] In the meantime, the party will lay the ideological groundwork for the liberation of Palestine by continuing to delegitimise the Israeli state through its anti-normalisation campaign.[208] Furthermore, it will also contribute to this groundwork by maintaining its opposition to the naturalisation of the Palestinians, on the grounds that their permanent resettlement in Lebanon would bar their return to Palestine and legitimise Israel's occupation of their homes.[209]

In this manner, Hizbu'llah has injected its intellectual discourse with a sense of realism, which has permitted it to adapt to political developments without compromising the rejectionist underpinnings of its intellectual structure. In so doing, the party has also carved out a significant political role for itself for the post-withdrawal future.

8   Anti-Judaism

The Identification of Zionism with Judaism

On the surface Hizbu'llah appears to distinguish between Judaism and Zionism, which it claims to identify exclusively with the state of Israel. As enunciated by Fnaysh, the secular character of the Zionist movement attests to its dissociation from Judaism and Jewish religious law. The only relation between the two doctrines lies in the Zionist exploitation of Jewish *"asabiyya'* (tribal solidarity) to garner mass Jewish support for its political movement.[1] It is this 'political project' which the party views as abhorrent, rather than Judaism per se.[2]

For Hizbu'llah, Judaism is a 'divine religion' whose adherents are regarded as 'People of the Book', and thus accorded the same religious and legal rights in Islam as Christians.[3] So long as the Jews observe their religious beliefs and rituals without 'transforming them into political products that lead to the domination of others', Hizbu'llah 'has no objection to them'.[4] The party claims 'to have no problem' with the original Jewish inhabitants of Palestine, but only with those who emigrated there after 1948.[5]

Hizbu'llah therefore distinguishes between Zionist Jews and 'ordinary Jews',[6] who are culturally assimilated into their respective societies and whose affiliation to Judaism is devoid of any political or nationalist implications. These latter Jews abide by their religious law but do not seek to impose their own state 'at the expense of others'.[7]

Consequently, the Jews' interpretation of the Torah is 'not monolithic', but varied.[8] To some extent, the acknowledgement of the Jews' ideological heterogeneity is bolstered by Qasim's claim that a 'small number' of Jews are not Zionists.[9] Despite the original intent of this assertion, however, it can also be taken as an indication of the party's conviction that the number of Jews who actually digress from the Zionist mainstream is negligible. As a result, the purported distinction between Zionism and Judaism, which is contingent upon the assumption that not all Jews are Zionists, loses its cogency since it is believed that most Jews do in fact subscribe to Zionism as an ideology.

This view is further underlined by Qasim's interpretation of the following Qur'anic verse: 'Strongest among men in enmity to the believers wilt thou find the Jews' (5:85). In Qasim's understanding, this verse does not apply to 'every single Jew', but to 'the over-whelming majority' who are Zionists.[10] While the underlying aim of this exegesis was to exculpate the small number of Jews who 'are not evil', it also betrays the party's undeclared supposition that very few Jews are not Zionists. It is supposed that, had God excluded a large portion of the Jews, or at least a significant minority of them, from His condemnation, then He would have not made the gener-alisation that 'the Jews', as opposed to a segment of the Jewish community, were the most hostile of men to the believers.

In effect, Hizbu'llah's professed distinction between Judaism and Zionism is merely an attempt to give the benefit of the doubt to the small number of non-Israeli Jews who oppose Zionism. To all intents and purposes, the negligible number of anti-Zionist Jews has enabled Hizbu'llah to closely identify Judaism with Zionism. It has also con-tributed to the use of the term 'Jewish' as an epithet for 'Zionist'[11] and to the usage of both terms interchangeably.[12]

One may contend that the synonymy of the two terms in Hizbu'llah's lexicon, and the general equation of Zionism with Judaism, merely signify that all Zionists are necessarily Jews (although, doubtless the party would admit to the existence of non-Jewish Zionists) rather than indicate that all Jews are Zionists. However, to do so would be to ignore the party's extensive derogation of Judaism as a religion, irrespective of its Zionist offshoot. In light of the party's anti-Judaism, its claim to differenti-ate Judaism from Zionism becomes purely academic. Even if some Jews do not espouse Zionism, their religion is still rejected. Whether or not Jews champion Zionism is therefore immaterial, for their religion is held responsible for the birth of Zionism. That the over-whelming majority of Jews happen to be Zionists, by Hizbu'llah's reckoning, only highlights the Judaic origins of Zionism and greatly facilitates the close identification between two doctrines which are perceived to be equally iniquitous.

More than anything else, it is the biblical roots of the Zionist project that has been conducive to the equation of Zionism with Judaism. Just as Israel is considered the geodemographic product of Zionism, Zionism is considered the political outgrowth of Judaism. Thus, even though Fnaysh claims that Zionism is unrelated to Judaism by dint of its secular character, his depiction of Zionism as a 'Torah and Talmudic' ideology[13] is indicative of his linkage between Judaism and Zionism. Zionist ideology may be essentially secular in character, but its origins are distinctly religious.

The Zionist call for the restoration of the Jewish 'National Home' in Palestine was, after all, inspired by God's promise of the land of Canaan to Abraham and his descendants (Genesis 17:8). Moreover, the biblical etymology of the word 'Zionism', which is a derivative of the term 'Zion', further illustrates the religious origins of Zionist ideology. Captured in 1000 BCE by King David, Zion (or what is now called the Temple Mount) came to constitute the core of the City of David and was sanctified as the 'holy hill' of God (Psalms 2:6). After the fall of Jerusalem in 70 CE, Zion came to symbolise the hope of reconstructing the Jewish National Home in Palestine. It is against this biblical backdrop that Fnaysh claims that the 'theory of the historic right' to the 'Promised Land' constitutes the doctrinal basis of the Zionist claim to the land of Palestine.[14] All that Zionism did was 'to promote' this existing 'theory', and to translate it into operational terms.[15]

The association between Zionism and Judaism is also self-evident in the fact that Israel is the only country in the world to grant citizenship according to the criterion of religion, irrespective of the criteria of ethnicity or nationality.[16] That Israel is comprised of diverse ethnic groups bound together 'by their Talmud and Jewish fanaticism'[17] further underscores the Judaic essence of Zionism and Israel for Hizbu'llah. Accordingly, the party not only refers to Israel as 'the Zionist entity', but also as 'the Jewish entity'.[18]

Bearing these considerations in mind, it becomes easier to discern Hizbu'llah's attempts to Judaise Zionism and the Israeli state, as when it proclaims that 'the dreams of the Israelites are over'.[19] These attempts are also manifest in the party's transference of negative Jewish traits to Zionism and Israeli society. This tendency is best exemplified in one of Nasru'llah's diatribes against Israel: 'If we searched the entire world for a person more cowardly, despicable, weak and feeble in psyche, mind, ideology and religion, we would not find anyone like the Jew. Notice, I do not say the Israeli.'[20] Nasru'llah does not mean that these traits do not apply to the Israeli. For Hizbu'llah, they define the very essence of the Israeli, but only insofar as he has inherited them from his Judaic background, in which they originate.

Another Jewish legacy that is invariably invoked by the party is the Israelis' 'racist superiority'.[21] It believes that, in conformity with their biblical beliefs, the Israelis see themselves as God's 'chosen people' and accordingly view non-Jews or 'gentiles' as racially inferior to them. Their religious ideology instructs them to treat the gentiles as 'animals' and is responsible for their aggression.[22] Zionist society is therefore 'originally based on the doctrine of war and the killing of gentiles'[23] and the 'slaying of Prophets'.[24] Based on this portrayal, Baruch Goldstein's massacre of 29 Palestinian worshippers at the Ibrahimi Mosque in Hebron in February 1994 is not viewed by the party as an instance of human insanity, but is cited as an example of the belligerence that is intrinsic to Judaism as opposed to Zionism. [25]

Hizbu'llah believes that, as a people who are 'stained with aggression, depravity and the shedding of blood', the Israeli Jews cannot be trusted to make peace with the Arabs.[26] For Hizbu'llah, not only is their untrustworthiness attributable to their inherent aggression, which is reflected in their characteristically violent history, but also to their notorious deceit and treachery, as revealed in the Qur'an, the Old Testament and the New Testament.[27] According to Nasru'llah, their worship of the golden calf during Moses' 40-day absence, after having given him their Covenant (2:92), coupled with their frequent violations of their pacts with the Prophet Muhammad (8:56–8), renders them a people 'renowned for breaching covenants and promises, even with God and the prophets'.[28] Therefore, any covenant made with them would only be breached once they had made the necessary preparations for war.[29]

Anti-Zionism versus Anti-Judaism

Having deliberated the confluence of Judaism and Zionism in the thought of Hizbu'llah, the differentiation between the party's anti-Zionism and anti-Judaism becomes much harder to establish. In part, this is due to the sizeable impact the Zionist state has had on Hizbu'llah's perception of the Jews, which reveals itself in the tendency to transfer negative Israeli attributes onto the Jews as a whole. But since the Zionist state is ultimately traceable to Judaism in the mind of Hizbu'llah, the blurring of the distinction between its anti-Zionism and its anti-Judaism is, above all else, attributable to the Judaic roots of Zionism. Hizbu'llah's anti-Judaism therefore emerges as intrinsic a part of its intellectual structure as is its anti-Zionism.

As central an intellectual construct as Hizbu'llah's anti-Judaism is, however, one cannot conclude that this renders it an anti-Semitic movement. In fact, it would be a gross fallacy to claim that contemporary Islam is anti-Semitic, as some researchers on Arab and Islamic anti-Semitism tend to take for granted.[30] Still, it must noted that the fallacy does not stem from the fact that the Arabs are also believed to be Semites by virtue of their descent from Noah's son, Shem, but from the racial connotations of the term 'Semite'.

Even if the concept of anti-Semitism applies only to the Jewish descendants of Shem, the usage of the term 'Semite' rather than 'Jew' necessarily implies that it refers to the derogation of the Jews as a race and not as a religious community. The principal factor that has contributed to the confusion between the two is that Jewish Zionists consider the Jews to be both a religion and a race and therefore equate anti-Judaism with anti-Semitism.

Neither traditional nor contemporary Islam anathematises the Jews as a race – after all, Islam hails itself as a universal religion that does not recognise racial and ethnic boundaries – but as the adherents of a religion berated by Islam. Islam's vilification of Jews, or what I have chosen to call Islamic anti-Judaism, emanates from its excoriation of the genesis, history and religious convictions of the Jewish faith, not the Jewish race. Although traditional European anti-Semitism also draws its vituperation of the Jews from religious scripture and invokes Jewish religious history, the subject of its vituperation is the Jewish race not the Jewish faith. Martin Luther's invective against the Jews in a pamphlet published in 1543, 'Concerning the Jews and their Lies', is illustrative of this point: 'What shall the Christians do with this damned, rejected race of Jews? Since they live among us and we know about their lying and blasphemy and cursing, we cannot tolerate them.'[31]

As the founder of the Protestant Reformation, Luther's remarks bore distinctly religious overtones, which are also evident in his castigation of the Jews for misinterpreting their Scriptures. But, in the final analysis, his designation of the Jews as a 'race' betrayed the anti-Semitic nature of his attitude towards them.

Thus, it is neither the doctrinal basis of Hizbu'llah's enmity towards the Jews nor its vilification of Jewish religious history, nor even its use of religious idiom to derogate the Jews generally, that distinguishes its anti-Judaism from anti-Semitism. Rather, it is its abomination of the Jews as a religious community as opposed to a racial group which sets the two apart. This distinction is a critical one. In the case of the former, the Jews are anathematised for their religious beliefs, while in the case of the latter, they are abhorred for belonging to a certain race.

The grounds for this distinction are most clearly, albeit unwittingly, expressed in the definition of anti-Semitism advanced by Charles Y. Glock and Rodney Stark. For them, anti-Semitism refers to 'the hatred and persecution of Jews as a group. Not the hatred of persons who happen to be Jews, but rather, the hatred of persons because they are Jewish.'[32] It is their innate Jewishness, rather than their conviction in Judaism, which incurs the detestation of others.

The subtext here is that, for the anti-Semite, the evil innate in the Jew is incontrovertible as dictated by his racial origins. For the anti-Jew, the Jew's evil nature is something acquired from his Judaism, and as such, is revocable upon the renunciation of his faith (provided of course that he does not espouse Zionism). Perhaps the closest thing to an official substantiation of this inference is Ra'id's claim that 'we cannot say that this religious group was born evil. No one is born evil. The source of evil in deviant Judaism lies in its illusion of racial superiority.'[33] He thinks the Jews are not evil because they are Jews but because they subscribe to a deviant and racist Judaism.

Notwithstanding the conceptual differences, the similarities between anti-Semitism and anti-Judaism must not be overlooked either. The two predominant features of Islamic anti-Judaism correspond neatly with the two defining criteria of anti-Semitism: the demonisation of Jews[34] and the ascription of a universal plot against God and mankind to them.[35] Thus, the anti-Judaism of Hizbu'llah is as vituperative against Jews, if not more than, conventional anti-Semitism.

The Islamic Roots of Hizbu'llah's Anti-Judaism

Although Zionism and Judaism are synonymous in Hizbu'llah's lexicon, the resulting confluence of the party's anti-Zionism and anti-Judaism does not render the latter contingent upon the former. While there may be some truth in the contention propounded by some scholars that the conflict with Zionism has been the chief cause of Arab anti-Semitism,[36] in the case of contemporary Islam, and Hizbu'llah in particular, it would be more appropriate to state that Zionism has greatly impacted on an existing, yet latent, anti-Judaism. Although this might be hard to determine, especially since Hizbu'llah owes its birth to Israel's occupation of Lebanon, and hence to Zionism, the anti-Judaism of Hizbu'llah is detached from Zionism insofar as Islam is staunchly anti-Judaic.

This assertion flies in the face of Bernard Lewis' predication that traditional Islamic anti-Judaism does not resemble contemporary Islamic and Arab anti-Semitism. As propounded by Lewis, traditional Islam exhibited a 'normal' type of 'prejudice' that often generated a 'normal' or 'conventional' persecution, in contradistinction to the 'demonological beliefs and conspiratorial fantasies' that characterise Christian anti-Semitism, which were later mirrored by the Arab and Islamic world.[37]

In the first place, and in light of the above-cited reasons, Lewis makes the crucial mistake of designating Islamic anti-Judaism as anti-Semitism. In the second place, Lewis commits the equally grave error of depicting traditional Islam as more tolerant of Jews and the Judaic faith than its modern-day version, thereby implying that Zionism was the cause of Arab-Islamic anti-Semitism.

As odious as Zionism is to Hizbu'llah, the party insists that its strong aversion to Judaism is unrelated to its abomination of Zionism, and hence exists irrespective of the existence of Zionism. According to Hizbu'llah's interpretation of the Qur'an and the Old and New Testaments, from time immemorial the Jews have continuously demonstrated their quintessentially evil nature. Qasim expresses this view succinctly: 'The history of Jews has proven that, regardless of the Zionist proposal, they are a people who are evil in their ideas.' From the very origins of their existence, the Jews 'created mischief for people' wherever they went.[38] For 'Abbas al-Mussawi, this Qur'anic interpretation of Jewish history shows that the problem with the Jews does not lie in their occupation of Lebanon, and presumably not in their usurpation of Palestine either, but in their religious creed.[39]

Based on these statements and on several Qur'anic verses, one can propound the thesis that Zionism merely brought Hizbu'llah's latent anti-Judaism, which is rooted in a vehemently anti-Judaic Islamic tradition, to the fore.[40] Contemporary Islamic anti-Judaism is merely a politicised (though by no means radicalised) and militant expression of traditional Islamic anti-Judaism, which, upon a close Qur'anic exegesis, appears as hostile towards the Jews as the alleged anti-Semitism of contemporary Islam, and by extension, of Hizbu'llah.

If we are to employ Lewis' criteria for anti-Semitism, we would be led to the ineluctable conclusion that Islamic anti-Judaism closely resembles anti-Semitism in that it both demonises the Jews and, according to at least to one Qur'anic verse, accuses them of conspiring against humanity. The following excursus will strive to illustrate Islam's deep-rooted animosity towards the Jews by examining several Qur'anic verses which pertain to the Jews or the Children of Israel.[41] The objective of this analysis is to show that, while Hizbu'llah's anti-Judaism is to a considerable extent influenced by Zionism, it is not contingent upon it.

One of the most telling verses in this respect, and one frequently cited by the party as proof of the Qur'an's enmity towards the Jews,[42] is the following:

> Strongest among men in enmity to the believers wilt thou find the Jews and Pagans; and nearest among them in love to the believers wilt thou find those who say, 'We are Christians'; because amongst these are men who are devoted to learning, and men who have renounced the world, and they are not arrogant. (5:82)

On the most explicit level, this verse reveals God's immense dislike of the Jews. As the people who display the strongest enmity towards the Muslim believers, the Jews are clearly the Muslims' greatest enemy. Implicit in their designation as such is God's perception of them as His greatest enemy, for the enemy of those who believe in, and thereby represent God's revelation, is surely God's enemy too.

This portrayal of the Jews is expressed in two other verses, (2:97–8), whereby God declares that He is an enemy to whoever is an enemy to the angel Gabriel. In Qur'anic exegetical circles, this is widely believed to signify the Jews, in light of their consideration of Gabriel as their enemy. It is on this scriptural basis that Hizbu'llah depicts the Jews as a people 'whose blood is full of enmity towards mankind',[43] and more derogatory still, as 'the enemies of God and the messages' as well as 'humankind'.[44]

Also implicit in the above-cited verse is the equation of the Jews with the idolaters insofar as both are designated as the enemies of believers in the same breath. This inference is supported by Verse 51 of 'Women' which accuses the Jews of believing in 'idols' and of claiming that the idolaters are on a sounder path than the believers. In another verse (2:96) they are unequivocally likened to the idolaters, to the extent that they are deemed, 'of all people the most greedy for life – even more than the idolaters'. As discussed previously, the reluctance to die is construed by the party as a manifestation of the much-maligned trait of cowardice, which Hizbu'llah regularly ascribes to the Israelis. Hizbu'llah believes that the Jews exhibit a far greater degree of this despicable trait than the anathematised pagans, thus confirming the equation between the two groups.

The far-reaching moral implications of these verses lie in their demotion of the status of the Jews to that of blasphemers. But it is not only this inference that induces Nasru'llah to invoke the Qur'an's reference to the Jews' blasphemy. His assertion that God 'imprinted blasphemy' on the Jews' hearts[45] refers to Verse 88 of 'The Cow', which refers to the Children of Israel: 'They say our hearts are the wrappings (which preserve God's word) nay God's curse is on them for their blasphemy. Little is it they believe.'

The blasphemy of the Jews, and the consequent identification of them with the idolaters, was attributable to their disobedience to God and His Messengers, which incurred God's wrath upon them:

And abasement and poverty were pitched upon them [the Children of Israel], and they were laden with God's wrath; that because they had disbelieved the signs of God and slain the prophets unrightfully; that because they disobeyed, and were transgressors. (2:58)

These three attributes of disbelief, disobedience and aggression are recurrent themes in the Qur'an, as evidenced by the numerous renditions of the Jews' characteristic rejection of God's signs and the revelations conveyed to them by His Messengers. With regard to the Children of Israel, the Qur'an vituperates:

And We gave Moses the Book and followed him up with a succession of Messengers; We gave Jesus the son of Mary clear signs and strengthened him with the Holy Spirit. Is it that whenever there comes to you a Messenger with what you yourselves desire not, you are puffed up with pride? Some you called impostors and others you slew. (2:87)

Although they had already received the Ten Commandments and the Law from Moses, the Israelites betrayed him by worshipping a golden calf they had constructed whilst he was away on Mount Sinai

(2:92–3). Upon Moses' intercession, God forgave them, but their unbelief and disobedience of His signs continued unabated.

Had they adhered to their Torah – which God berates them for not doing (5:66) – they would not have rejected Jesus and then Muhammad, whose advent the Prophet Moses foretold, as intimated by the following verse: 'And when there comes to them a Book from God [the Qur'an], confirming what was with them … when there comes to them that which they should have recognised, they refuse to believe in it' (2:89). Over and above this, they continuously violated their pacts with Muhammad, as stated in Verse 56 of 'The Spoils', and fought him at the Battle of Khaybar, where they were vanquished by him.

It is against this historical and scriptural backdrop that Hizbu'llah's struggle against Israel can be viewed as a continuation of Muhammad's conflict with the Jews of his day. In fact, many Hizbu'llah rallies feature the popular victory call: *'Khaybar, Khaybar ya Yahud, jayshu Muhammad sawfa ya''ud'* ('Khaybar, Khaybar, oh Jews, the army of Muhammad will return'). The parallels drawn between the Battle of Khaybar and the resistance to the Israeli occupation are symptomatic of the historicism employed by the party in its depiction of its struggle with Israel. Even prior to the emergence of Zionism, the Jews were virulently opposed to Islam. For Hizbu'llah, their occupation of Palestine and Lebanon is an extension of their enmity toward the Muslims and a confirmation of their deeply entrenched racist superiority.

Just as Israel's aggression against the Arab-Islamic world is attributed by the party to the Israelis' perception of the Arabs and Muslims as religiously, culturally and racially inferior to them, Nasru'llah interprets the pre-Zionist Jews' rejection of Muhammad's revelation as a stereotypically racist response on their part. When they discovered that Muhammad was 'a Hashemite Arab Prophet rather than one of the Sons of Israel, their racism made them fight him'.[46]

Although the Qur'an does not characterise the Jews as racist, Hizbu'llah's portrayal of them as such is facilitated by the coincidence of race and religion in Judaism. The Torah and Talmud teach the Sons of Israel that the 'other' is a 'subhuman' created 'to serve' them, 'God's Chosen People', thereby rendering Muslims and Christians 'their slaves'.[47] Judaism is therefore an inherently racially exclusionary religion that believes in the racial supremacy of the Sons of Israel and their descendants over other races and religions.

However, it is unlikely that Hizbu'llah would dispute the claim that the Jews' opposition to Muhammad was as much a product of their inveterate arrogance and perfidy, as it was of their racism. The very fact that the party adduces the Jews' violation of their covenants with their own Prophets and Messengers, who were of the same race as them, corroborates this assumption.[48]

The Qur'an states as much in Verse 2 of 'The Cow': 'Is it not (the case) that every time they make a Covenant, some party among them throw it aside?' The same case is made in Verse 93 of the same *Sura*, in which God censures the Children of Israel for breaking their Covenant with Moses. Hizbu'llah believes it is no wonder that a people who betray their own Prophets and who defame them in their holy books display 'this level of animosity' towards the Hashemite Prophet of Islam.[49]

As recurrent as the themes of Jewish deceitfulness and treachery in Hizbu'llah's intellectual discourse, is the theme of Jewish aggression. The party frequently utilises the Qur'an's repeated reference to the Jews' habitual slaying of prophets as an exemplification of their unparalleled depravity and aggression.[50] Their depiction as the 'slayers of the Prophets and Messengers' is derived from several Qur'anic verses (such as 2:61, 4:155 and 5:70, to name but a few) which decry the Jews' slaying of Messengers, in addition to the following verse: 'They [the Jews] said (in boast), "We killed Christ Jesus the son of Mary, the Messenger of God"' (4:157).

Because of their disobedience, disbelief, and aggression towards God's Messengers, the Jews brought upon themselves God's curse, according to Verse 58 of 'The Table'. Also quoted above is Verse 88 of 'The Table' whereby God declared his curse upon the Children of Israel for their overall blasphemy. Even David and Jesus are reported in the Qur'an to have cursed the Children of Israel for their 'disobedience' and 'excesses' (5:78).

Like anyone subject to God's curse, the ultimate fate of the Jews is Hell. Such a punishment is implied in Verse 86 of 'The Table', which is a continuation of the verse that differentiates the Jews from the Christians and equates them with the idolaters. After discussing Christian piety, and intimating that the Christians will be rewarded with an eternal life in Paradise in the intermediate verses, Verse 86 asserts that 'those who reject Faith and belie Our Signs, they shall be the companions of Hell-Fire'. This must be with reference to the Jews and pagans for they are the ones who are contrasted with the Christians in Verse 82. Their portrayal in other verses as those who reject God's Messengers and signs lends further weight to this inference, as does Verse 41 of 'The Table', which affirms that the hypocrites and Jews will suffer 'a heavy punishment in the Hereafter', which clearly denotes Hell.

Thus, the rejection of God's Messengers rendered the Jews blasphemers in God's eyes, placing them on a par with the idolaters. As such, they incurred God's wrath and curse upon themselves, and earned His damnation of them. The logical conclusion of all this is that the Jews are necessarily evil beings in the Qur'anic dispensation – a verdict which restates the original postulation on the Qur'an's demonisation of the Jews.

But this verdict is not only based on deductive logic, but is also grounded in several Qur'anic verses, which explicitly characterise the Jews as evil. Verses 79 and 80 of 'The Table', for example, refer to the Children of Israel's 'evil' works and deeds, while Verse 51 of 'Women' accuses them of believing in 'evil'. Another verse (5:63) queries why their Rabbis do not prevent them from speaking 'sinful' words, and concludes that their works are essentially 'evil'. They are even associated with 'Satans' in Verse 102 of 'The Cow' in that 'they followed what the Satans recited over Solomon's Kingdom'.

The Qur'an's depiction of the Jews as evil is echoed by Hizbu'llah, to the extent that Ra'id speaks of the 'source of evil' in Judaism,[51] and Qasim portrays the Jews as a people 'who are evil in their ideas'.[52] In neither of these statements are a portion of the Jews excepted from their characterisation as iniquitous. Yet at least one Qur'anic verse exempts part of the Jewish community from the overall designation of the Jews as evil. One such example is Verse 66 of 'The Table' which proclaims that: 'There is from among them [the People of the Book] a party of the right course; but many of them follow a course that is evil.'

However, the pervasive reference to them as 'the Jews' and 'the Children of Israel' in the aforementioned verses, as well as in many others, leads to the inevitable conclusion that this 'party' of them who are not evil is too insignificant a number to warrant the substitution of the term 'the' for the term 'many' whenever they are demonised. Accordingly, the term 'many' actually means the overwhelming majority. Verse 46 of 'Women' corroborates this point – 'they [the Jews] believe not, save but a few' – a clear indication that only a minority of them are not evil blasphemers.

On the other hand, it could well be that the party among the People of the Book who follow the 'right course', referred to in Verse

66 of 'The Table', consists solely of Christians, while the 'many' who are evil may be an allusion to the People of the Book who happen to be Jews. A varying interpretation of Verse 46 of 'Women' also points in the same direction. Some Qur'anic translators, such as Maulvi Sher Ali and M.H. Shakir, interpret the phrase '*Fa la yu'minun illa qalilan*' to mean 'so they do not believe but a little', rather than 'they believe not save but a few'. According to this different interpretation, all of the Jews, without exception, are deemed disbelievers. But in the final analysis, whether one adopts the former or latter interpretation of these two verses, the implication remains the same: few, if any, Jews are viewed favourably by God.

This argument is also buttressed by the following verse, which is cited by Nasru'llah at one of the party's public rallies.[53]

The Jews say: 'God's hands are fettered.' Fettered are their hands and they are cursed for what they have said. Nay but His hands are outspread. He expends how He will. And what has been sent down to thee from thy Lord will surely increase many of them in insolence and unbelief; and We have cast between them enmity and hatred, till the Day of Resurrection. As often as they light a fire for war, God will extinguish it. They (ever) strive to do mischief on earth. And God loveth not those who do mischief. (5:64)

Aside from the term 'the Jews' at the beginning of the verse, which denotes that almost all Jews are iniquitous, other elements of this verse point to such a generalisation. As in Verse 66 of 'The Table', the true purport of 'many of them' is the overwhelming majority of them, thereby signifying that practically all the Jews during the Prophet's era were insolent and blasphemous.

But the generalisation does not only relate to the Jews of Muhammad's time, but to all Jews throughout history. This is evinced by God's pledge to sow internal strife amongst them 'until the Day of Resurrection'. In other words, God's detestation of them will persist until the end of time by virtue of their transhistorical depravity. Such an inference can also be discerned from the phrase 'as often as they light a fire for war God will extinguish it', implicit in which is the perpetuation of God's execration of them for their enduring aggression. In effect, the Jews of yesterday, today, and the generations to come, are necessarily included in those who are cursed, damned and generally demonised in the Qur'an. According to such a Qur'anic exegesis, there is no distinction between pre-

Zionist, non-Zionist or Zionist Jews – a conclusion which lends further credence to the original hypothesis that the anti-Judaism of Hizbu'llah is not a product of Zionism.

One could even theorise that, for Hizbu'llah, this verse is a clear demonstration of God's foreknowledge of the Jews' Zionism, in that it avers that, 'they (ever) strive to do mischief on earth'. In all likelihood, 'Abbas al-Mussawi's reference to the Jews' proclivity to 'create mischief for people',[54] which most probably springs from this excerpt, is an attempt to trace Jewish Zionism, which is but one manifestation of such mischief, to a primordial Jewish trait or disposition. On closer inspection, this disposition to 'strive to create mischief' or '[exert] effort for corruption' as it is translated by other interpreters of the Qur'an, closely corresponds to that other criterion of anti-Semitism, and hence of Islamic anti-Judaism – the attribution of a universal plot against mankind to the Jews.

The allusion to such a plot can be elicited from the terms 'strive' and 'create mischief/corruption'. To the extent that the term 'strive' denotes an active effort or exertion, and the term 'mischief' or 'corruption' denotes evil-doing or harm unto others, the Qur'anic depiction of the Jews as a people who '(ever) strive to create mischief on earth' represents an active and concerted effort on the part of the Jews to inflict evil or harm onto others. Moreover, insofar as this mischief is directed at 'the earth' in its entirety, humanity as such is the object of the Jews' evil-doing. This active and concerted effort to cause evil to befall the entire earth means that the Jews are conspiring against humanity.

While the theme of a universal Jewish conspiracy is mainly confined to the party's strictures on the Zionist 'plot', the Holocaust is considered another exemplification of the Jewish conspiracy against mankind, in the intellectual discourse of Hizbu'llah. This accusation betokens the party's intent to show the Jews' victimisation as a façade designed to elicit world sympathy for the cause of a National Home for the Jews in Palestine and to exploit the Holocaust as a means of continuously troubling the world's collective consciousness. As queried by Nasru'llah: 'Why would God single out the Jews from the 40 million [people] of other nationalities and religions [who were killed in the Second World War] to remain a cause which necessitates the apologies and compensation of various governments?'[55]

Hizbu'llah's designation of the Holocaust as a Jewish conspiracy centres on two principal arguments. First is its claim that the six million Jews purported to have been killed by the Nazis is a highly exaggerated figure.[56] Accordingly, the party denounces the indictment of Roger Garaudy, the French author of *The Founding Myths of Israeli Politics*, who was put on trial for declaring that the number of Jews killed by the Nazis was far less than six million.[57]

Second, is the party's contention that the Holocaust was either fabricated, or orchestrated, by the Jews – an argument, which is categorised as yet another benchmark of anti-Semitism.[58] Proponents of the former view, such as Nasru'llah, argue that, since the Jews have never been able to prove the existence of the infamous gas chambers, there is no evidence to indicate that they were actually massacred by the Nazis.[59] This view is echoed by another party official, who expounds that the Jews who died during the Second World War were but some of the 160,000 civilians who died as result of the US' bombing of Germany. The corpses of those killed were then 'exploited by the Jews, who claimed that they were the product of the gas chambers'.[60]

Others in the party accuse some Jews of having 'collaborated' with the Nazis in the killing of their brethren.[61] As explicated by Ra'id, 'from what we know about the Jews, their tricks and their deception, we do not think it unlikely that they partook in the planning of the Holocaust'.[62] At minimum, they 'prepared the foreground which incited the Nazis to the Holocaust killings, so that they could serve their settlement project in Palestine'.[63] Whether the Jews concocted or stage-managed the Holocaust in order to serve their Zionist project, their ability to have deceived the entire world into believing that their victimisation was genuine, renders both acts tantamount to a universal Jewish conspiracy against mankind.

Judaism as a 'Deviation' from the Revelation of Moses

Insofar as Hizbu'llah's demonisation of the Jews issues from a Qur'anic reading of the Jews' history of aggression, disbelief, treachery and conspiratorial predilection, the party is effectively demonising their religious convictions, which are believed to be the underlying cause of Jewish depravity. Hizbu'llah is therefore imputing Judaism with the responsibility for corrupting its adherents. But this is not to be confused with the revelation of Moses, which represents authentic Judaism for Hizbu'llah. Rather, it is the 'counterfeit' 'deviant' Judaism which is the subject of Hizbu'llah's vituperation, and hence the basis of its anti-Judaism.[64]

The party's theory on Jewish 'deviance' is anchored in several Qur'anic verses which signify that the Jews both departed from and falsified the revelation of Moses embodied in the Torah. In Verse 66 of 'The Table', for example, the Jews are castigated for not having 'stood fast by the Torah, the Gospel and all the revelations that were sent to them from their Lord'. Their failure to adhere to the Torah – insofar as it foretold the coming of Jesus and Muhammad – was not only a product of their rejection of the revelations that succeeded that of Moses, but also a product of their non-compliance with their own Book, prior to any other revelations.

The Qur'an contains numerous verses which suggest that the Jews concealed the truth of their Scriptures. In the continuation of Verse 40 of 'The Cow', which addresses the Children of Israel, Verse 42 cautions them not to 'cover truth with falsehood nor to conceal the truth' when they 'know (what it is)'. A section of Verse 91 of 'Cattle' is even more explicit in this regard: 'Say: Who then sent down the Book which Moses brought? A light and guidance to man: But ye make it into (separate) sheets for show, while ye conceal much (of its contents)'.

As well as being accused of deliberately concealing parts of the Old Testament and fragmenting its contents, the Jews are also accused of having changed its substance through a process of distortion and forgery. Verse 75 of 'The Cow' speaks of 'a party of them [the Children of Israel]' who had 'heard the word of God and perverted it knowingly after they had understood it'.

In a similar vein, the following excerpt from Verse 13 of 'The Table' affirms: 'They [the Children of Israel] change the words from the right places and forget a good part of the Message that was sent them.' This is echoed by Verse 46 of 'Women' which unequivocally asserts: 'Of the Jews there are those who displace words from their right places.' Bearing these verses in mind, the identity of those who are signified in the following verse, becomes obvious: 'Then woe to those who write the Book with their own hands and then say: "This is from God," to traffic with it for a miserable price!' (2:79).

But despite the Qur'anic leitmotif of Jewish deviance, precisely when Judaism digressed from its pristine and authentic form remains a point of conjecture. Fayyad speculates that the deviation from Moses' message must have occurred in the interim between Jesus' Prophethood and Muhammad's. What leads him to this conclusion is the Qur'anic reference to the 'Children of Israel' from the era of Moses until the era of Jesus, and its reference to them as 'the Jews' during Muhammad's time. As construed by Fayyad, the replacement of the former term with the latter is symptomatic of the Children of Israel's digression from their Torah,[65] which presumably induced God to call them by another name. Why God waited until they rejected Jesus' revelation to brand them 'Jews', when they had clearly displeased Him way before then, is unclear.

Fayyad's theory does not deny that the 'Children of Israel' were anathematised by God, or that they were disassociated from the 'demonic' Jewish mentality depicted in the previous section, only that they fared a little better than 'the Jews' to the extent that some verses in the Qur'an do not generalise that all of them were unbelievers. Although Fayyad does not offer any examples, one could assume that the following verse is demonstrative of his reasoning:

> Oh ye who believe! Be ye helpers of God: As said Jesus the son of Mary to the Disciples, 'Who will be my helpers to (the work of) God?' Said the Disciples, 'We are God's helpers!' Then a portion of the Children of Israel believed and a portion disbelieved. (61:14)

If this is Fayyad's criterion for distinguishing between the 'Children of Israel' and 'the Jews', then it follows that he interprets Verse 66 of 'The Table' and Verse 46 of 'Women' in the above-cited manner, which does not exempt any of the Jews from the charge of unbelief. Such an assumption also flows from his equation of the Jews with deviance. If the Jews are the aberrant descendants of the Children of Israel, then none of them can be exempted from the charge of unbelief.

The corollary of all this is that the Jews 'are not the original People of the Book', as declared by Ra'id.[66] Still, it is unlikely that Ra'id, or anyone else in Hizbu'llah, would dispute the reasoning that, even if they are not the 'original' People of the Book (i.e. the Children of Israel), they are a People of the Book nonetheless, as falsified a Book as it may be.[67] After all, the concept of the People of the Book was coined during the Prophet Muhammad's era, when the term 'Children of Israel' had fallen out of use and was replaced by 'the Jews'. The concept of the People of the Book was therefore applicable to the Christians and Jews, as evinced by the following Qur'anic verse: 'Say [God to Prophet Muhammad]: "Oh People of the Book! Ye have no ground to stand upon unless ye stand by the Torah and the Gospel, and all the revelation that has come to you from your Lord"' (5:68).

According to this Qur'anic basis, Islamic jurisprudence deals with the Jews as a People of the Book, unmindful of their deviance from pristine Judaism and their consequent categorisation as unbelievers. In point of fact, this is precisely how Islamic jurisprudence deals with other religious communities, including Muslims. Its deliberations do not distinguish between Muslim believers and unbelievers, but apply to both in an identical manner. Herein lies the discrepancy between Islamic ideology and Islamic law. The former deals with the individual on the basis of his religious beliefs, whereas the latter deals with him on the more superficial basis of his religious label.

On strictly doctrinal grounds, a male Muslim is permitted to marry a Jewish woman, insofar as Verse 5 of 'The Table' stipulates that it is lawful for the believer to marry 'chaste women among the People of the Book'. For Hizbu'llah, however, the notion of intermarriage between Jews and Muslims is inconceivable. Although marriage to Jews is sanctioned in Islamic law, it is proscribed in the Islamic ideology of Hizbu'llah. In this respect, the anti-Judaism of Hizbu'llah is more fervent than the anti-Judaism of the Qur'an.

However, the party is compelled to abide by the dictates of Islamic jurisprudence and recognise the Jews as a People of the Book, who despite their demonisation in the Qur'an cannot be the subjects of a *jihad* on that account alone.[68] As they are People of the Book, Hizbu'llah is compelled to grant Jews the religious, legal, cultural and political rights entitled to them under Islamic law. This reveals itself in Fnaysh's affirmation that, even as deviants, 'Islam guarantees the rights of Jews',[69] and in the party's invocation of the Prophet's treatment of the Jews of his time, as well as the contemporary Iranian model, as instances of socio-political inclusion and the institutionalisation of Jewish rights.[70]

But what the party is not compelled to accept is close social interaction between Jews and Muslims. Legal recognition and political inclusion clearly do not translate themselves into social integration in the thought of Hizbu'llah, the upshot of which is an enforced toleration of an anathematised people. This manifests itself in the party's reassurance to non-Zionist Jews that, 'in spite of all their faults',[71] Hizbu'llah is willing to condone Jews in its midst and does not believe that any harm should come to them.[72]

It is also manifest in the concept of '*al-tasakun al-barid*' ('cold cohabitation') between Muslims and Jews, envisaged by Fayyad.

Under such an arrangement, the Jews would be left to live in peace because the conflict between Islam and the Jews is essentially ideological as opposed to existential, as in the case of Zionism. However, there would be no normalisation of relations with them, hence the coldness of this cohabitation.

Furthermore, Fayyad is keen to emphasise that the choice of term 'cohabitation' itself betokens the irreconcilability of relations between the two. Derived from the verb '*sakan*' (to inhabit), the concept of *tasakun* denotes a shared inhabitancy between two or more communities, which for Fayyad does not in any way signify a sense of communal '*ta'ayush al-mushtaraq*' (co-existence). This latter concept denotes the existence of common denominators, aside from shared inhabitancy, which renders it inapplicable to Jews and exclusive to Christians.[73]

Conclusion

Over the course of time, Hizbu'llah has evolved from an essentially military organisation into a military-cum-political movement bound together by an intellectual structure founded on various religious, moral and political pillars. These pillars have had to interact with an ever changing socio-political reality, which in several cases has necessitated their reformulation. But rather than entail a relinquishment of these pillars, this reformulation has involved an earnest attempt by the party to preserve them as moral absolutes, whilst adapting itself to various political developments by means of a relative moral outlook.

Therefore, Hizbu'llah has striven to strike a delicate balance between the ideal and the real in a fairly consistent manner. It has done this by confining its adaptation, and at times embrace, of reality to the political realm, whilst limiting its strategic goals to the intellectual realm. By means of this over-rationalisation, Hizbu'llah has been able to both ensure its political survival and develop its political thought without severely compromising its principles or losing its intellectual consistency – an ability which distinguishes the party from most other Islamic groups which, in the face of political reality, have either remained ideologically rigid or severely compromised their principles.

The envisagement of Hizbu'llah's future political role must therefore take account of the complex interaction between its intellectual structure and the political developments at hand. Since this text was written, several political developments have unfolded which have impacted on the party, first among which has been Israel's unilateral withdrawal from Lebanese territory, save for the disputed Shiba' Farms, between 22 and 24 May 2000.

Although Hizbu'llah's victory over Israel appeared to have deprived it of a military *raison d'être*, and by implication, a geostrategic role, the party soon made it clear that its resistance was far from over. Hizbu'llah's threat to persist in its struggle against Israel until the Shiba' Farms were liberated and the remaining 19 Lebanese prisoners held in Israeli jails were freed was effectively carried out when the Islamic Resistance planted two roadside bombs against Israeli troops stationed in the Shiba' Farms in October and November 2000.

Hizbu'llah's military operations were given a new lease of life by the Lebanese government's declaration of an incomplete Israeli withdrawal, upon which Hizbu'llah had made the continuation of its resistance activity contingent. Yet despite the Lebanese state's call for the retrieval of the Shiba' Farms, and its submission of documented evidence to the UN, which supposedly proves that the Farms fell under Lebanese jurisdiction in the past, as corroborated by Syria, the government's previous muteness on the issue points to Syria's hand in giving it prominence.

Viewed from Syria's perspective, the Shiba' issue could serve as an invaluable trump card in its peace negotiations with Israel by providing it with a means with which to threaten Israel if it does not return the Golan Heights to Syria. It would most likely do this by officially relinquishing the Farms to Lebanon in a written document, thereby rendering Israel's withdrawal from Lebanon incomplete both on the international and local levels. This would have the effect of bestowing international legitimacy on Hizbu'llah's military campaign to liberate the area, which it now lacks. In turn, the legitimisation of such a campaign by the international community would inevitably result in the escalation of Resistance attacks against Israeli troops in the Shiba' region.

To that effect, Hizbullah's attacks on Shiba' serve Syria's interests in the peace negotiations. That is not to say, however, that the party has nothing to gain from the prolongation of its resistance activity. By giving Hizbu'llah a sufficient excuse to strike at Israeli military targets, the Shiba' issue has permitted the Islamic Resistance to continue to pursue the debilitation of its enemy, and by implication, the liberation of Palestine. The preservation of this geostrategic role is not only evidenced by the party's sporadic attacks on Israeli forces in Shiba', but also by its capture of three Israeli soldiers from the Shiba' Farms on 7 October 2000, and its abduction of a retired Israeli colonel from Lebanon several days later.

Timed to coincide with the onset of the revitalised *Intifada* (uprising), which began on 28 September 2000, the abductions were clearly aimed at supporting the Palestinian cause, as confirmed by Nasru'llah's pledge to assist the Palestinians in their uprising just three days before the first abduction. Yet despite the execution of the abductions at such a crucial juncture in time, the meticulous planning they entailed months ahead of the *Intifada* is indicative that they were not contingent upon its outbreak. The logical conclusion of this assertion is that Hizbu'llah was intent on reactivating its military role in a situation of relative calm, thereby signifying that Israel's near complete withdrawal from the South had done nothing to temper the movement's struggle against its long-standing foe or to dampen its resolve to liberate Palestine.

As one of the central demands for the release of the four Israeli captives, Hizbu'llah's call for the release of the 1600, mainly Palestinian, Arab prisoners held in Israel is a reaffirmation of its pledge to contribute to the liberation of Palestine. Moreover, by capturing Israeli soldiers on what it claims to be Lebanese land, Hizbu'llah has been able to actively assist the Palestinians in the pursuit of their cause, without having to encroach on Israeli territory per se, and run the risk of inflicting even greater repercussions on Lebanon. In effect, Hizbu'llah's abductions represent a symbolic step towards the liberation of the pan-Islamic emblem of Jerusalem, yet one which does not pose a direct threat to the existence of the Israeli state.

The intent to perpetuate its struggle against Israel explains the seemingly absurd electoral alliances Hizbu'llah made in the parliamentary election of September 2000, which neither accrued it a higher number of votes nor benefited its popular image as an ideologically 'pure' movement. The party's last minute decision to exchange votes with the former commander of the once pro-Israeli Lebanese Forces, Eli Hobayqa, in the Ba'bda-'Alay constituency, and its inclusion of another former member of the Lebanese Forces on its electoral list for the Ba'lbakk-Hirmil district, were clearly forged at Syria's behest.

While both alliances were undoubtedly motivated by considerations of political survival in the face of Syrian pressure, the pursuit of institutional longevity on Hizbu'llah's part should also be viewed as an attempt to ensure the continuation of its resistance activity. By bowing to Syrian pressure and subjecting itself to the charge of ideological dilution, Hizbu'llah was in fact buying its Islamic Resistance a renewed dose of freedom to act on the southern front.

Such a strategy is reminiscent of the party's alliance with Amal in the 1992 and 1996 elections at Syria's prompting, which also served this purpose. Its self-imposed alliance with Amal in all the constituencies it ran for in the 2000 election was a carefully deliberated attempt to maintain the necessary degree of calm required for the manoeuvrability of its Resistance.

In effect, the relationship between Syria and Hizbu'llah is one based on common strategic interests. Thus, although Syria has tried to curb the party's growth in the past, it is unlikely to seek its decimation in the future when it clearly provides Syria with an invaluable trump card in the peace negotiations with Israel. Accordingly, Syria will continue to provide the party with the necessary political backing to pursue its military aspirations. In turn, Hizbu'llah will continue to condone the Syrian political 'ceiling' by viewing it as the price it must pay for the attrition of Israel.

The party's subordination of its domestic political goals to its geostrategic military ones was not only evident in its submission to Syrian interests in the parliamentary election, but also in its non-pursuit of a cabinet post in the new Hariri administration, which was inaugurated in October 2000. Unlike its relationship with previous Hariri administrations, Hizbu'llah refrained from passing a vote of no confidence in the third Hariri government, but chose instead to abstain from voting on account of the perceived 'improvement' in its political programme. Hizbu'llah's reluctance to pursue a cabinet post was not attributable to its stand on the new administration, but to its resistance strategy.

As a chief concern of the party's, the quest for political and administrative reform would figure prominently in any ministerial portfolio held by Hizbu'llah. Insofar as such a reformist crusade would necessarily generate antagonism towards the party from several political quarters, and accordingly, diminish support for its Resistance, Hizbu'llah would be disinclined to embark on an endeavour that would ultimately cost it its resistance priority.

None of this is to say, however, that Hizbu'llah's domestic political role will be any less efficacious than it has been in the past. The party will continue to pursue political and administrative reform, though from the less threatening parliamentary arena. It will persist in its drive for the abolition of political sectarianism and the institution of a 'citizen's democracy' in its place, the development of deprived regions, and its political and cultural crusade against the normalisation of ties with Israel, in the event of a Lebanese-Israeli peace agreement.

In short, Hizbu'llah's political programme will be an essentially secular one that will closely correspond to the agendas of leftist and nationalist political forces. Hizbu'llah will therefore remain an Islamic party on the intellectual level, but will most likely become a semi-secularised one on the national political level.

As a form of political adaptation, the dual strategy of confining the quintessentially Islamic and unattainable to the intellectual realm, and the secular and attainable to the national political realm is, to all intents and purposes, an ultimately precarious one. The conjoining of the party's Islamic state ideal with its political endorsement of democracy, its intellectual commitment to the concept of the *Wilayat al-Faqih* with its submission to the authority of the Lebanese state, the paramountcy of its Islamic identity with its nationalism, and the consecration of its goal of liberating Jerusalem with its tacit acceptance of the peace negotiations, typifies a marriage between the intellectual and political which cannot persist indefinitely.

Thus, although Hizbu'llah has succeeded in striking an artful balance between its intellectual structure and political discourse for the time being, at the end of the day, the party will have to tip the balance in favour of either one. Judging by the continued subordination of its domestic political role to its geostrategic concerns, it seems as though Hizbu'llah has chosen to accord its Lebanese identity and role as an influential local political force secondary status to its Islamic identity and role as a revolutionary exemplar for the *umma*.

Appendix One:
Miladi Equivalents to Hijri Years

First day of Hijri year	Miladi equivalent
1 Muharram 1404	8 October 1983
1 Muharram 1405	27 September 1984
1 Muharram 1406	16 September 1985
1 Muharram 1407	6 September 1986
1 Muharram 1408	26 August 1987
1 Muharram 1409	14 August 1988
1 Muharram 1410	3 August 1989
1 Muharram 1411	23 July 1990
1 Muharram 1412	13 July 1991
1 Muharram 1413	2 July 1992

Appendix Two: List of Hijri Months

Month number	Hijri month
1	Muharram
2	Safar
3	Rabi' al-Awwal
4	Rabi' ath-Thani
5	Jamad al-Awwal
6	Jamad ath-Thani
7	Rajab
8	Sha'ban
9	Ramadan
10	Shawwal
11	Dhu al-Qa'da
12	Dhu al-Hujja

Glossary

aya – verse

Faqih (pl. *fuqaha*) – an expert on Islamic jurisprudence (*fiqh*) who has achieved the necessary level of competence to practice legal rationalism, known as *ijtihad*

fatwa – religious edict issued by a *marja' at-taqlid*

infitah – openness or opening up

hadiths – the body of traditions about the Prophet Muhammad which form a supplement to the Qur'an

Hala al-Islamiyya al-Shi'yya – the Islamic Shi'ite situation

Hizbu'llah – the party of God

Intifada – uprising

jihad – although the conventional translation of this term is 'holy war', it is conceptualised by Hizbu'llah to mean any defensive act, whether military or otherwise, which exerts effort in God's cause

Mahdi – the Twelfth Shi'ite Imam who is believed to have been in occultation since 874 CE and whose eventual return (*raj'a*) is anticipated

Majlis al-Shura – the Decision-Making Council, Hizbu'llah's highest decision-making body

marja' at-taqlid – a prominent *mujtahid* who serves as a model of emulation for all his followers

mujahidin (sing. *mujahid*) – those who engage in a defensive *jihad*

mujtahid – same as *faqih*

Pasdaran – Iran's Revolutionary Guards Corps

Shari'a – the Islamic code of religious law

sura – chapter

thawabit – fixed principles that are impervious to change

'ulama – the religiously learned class

umma – the community of Muslim believers

wajib al-shari' – religious legal obligation

Wali al-Faqih – leader jurisprudent

Wilayat al-Faqih – the guardianship of the governance of the jurisprudent

Notes

Introduction

1. Although both Israel and the UN regard the Farms as Syrian territory, which Israel has occupied since 1967, both the Lebanese government and Syria maintain that the Farms belong to Lebanon.
2. As suggested by the title of this book, this work does not employ the concept of ideology but prefers to utilise the notion of intellectual structure. Since the concept of ideology not only denotes a political and social vision but an economic one as well, it cannot be applied to Hizbu'llah which has not, to date, formulated a comprehensive economic programme. What the party has formulated are a series of social and political ideas, which constitute the pillars of its intellectual structure. Accordingly, Hizbu'llah does not refer to its social and political vision as 'our ideology', but chooses instead to call it 'our political thought', 'our intellectual discourse' or 'our intellectual structure'.
3. Most of these interviews and speeches have been provided by Manar Television's archives department. Since the archives department has not documented the precise dates of most of these interviews and speeches, I have only been able to cite the month and year in which they were made.
4. See Magnus Ranstorp, *Hizb'allah in Lebanon: The Politics of the Western Hostage Crisis*, with a foreword by Terry Waite (New York: St. Martin's Press, 1997), p. 37 and p. 42; Nizar Hamzeh, 'Clan Conflicts, Hezbollah and the Lebanese State', *Journal of Social, Political and Economic Studies* 19, no. 4 (Winter 1994), p. 441; Judith Miller, 'Faces of Fundamentalism: Hassan Turabi and Muhammad Fadlallah', *Foreign Affairs* (November–December 1994), p. 126; Mary-Jane Deeb, 'Militant Islam and the Politics of Redemption', *AAPSS*, p. 524 (November 1992), p. 63; Gabriel A. Almond, Emmanuel Sivan and R. Scott Appleby, 'Fundamentalism: Genus and Species', in *Fundamentalisms Comprehended*, eds Martin E. Marty and R. Scott Appleby, *The Fundamentalist Project*, vol. 5 (Chicago and London: University of Chicago Press, 1995), p. 141.
5. Al-Sayyid Husayn al-Mussawi, interview by author, tape recording, southern suburbs of Beirut, 21 August 1997.
6. Ibid.
7. Shaykh Subhi al-Tufayli quoted in Hala Jaber, *Hezbollah: Born With a Vengeance* (London: Fourth Estate, 1997), p. 68.
8. 'Ali Fayyad, interview by author, tape recording, Beirut, 2 March 1997.
9. Jaber, p. 67 and Chibli Mallat, *Shi'i Thought from the South Lebanon*, Papers on Lebanon, vol. 7 (Oxford: Centre for Lebanese Studies, 1988), p. 28.
10. Jaber, *Hezbollah*, p. 67

11. Ibid.
12. Martin Kramer, 'Redeeming Jerusalem: The Pan-Islamic Premise of Hizballah', in *The Iranian Revolution and the Muslim World*, ed. David Menashri (Boulder, CO: Westview Press, 1990), p. 122.
13. Samuel Huntington, *Political Order in Changing Societies* (Clinton, MA: The Colonial Press Inc., 1973), p. 33.
14. Muhsin Ibrahim quoted in Elizabeth Picard, 'Political Identities and Communal Identities: Shifting Mobilization Among the Lebanese Shi'a Through Ten Years of War, 1975–1985', in *Ethnicity, Politics and Development*, eds Dennis L. Thompson and Dov. Ronen (Boulder, CO: Lynne Rienner Publishers, 1986), p. 164.
15. Fuad Ajami quoted in Hilal Khashan, *Inside the Lebanese Confessional Mind* (Lanham, MD: University Press of America, 1992), p. 44.
16. See Nazih Ayubi, *Political Islam: Religion and Politics in the Arab World* (London and New York: Routledge, 1991), p. 176; and Valerie Hoffmann, 'Muslim Fundamentalists: Psychosocial Profiles', in *Fundamentalisms Comprehended*, p. 209.
17. Majed Halawi, *A Lebanon Defied: Musa al-Sadr and the Shi'a Community* (Boulder, CO: Westview Press, 1992), p. 101.
18. Joseph Olmert, 'The Shi'is and the Lebanese State', in *Shi'ism, Resistance and Revolution*, ed. Martin Kramer (Boulder, CO: Westview Press, 1987), p. 192.
19. Augustus Richard Norton, 'Shi'ism and Social Protest in Lebanon', in *Shi'ism and Social Protest*, eds Juan R.I. Cole and Nikki R. Keddie (London: Yale University Press, 1986), p. 160.
20. John L. Esposito, *The Islamic Threat: Myth or Reality?* (New York: Oxford University Press, 1992), p. 13.
21. See Robin Wright, *Sacred Rage: The Crusade of Modern Islam* (New York: Linden Press/Simon and Schuster, 1995), p. 75; and Helena Cobban, 'The Growth of Shi'i Power in Lebanon and its Implications for the Future', in *Shi'ism and Social Protest*, p. 142.
22. Cobban, 'The Growth of Shi'i Power in Lebanon', p. 143.
23. David McDowell, *Lebanon: A Conflict of Minorities* (London: Minority Rights Group, 1983), p. 3.
24. Muhammad Fnaysh, interview by author, tape recording, Beirut, 15 August 1997.
25. *Al-'Ahd*, 21 November 1997.
26. *Al-Hawadith*, 19 March 1999.
27. *South Lebanon 1948–1986: Facts and Figures* (Beirut: Dar Bilal, 1986), p. 35.
28. Ibid., p. 26.
29. Stuart Colie, 'A Perspective on the Shi'ites and the Lebanese Tragedy', in *The Middle East Reader*, ed. Michael Curtis (New Brunswick, NJ: Transaction, 1986), p. 118.
30. Cobban, 'The Growth of Shi'i Power in Lebanon', p. 147.
31. Anoushiravan Ehteshami and Raymond A. Hinnebusch, *Syria and Iran: Middle East Powers in a Penetrated Regional System* (London and New York: Routledge, 1997), p. 120.

32. Chris Mowles, 'The Israeli Occupation of South Lebanon', *Third World Quarterly* 8, no. 4 (October 1986), p. 1357.
33. Ibid., pp. 1355–6.
34. Ibid., p. 1356.
35. Martin Kramer, 'Redeeming Jerusalem', p. 108.
36. Shimon Shapira, 'The Origins of Hizballah', *Jerusalem Quarterly*, no. 46 (Spring 1988), p. 116.
37. Martin Kramer, 'The Oracle of Hizballah: Seyyid Muhammad Husayn Fadlallah', in *Spokesmen for the Despised: Fundamentalist Leaders in the Middle East*, ed. R. Scott Appleby (Chicago: University of Chicago Press, 1997), p. 100.
38. Shapira, 'The Origins of Hizballah', p. 116.
39. Shaykh Na'im Qasim, interview by author, tape recording, southern suburbs of Beirut, 17 March 1998.
40. Kramer, 'The Oracle of Hizballah', p. 101.
41. Ibid., p. 105.
42. Jaber, *Hezbollah*, p. 68.
43. Mallat, *Shi'i Thought from South Lebanon*, concurs at p. 28.
44. Husayn al-Mussawi, 21 August 1997.
45. Abdulaziz Sachedina, 'Activist Shi'ism in Iran, Iraq and Lebanon', in *Fundamentalisms Observed*, eds Martin E. Marty and R. Scott Appleby, *The Fundamentalist Project*, vol. 1 (Chicago and London: University of Chicago Press, 1991), p. 448.
46. Fnaysh, 15 August 1997.
47. Kramer, 'Redeeming Jerusalem', p. 106.
48. Ibid., p. 109.
49. Ibid., p. 110.
50. Mahmud A. Faksh, 'The Shi'a Community of Lebanon: A New Assertive Political Force', *Journal of South Asian and Middle East Studies* 14, no. 3 (Spring 1991), p. 48.
51. 'Ali Fayyad, 2 March 1997, and Husayn al-Mussawi, 21 August 1997.
52. Fnaysh, 15 August 1997.
53. This contradicts Ranstorp's assertion, *Hizb'allah in Lebanon*, p. 73 that the first *Shura* was formed in 1986.
54. Fnaysh, 15 August 1997. See also al-Sayyid Hassan Nasru'llah, *'Ala al-Hawa*, Orbit TV, May 1997.
55. See Shapira, 'The Origins of Hizballah', p. 124 (but he makes no mention of the committee).

Chapter 1

1. See *al-Burnamij al-Intikhabili li Hizb'ullah* for 1992, p. 1, and 'Text of Open Letter Addressed by Hizballah to the Downtrodden of Lebanon and the World', in *Amal and the Shi'a: Struggle for the Soul of Lebanon*, Augustus Richard Norton (Austin, TX: University of Texas Press, 1987), p. 167.
2. Emile Sahliyeh, 'Religious Fundamentalisms Compared: Palestinian Islamists, Militant Lebanese Shi'ites and Radical Sikhs', in *Fundamentalisms Comprehended*, vol. 5, *The Fundamentalist Project*, eds Martin E.

Marty, R. Scott Appleby (Chicago: University of Chicago Press, 1995), p. 148.

3. David George, 'Pax Islamica: an Alternative New World Order?' in *Islamic Fundamentalism*, no. 2, Twayne's Themes in Right Wing Politics and Ideology Series, ed. Youssef Choueiri (Boston: Twayne, 1990), p. 82.

4. James Piscatori, *Islam in a World of Nation-States* (Cambridge: Cambridge University Press, 1986), p. 116.

5. George, 'Pax Islamica', p. 83.

6. Ibid., p. 82.

7. See As'ad AbuKhalil, 'Ideology and Practice of Hizballah in Lebanon: Islamization of Leninist Organizational Principles', *Middle Eastern Studies* 27, no. 3 (July 1991), p. 395.

8. Ervand Abrahamian, *Khomeinism: Essays on the Islamic Republic* (London: I.B. Tauris, 1993), p. 31.

9. Ervand Abrahamian, 'Khomeini: A Fundamentalist?' in *Fundamentalism in Comparative Perspective*, ed. Lawrence Kaplan (Amherst: University of Massachusetts Press, 1992), p. 121.

10. Al-Sayyid 'Abbas al-Mussawi, 'Min Jibshit illa al-Nabishit' (speech on day of his assassination), Biqa', al-Manar TV, 16 February 1992.

11. Ibid.

12. Al-Sayyid Hassan Nasru'llah, Nabatiyyeh, al-Manar TV, September 1996.

13. Al-Sayyid 'Abbas al-Mussawi, Beirut, in *Amiru'l-Zakira*, Sha'ban 1413, comp. Hizb'ullah, al-Wahda al-'Ilamiyya al-Markaziyya (n.p.: Manshurat al-Wala', 1993), p. 231.

14. Al-Sayyid Hassan Nasru'llah, ''*Ashura* Speech', southern suburbs of Beirut, al-Manar TV, 12 May 1997.

15. Ibid.

16. 'Constitution of the Islamic Republic of Iran', *Middle East Journal* 34 (1980), Principle 154.

17. Ibrahim al-Amin al-Sayyid, quoted in *al-'Ahd*, 21 Dhu al-Qa'da 1404.

18. Muhammad Fnaysh, 15 August 1997.

19. Husayn al-Mussawi, 21 August 1997.

20. Ibid.

21. 'Abbas al-Mussawi, Beirut, *Amiru'l-Zakira*, 21 Muharram 1409, p. 209.

22. al-Amin quoted in *al-'Ahd*, 21 Dhu al-Qa'da 1984.

23. Ibid.

24. Based on the scheme adopted by Gabriel A. Almond, Emmanuel Sivan and and R. Scott Appleby, 'Fundamentalism: Genus and Species', in *Fundamentalisms Comprehended*, vol. 5, *The Fundamentalist Project*, eds Martin E. Marty and R. Scott Appleby (Chicago: University of Chicago Press, 1995) p. 407.

25. As'ad AbuKhalil, 'The Incoherence of Islamic Fundamentalism: Arab Islamic Thought at the End of the Twentieth Century', *Middle East Journal* 48, no. 4 (Autumn 1994), p. 679.

26. Ibid., p. 678.

27. Fnaysh, 15 August 1997.

28. Emmanuel Sivan, 'Eavesdropping on Radical Islam', *Middle East Quarterly* 2, no. 1 (March 1995), p. 18.
29. Fnaysh, 15 August 1997.
30. Nasru'llah, *Kalam al-Nas*, C33 TV, May 1996.
31. Husayn al-Mussawi, 21 August 1997.
32. 'Ali Fayyad, 2 March 1997.
33. Husayn al-Mussawi, 21 August 1997.
34. Fnaysh, 15 August 1997.
35. Shaykh Na'im Qasim, 17 March 1998.
36. Muhammad Muhsin, interview by author, tape recording, Beirut, 3 March 1997.
37. 'Open Letter', p. 184.
38. Ibid., p. 173
39. Ibid., p. 184.
40. Fnaysh, 15 August 1997.
41. Abbas Kelidar, 'The Shi'i Imami Community and the Politics of the Arab East', *Middle East Studies* 19 (January 1983), p. 3.
42. Norman Calder, 'Accommodation and Revolution in Imami Shi'i Jurisprudence: Khumayni and the Classical Tradition', *Middle Eastern Studies* 18, no. 1 (1982), p. 3.
43. Giovanni Sartori, *Parties and Party Systems,* vol. 1 (London: Cambridge University press, 1977), p. 133.
44. Yussef Meri', interview by author, tape recording, Beirut, 10 April 1998.
45. Hassan Nasru'llah, *al-Haki Baynatna*, MTV, July 1998.
46. See al-Sayyid Hassan Nasru'llah quoted in *al-'Ahd*, 21 Nov 1997 and Muhammad Fnaysh, *Wujhat Nazar*, Future TV, 2 July 1997.
47. Hassan Nasru'llah quoted in *al-'Ahd*, 21 November 1997.
48. Hassan Nasru'llah quoted in *al-'Ahd*, 25 February 1994.
49. Husayn al-Mussawi, 21 August 1997.
50. Nasru'llah quoted in *al-'Ahd*, 21 November 1997.
51. Meri', 10 April 1998.
52. *Al-'Ahd*, 19 September 1997.
53. Youssef Choueiri, 'The Political Discourse of Contemporary Islamist Movements', in Choueiri, *Islamic Fundamentalism*, p. 21.
54. These are the reasons for its oppression as cited by Husayn al-Mussawi, 21 August 1997, and Qasim, 17 March 1998, in personal interviews.
55. Husayn al-Mussawi, 21 August 1997.
56. Ibid.
57. Qasim, 17 March 1998.
58. *Al-Maokif*, n.d., p.4.
59. *Al-'Ahd*, 21 November 1997.
60. Qasim, 17 March 1998.
61. Ibid.
62. *As-Safir*, 24 August 1998.
63. Meri', 10 April 1998.
64. Hassan Nasru'llah, *Kalam al-Nas*, LBC, March 1997.
65. *Al-'Ahd*, 21 November 1997.
66. Al-Sayyid 'Abbas al-Mussawi, Beirut, *Amiru'l-Zakira*, Rabi' ath-Thani 1405, p. 189.

67. Nasru'llah, LBC, March 1997.
68. Al-Sayyid Hassan Nasru'llah, *'Ala al-Hawa*, Orbit TV, May 1997.
69. *Al-'Ahd*, 21 November 1997.
70. Husayn al-Mussawi, 21 August 1997.
71. Fayyad, 2 March 1997.
72. Fnaysh, 15 August 1997 and Meri', 10 April 1998.
73. Meri', 10 April 1998.
74. *Al-'Ahd*, 21 November 1997.
75. Fayyad, 2 March 1997.
76. *Al-'Ahd*, 21 November 1997.
77. Shaykh Subhi al-Tufayli quoted in *al-'Ahd*, 21 Sha'ban 1407.
78. Al-Sayyid Hassan Nasru'llah, 'Jerusalem Day', southern suburbs of Beirut, al-Manar TV, March 1997.
79. See Nasru'llah, LBC, March 1997, and Nasru'llah, Orbit TV, 7 February 1997.
80. Nasru'llah, LBC, March 1997.
81. Meri', 10 April 1998.
82. Qasim, 17 March 1998. See also Nasru'llah, MTV, July 1998 and *al-'Ahd*, 21 November 1997.
83. 'Open Letter', p. 175.
84. Ibid., p. 176.
85. This phrase is used in ibid., p. 176.
86. Ibid., pp. 175–6.
87. These terms are borrowed from Sartori, *Parties and Party Systems*, p. 133.
88. Ibid., p. 132.
89. These terms are adapted from Milbraith and Goel quoted in Nahfat Nasr and Monte Palmer, 'Alienation and Political Participation in Lebanon,' *International Journal of Middle East Studies* 8 (1977), p. 509.
90. Hizbu'llah, al-Maktab as-Siyasi, Lijnat al-Tahlil wal-Dirasat, *Wathiqat al-Ta'if: Dirasa fi al-Madmun* (n.p., 1989), p. 5 and p. 53.
91. Ibid., p. 13 and p. 39.
92. For example, the Sunni premier would not be free to choose his ministers, but would require the approval of the president, ibid., p. 45.
93. Ibid., p. 12 and p. 51.
94. Ibrahim al-Amin al-Sayyid (address to parliament, Beirut, February 1997), al-Manar TV.
95. Magnus Ranstorp, *Hizbu'llah in Lebanon: The Politics of the Western Hostage Crisis* (New York: St. Martin's Press, 1997), p. 143.
96. Nasru'llah, LBC, March 1997.
97. 'Ali Fayyad, interview by author, tape recording, Beirut, 18 February 2000. See also Matts Warn, 'A Voice of Resistance: The Point of View of Hizballah', Advanced Course in Political Science, May 1997 (Department of Political Science, Stockholm University, Stockholm), p. 48.
98. As charged by May Chartouni-Dubarry, 'Hizballah: From Militia to Political Party', in *Lebanon on Hold: Implications for Middle East Peace*, eds Nadim Shehadi and Rosemary Hollis (London: Royal Institute of International Affairs; Oxford: Centre for Lebanese Studies, 1996), p. 60.
99. Fayyad, 18 February 2000.

100. Muhammad Ra'id, interview by author, tape recording, Beirut, 9 March 1998.
101. Ibid.
102. Fayyad, 18 February 2000.
103. Nasru'llah, LBC, March 1997.
104. Ibrahim al-Amin al-Sayyid, al-Manar TV, February 1997.
105. Qasim, 17 March 1998.
106. Ibid.
107. *Al-'Ahd*, 21 November 1997.
108. Husayn al-Mussawi, 21 August 1997.
109. 'Open Letter', p. 176.
110. Muhsin, 1 March 1997.
111. Fayyad, 2 March 1997.
112. Nasru'llah, al-Manar TV, September 1996.
113. These terms are adapted from Giovanni Sartori, 'Opposition and Control: Problems and Prospects', *Government and Opposition* 1, no. 1 (Winter 1966), p. 151.
114. Augustus Richard Norton, 'Hizballah: From Radicalism to Pragmatism?' *Middle East Policy* 5, no. 4 (January 1998), p. 156.
115. An observation which has also been noted by Chartouni-Dubarry, 'Hizballah', p. 61.
116. Nilufer Gole, 'Authoritarian Secularism in Islamist Politics: The Case of Turkey', in *Civil Society in the Middle East*, ed. Augustus Richard Norton, vol. 2 (Leiden, New York, Cologne: EJ Brill, 1996), p. 29, applies these terms to Turkey's Refah party, which I also found applicable to Hizbu'llah.
117. See Nasru'llah, al-Manar TV, September 1996, for a summary of such issues and Chartouni-Dubarry, 'Hizballah', p. 61.
118. As defined by Sartori, 'Opposition and Control', p. 151.
119. Ibid.
120. See, for example, Gole, 'Authoritarian Secularism in Islamist Politics', p. 29.
121. Qasim, 7 March 1998, and Ra'id, 9 March 1998.
122. Husayn al-Mussawi, 21 August 1997; Ra'id, 9 March 1998; Qasim, 7 March 1998, who prefers the term 'constitutional'.
123. Husayn al-Mussawi, 21 August 1997. See also al-Sayyid Hassan Nasru'llah, southern suburbs of Beirut, al-Manar TV, 8 August 1997.
124. Fnaysh, 15 August 1997.
125. Qasim, 17 March 1998.
126. Fnaysh, 15 August 1997.
127. *Harmun*, 27 December 1998.
128. *Nida' al-Watan*, 14 December 1998.
129. *Harmun*, 27 December 1998. See also *al-Massira*, 21 December 1998, for Hizbu'llah's positive assessment of Lahhud.
130. *Daily Star*, 22 December 1998.
131. *Harmun*, 27 December 1998.
132. Al-Sayyid Hassan Nasru'llah quoted in *al-Hawadith*, 19 March 1999.

Chapter 2

1. Muhammad Husayn Fadlu'llah, 'Islamic Unity and Political Change: Interview with Shaykh Muhammad Hussayn Fadla'llah', interview by Mahmoud Soueid, *Journal of Palestine Studies* 25, no. 1 (Autumn 1995), p. 64.
2. Husayn al-Mussawi, 21 August 1997.
3. 'Abd al-Hamid al-Mutawali quoted in *al-'Ahd*, 20 Rabi' al-Awwal 1407.
4. Ibrahim al-Amin al-Sayyid, quoted in *al-'Ahd*, 26 Sha'ban 1405 .
5. Foreign Relations' Unit, *Hizballah: View and Conceptions*, (n.p., n.d.), p. 2.
6. Husayn al-Mussawi, 21 August 1997.
7. William E. Shepard, 'Islam and Ideology: Towards a Typology,' *International Journal of Middle East Studies* 19 (1987), p. 308.
8. *Al-'Ahd*, 3 Rabi' ath-Thani, 1407.
9. See Ayatu'llah Seyyid Ruhu'llah Mussawi Khumayni, 'Khomeini', in *Expectation of the Millennium: Shi'ism in History*, eds Seyyed Hossein Nasr, Hamid Dabashi and Seyyed Vali Reza Nasr (Albany: State University of New York Press, 1989), p. 358; Sami Zubaida, *Islam: The People and the State* (London and New York: I.B. Tauris and Co. Ltd, 1993), p. 16; Norman Calder, 'Accommodation and Revolution in Shi'i Jurisprudence: Khumayni and the Classical Tradition', *Middle Eastern Studies* 18, no. 1 (1982), p. 9.
10. Calder, 'Accommodation and Revolution', p. 10.
11. 'Ali Fayyad, 2 March 1997.
12. Al-Sayyid Hassan Nasru'llah's view cited in Ghassan 'Azi, *Hizb'ullah: Min al-Hilm ila al-Waqi'yya al-Siyasiyya* (Kuwait: Qurtas Publishing, 1998), p. 77.
13. Husayn al-Mussawi, 21 August 1997.
14. *Al-'Ahd*, 23 Shawwal 1405.
15. Al-Sayyid Husayn al-Mussawi quoted in Martin Kramer, 'Hizballah: The Calculus of Jihad', *Bulletin: The American Academy of Arts and Sciences* 47, no. 8 (May 1994), p. 30.
16. Judith Harik, 'Between Islam and the System: Sources and Implications of Popular Support for Lebanon's Hizballah', *Journal of Conflict Resolution* 40, no. 1 (March 1996) p. 56 and p. 61.
17. Husayn al-Mussawi, 21 August 1997.
18. Yussef Meri', 10 April 1998. See also al-Sayyid Hassan Nasru'llah, MTV, July 1998, and Nasru'llah, Orbit TV, May 1997.
19. 'Text of Open Letter Addressed by Hizballah to the Downtrodden of Lebanon and the World,' in *Amal and the Shi'a: Struggle for the Soul of Lebanon*, Augustus Richard Norton (Austin, TX: University of Texas Press, 1987), p. 174
20. *Al-Maokif*, no. 29, p. 3.
21. See 'Open Letter', p. 175; Subhi al-Tufayli quoted in *al-'Ahd*, 10 Safar 1406; Nasru'llah, Orbit TV, May 1997; *Ad-Diyar*, 19 December 1993; Nasru'llah, MTV, July 1998.

22. See Khumayni, 'Khomeini', p. 357; Zubaida, *Islam*, p. 16. Mangol Bayat, 'The Iranian Revolution of 1978–79: Fundamentalist or Modern?' *Middle East Journal*, no. 1 (Winter 1983), p. 36, notes that Khumayni's use of the caliphate as proof of the enduring necessity of an Islamic government is, paradoxically, a Sunni argument.
23. Nasru'llah, LBC, March 1997.
24. See Nasru'llah, Orbit TV, May 1997, and *al-'Ahd*, 21 November 1997.
25. See *al-Maokif*, no. 22, p. 1, and Nasru'llah, Orbit TV, May 1997.
26. Husayn al-Mussawi, 21 August 1997, and Muhammad Muhsin, 1 March 1997.
27. Martin Kramer, 'Redeeming Jerusalem: The Pan-Islamic Premise of Hizballah', in *The Iranian Revolution and the Muslim World*, ed. David Menashri (Boulder, CO: Westview Press, 1990), p. 124.
28. *Al-'Ahd*, 10 Safar 1406.
29. See Nilufer Gole, 'Authoritarian Secularism in Islamist Politics: The Case of Turkey', in *Civil Society in the Middle East*, ed. Augustus Richard Norton, vol. 2 (Leiden, New York, Cologne: EJ Brill, 1996), p. 27, and John P. Entelis, 'Civil Society and the Authoritarian Temptation in Algerian Politics: Islamic Democracy Versus the Centralised State', in *Civil Society in the Middle East*, p. 48.
30. Muhammad Fnaysh, 15 August 1997.
31. I use the term Islamist rather than Islamic to denote a society that advocates the establishment of an Islamic state, as opposed to a society that is merely pious.
32. Nazih Ayubi, *Political Islam: Religion and Politics in the Arab World* (London and New York: Routledge, 1991), p. 156.
33. Ibid., p. 157.
34. Ruhu'llah Khumayni, *Islam and Revolution: Writings and Declarations of Imam Khomeini*, trans. and ed. Hamid Algar (Berkeley, CA: Mizan Press, 1981), p. 330.
35. Khumayni, *Writings and Declarations*, p. 330.
36. Ahmad al-Qattan quoted in Emmanuel Sivan, 'Eavesdropping on Radical Islam', *The Middle East Quarterly* 2, no. 1 (March 1995), p. 16.
37. *Al-'Ahd*, 20 Rabi'al-Awwal 1407.
38. Fadlu'llah quoted in Martin Kramer, 'The Oracle of Hizballah: Seyyid Muhammad Husayn Fadlallah', in *Spokesmen for the Despised Fundamentalist Leaders in the Middle East*, ed. R. Scott Appleby (Chicago: University of Chicago Press, 1997), p. 125.
39. *Al-'Ahd*, 13 Rabi' al-Awwal 1407.
40. Ibid.
41. Ibid.
42. Ibid. 20 Rabi' al-Awwal 1407.
43. Ibid. 13 Rabi' al-Awwal 1407.
44. Fadlu'llah quoted in Haleh Vaziri, 'Iran's Involvement in Lebanon: Polarization and Radicalization of Militant Islamic Movements', *Journal of South Asian and Middle Eastern Studies* 16, no. 2 (Winter 1992), p. 11
45. John O. Voll and John L. Esposito, 'Islam's Democratic Essence', *Middle East Quarterly* (September 1994), p. 8.

46. T.M. Aziz, 'Popular Sovereignty in Contemporary Shi'i Political Thought', *Muslim World* 36, nos. 3–4 (July-October 1996), p. 286.
47. Ibid.
48. *Al-'Ahd*, 17 Rabi' ath-Thani 1407.
49. Constitution of the Islamic Republic of Iran, Principle 96.
50. *Al-'Ahd*, 17 Rabi' ath-Thani 1407.
51. Anne Lambton, 'A Reconsideration of the Position of the Marja' al-Taqlid and the Religious Institution', *Studia Islamica* 20 (1964), p. 128.
52. Voll and Esposito, 'Islam's Democratic Essence', p. 6. It must be noted, however, that Sadr advocated the direct election of the *Faqih*, as reported by Aziz, 'Popular Sovereignty', p. 287.
53. Principle 6 of the Iranian Constitution.
54. Ayubi, *Political Islam*, p. 150.
55. John L. Esposito and John O. Voll, *Islam and Democracy* (New York and Oxford: Oxford University Press, 1996), p. 49.
56. Kramer, 'The Oracle of Hizballah', p. 157.
57. *Al-'Ahd*, 20 Rabi' al-Awwal 1407.
58. Constitution of the Islamic Republic of Iran, Principle 26.
59. Kramer, 'The Oracle of Hizballah', p. 157.
60. Ibid., p. 127.
61. Shaykh Na'im Qasim, 17 March 1998, and Nasru'llah, Orbit TV, May 1997.
62. Qasim, 17 March 1998, and Muhammad Ra'id, 9 March 1998. See also 'Ali Fayyad, *as-Safir*, 31 July 1998.
63. Fayyad, *as-Safir*, 31 July 1998.
64. Ra'id, 9 March 1998.
65. *As-Safir*, 18 August 1998. It is rumoured that the author of this article, Hassan Harb, is a pseudonym and that the author is in fact a prominent Hizbu'llah official.
66. Qasim, 17 March 1998. See also *al-'Ahd*, 25 February 1994.
67. Fnaysh, 15 August 1997.
68. Ibid.
69. Constitution of the Islamic Republic of Iran, Principle 64.
70. Ibid., Principle 144.
71. Sivan, 'Eavesdropping on Radical Islam', p. 22.
72. Constitution of the Islamic Republic of Iran, Principle 115.
73. Kramer, 'The Oracle of Hizballah', p. 27.
74. As declared by Ra'id, 9 March 1998; Fnaysh, 15 August 1997; Muhsin, 1 March 1997; Fayyad, 2 March 1997.
75. Fayyad, 2 March 1997.
76. Ra'id, 9 March 1998.
77. Muhsin, 1 March 1997. But one must note that there are a few Sunni advocates of the *Wilayat al-Faqih* concept who are party members.
78. Husayn al-Mussawi, 21 August 1997.
79. Fnaysh, 15 August 1997.
80. Ra'id, 9 March 1998.
81. While the party does not use the term 'Lebanonisation', it is widely used by Lebanese observers of the party. The party uses the term '*infitah*' to describe its post-Ta'if political role. See, for example al-Sayyid

Hassan Nasru'llah's use of this term in *al-'Ahd*, 21 November 1997, and *al-'Ahd*, 3 November 1995.

82. See Asl'ad AbuKhalil, 'Ideology and Practice of Hizballah in Lebanon: Islamization of Leninist Organizational Principles', *Middle Eastern Studies* 27, no. 3 (July 1991), p. 401 and Nizar Hamzeh, 'Lebanon's Hizballah: From Islamic Revolution to Parliamentary Accommodation', *Third World Quarterly* 14, no. 2 (1993), p. 324.

83. Hamzeh, 'Lebanon's Hizballah', p. 323.

84. Ibid., p. 325. Hamzeh also makes this case in 'The Islamic Spectrum of Lebanese Politics', *Journal of South Asian and Middle Eastern Studies* 16, no. 3 (Spring 1993), p. 40.

85. Even Nasru'llah admitted this on Orbit TV, May 1997.

86. By Nasru'llah's account on Orbit TV, May 1997, this debate lasted for eight months, while Fnaysh, 15 August 1997, maintains that it lasted for two years.

87. Fnaysh, 15 August 1997.

88. See Abdel Salam Sidahmed and Anoushiravan Ehteshami, 'Introduction' to *Islamic Fundamentalism*, no. 2, Twayne's Themes in Right Wing Politics and Ideology Series, ed. Youssef Choueiri (Boston: Twayne Publications, 1990), p. 14, where they claim that there can be 'a synthesis between Islamism and democracy' in light of this borrowing.

89. Voll and Esposito, 'Islam's Democratic Essence', p. 9.

90. Fnaysh, 15 August 1997.

91. Fayyad, 2 March 1997, and Fnaysh, 15 August 1997. See also Fadlu'llah, 'Islamic Unity and Political Change', p. 67.

92. Fnaysh, 15 August 1997.

93. See Nasru'llah, Orbit TV, May 1997, and Nasru'llah, MTV, July 1998.

94. Fnaysh, 15 August 1997.

95. Nasru'llah, MTV, July 1998.

96. Qasim, 17 March 1998. See also Nasru'llah, Orbit TV, May 1997, and Nasru'llah, MTV, July 1998.

97. *Al-'Ahd*, 21 November 1997.

98. As described by Ibrahim al-Amin al-Sayyid in *al-'Ahd*, 12 Muharram 1406.

99. See Nasru'llah, MTV, July 1998, and *as-Safir*, 31 July 1998.

100. Fayyad, 2 March 1997.

101. As reasoned by Ra'id, 9 March 1998, Meri', 10 April 1998, and anonymous party source, interview by author, tape recording, Beirut, 13 February 2000. This reasoning is also discerned by Kramer in 'Redeeming Jerusalem', p. 119.

102. 'Open Letter', p. 174 and p. 175.

103. *Al-'Ahd*, 21 November 1997. Fadlu'llah shares this view, as disclosed by Kramer, 'The Oracle of Hizballah', p. 158.

104. Qasim quoted in *al-Maokif*, no. 29, p. 4.

105. For a brief account of this see Kramer, 'The Oracle of Hizballah', p. 142 and Hala Jaber, *Hezbollah: Born with a Vengeance* (London: Fourth Estate Ltd, 1997), p. 32.

106. *Al-'Ahd*, 29 Jamad ath-Thani 1407.

107. Shaykh Subhi al-Tufayli and al-Sayyid Muhammad Husayn Fadlu'llah quoted in *al-'Ahd*, 29 Jamad ath-Thani 1407.

108. See Jaber, *Hezbollah*, p. 35 and Anoushiravan Ehteshami and Raymond A. Hinnebusch, *Syria and Iran: Middle East Powers in a Penetrated Regional System* (London and New York: Routledge, 1997), p. 134.

109. *Wathiqat al-Ta'if*, p. 53

110. Fnaysh, 15 August 1997.

111. *Al-Maokif*, no. 5, p. 8.

112. Fayyad, 2 March 1997. Nasru'llah also prefers to call it a 'development' rather than 'change', as disclosed on MTV, July 1998.

113. May Chartouni-Dubarry, 'Hizballah: From Militia to Political Party', in *Lebanon on Hold: Implications for Middle East Peace*, eds Nadim Shehadi and Rosemary Hollis (London: Royal Institute of International Affairs; Oxford: Centre for Lebanese Studies, 1996), p. 60.

114. Fayyad, 2 March 1997.

115. *Al-Maokif*, no. 27, p. 4.

116. Qasim quoted in *al-Maokif*, no. 6, p. 3.

117. Fayyad, 2 March 1997.

118. Term used by Hizbu'llah quoted in Chartouni-Dubarry, 'Hizballah', p. 61.

119. Source close to the party cited in *as-Safir*, 31 July 1998.

120. Nasru'llah, September 1996.

121. Ibid.

122. Chartouni-Dubarry, 'Hizballah', pp. 60–1.

123. Fayyad, 18 February 2000.

124. As distinguished by Sidahmed and Ehteshami, 'Introduction', p. 13.

125. Ibid.

126. Fnaysh, Future TV, 2 July 1997.

127. See, for example, al-Sayyid Hassan Nasru'llah, 'Jerusalem Day', 7 February 1997, for such criticisms.

128. Ra'id, 9 March 1998. See also *al-Maokif*, no. 15, p. 5.

129. Ra'id, 9 March 1998.

130. Muhammad Fnaysh, *Wajhan ila Wajh*, al-Manar TV, October 1997.

131. This term is used by Giles Trendle in 'Hizballah's Pragmatism and Popular Standing,' in Shehadi and Hollis, *Lebanon on Hold*, p. 66.

132. As argued by Trendle, 'Hizballah's Pragmatism', p. 66.

133. Fayyad, 2 March 1997.

134. Al-Sayyid Hassan Nasru'llah quoted in *al-Maokif*, no. 4, p. 3, and Ibrahim al-Amin al-Sayyid, quoted in *al-Maokif*, no. 3, p. 2.

135. As declared by Muhsin, 1 March 1997; Husayn al-Mussawi, 21 August 1997; Ra'id, 9 March 1998; Fnaysh, 15 August 1997. See also al-Sayyid Hassan Nasru'llah quoted in *al-Maokif*, no. 26, p. 1.

136. Husayn al-Mussawi, 21 August 1997.

137. This view is maintained by Augustus Richard Norton, 'Hizballah: From Radicalism to Pragmatism?', *Middle East Policy* 5, no. 4 (January 1998), p. 156, and Lisa Anderson, 'Fulfilling Prophesies: State Policy and Islamic Radicalism', in *Political Islam: Revolution, Radicalism or Reform?* ed. John L. Esposito (Boulder, CO: Lynne Reiner Publishers, 1997), p. 26.

138. As asserted by Fnaysh, 15 August 1997; Nasru'llah, MTV, July 1998; Nasru'llah, Orbit TV, May 1997.
139. Fayyad, 18 February 2000.
140. Ibid., and Fnaysh, 15 August 1997.
141. In theory, democracy can encompass parties espousing counter-ideologies such as Islam and communism, which ultimately seek to overturn democracy. In reality, however, the capacity for democracy to absorb counter-ideologies has been severely limited, as exemplified by the cases of the US where Communist parties are banned, the prohibition of Islamic parties in Turkey and the cancellation of elections in Algeria, which the FIS were poised to win.

Chapter 3

1. Ayatu'llah Khumayni, 'Khomeini', in *Expectation of the Millennium: Shi'ism in History*, eds Seyyed Hossein Nasr, Hamid Dabashi and Seyyed Vali Reza Nasr (Albany: State University of New York Press, 1989), p. 358.
2. Khumayni quoted in Norman Calder, 'Accommodation and Revolution in Imami Shi'i Jurisprudence: Khumayni and the Classical Tradition', *Middle Eastern Studies* 18, no. 1 (1982), p. 10.
3. Moojan Momen, *An Introduction to Shi'ite Islam: The History and Doctrines of Twelver Shi'ism* (New Haven and London: Yale University Press, 1985), p. 196.
4. Hamid Enayat, 'Khomeini', in Nasr et al., *Expectation of the Millennium: Shi'ism in History*, 1989), p. 338; and T.M. Aziz, 'Popular Sovereignty in Contemporary Shi'i Political Thought', *Muslim World* 36, nos 3–4 (July–October 1996), p. 277.
5. As cited by Ervand Abrahamian, 'Khomeini: A Fundamentalist?', in *Fundamentalism in Comparative Perspective*, ed. Lawrence Kaplan (Amherst: University of Massachusetts Press, 1992), p. 118; Sami Zubaida, *Islam: The People and the State* (London and New York: I.B. Tauris and Co. Ltd, 1993), p. 18; and Enayat, 'Khomeini', p. 338. I have chosen to use the Oxford University Press translation of the Qur'an for the proper *sura* and *aya* number.
6. See Enayat, 'Khumayni', p. 338, and Emmanuel Sivan, 'Sunni Radicalism in the Middle East and the Iranian Revolution', *International Journal of Middle East Studies* 21 (1989), p. 10.
7. Abrahamian, 'Khomeini: A Fundamentalist?', p. 118.
8. Mangol Bayat, 'Khomeini', in Nasr et al., *Expectation of the Millennium: Shi'ism in History*, pp. 351–2.
9. Ibid., p. 352.
10. Abdulaziz A. Sachedina, 'Activist Shi'ism in Iran, Iraq and Lebanon', in *Fundamentalisms Observed*, eds Martin E. Marty and R. Scott Appleby, *The Fundamentalist Project*, vol. 1 (Chicago and London: University of Chicago Press, 1991), p. 429.
11. Momen, *An Introduction to Shi'ite Islam*, p. 190.
12. Bayat, 'Khomeini', p. 353.
13. Enayat, 'Khomeini', p. 334.

14. Momen, *An Introduction to Shi'ite Islam*, p. 196.
15. Calder, 'Accommodation and Revolution', p. 16.
16. Gregory Rose, 'Velayet-e-Faqih and the Recovery of Islamic Identity in the Thought of Ayatollah Khomeini', in *Religion and Politics in Iran*, ed. Nikki Keddie (New Haven and London: Yale University Press, 1983), p. 170.
17. See Rose, 'Velayet-e-Faqih and the Recovery of Islamic Identity', p. 169, and Momen, *An Introduction to Shi'ite Islam*, p. 191.
18. Calder, 'Accommodation and Revolution', *An Introduction to Shi'ite Islam*, p. 16.
19. Enayat, 'Khomeini', p. 339.
20. Calder, 'Accommodation and Revolution', p. 14.
21. Ibid., p. 17.
22. Constitution of the Islamic Republic of Iran, Principle 5.
23. *Al-'Ahd*, 3 Rabi' ath-Thani 1407.
24. See Sivan, 'Sunni Radicalism', p. 9 and p. 12; Rose, 'Velayet-e-Faqih and the Recovery of Islamic Identity', p. 177; Zubaida, *Islam*, p. 17.
25. See Khumayni, 'Khomeini', p. 177; Enayat, 'Khomeini', p. 335; Calder, 'Accommodation and Revolution', p. 15; Sivan, 'Sunni Radicalism', p. 12.
26. Aziz, 'Popular Sovereignty', p. 277.
27. *Al-'Ahd*, 3 Rabi' ath-Thani 1407.
28. 'Ali Fayyad, 2 March 1997.
29. Momen, *An Introduction to Shi'ite Islam*, p. 248.
30. Enayat, 'Khomeini', pp. 341–2.
31. See Enayat, 'Khomeini', p. 342 and Aziz, 'Popular Sovereignty', p. 280.
32. Constitution of the Islamic Republic of Iran, Principle 110.
33. Ibid., Principle 112.
34. Ibid., Principle 110.
35. See al-'Ahd, 3 Rabi' ath-Thani 1407, and Zubaida, *Islam*, p. 17.
36. See al-'Ahd, 3 Rabi' ath-Thani 1407, and Calder, 'Accommodation and Revolution', pp. 9–10.
37. *Al-'Ahd*, 3 Rabi' ath-Thani 1407.
38. See Aziz, 'Popular Sovereignty', p. 279 and Enayat, 'Khomeini', p. 339.
39. See al-'Ahd, 3 Rabi' ath-Thani 1407, and Khumayni, *Islam and Revolution: Writings and Declarations of Imam Khomeini*, trans. and ed. by Hamid Algar (Berkeley, CA: Mizan Press, 1981), p. 342.
40. See the Constitution of the Islamic Republic of Iran, Principle 109, and al-'Ahd, 17 Rabi' ath-Thani 1407, for the required qualities and functions of the *Faqih*.
41. This comparison has been made by several scholars, including Aziz, 'Popular sovereignty', p. 287; Farhang Rajaee, 'Iranian Ideology and Worldview: The Cultural Export of Revolution', in *The Iranian Revolution: Its Global Impact*, ed. John L. Esposito (Miami: Florida International University Press; Gainsville, FL: Orders, University Press of Florida, 1990), p. 70; Anne Lambton, 'A Reconsideration of the Position of the Marja' al-Taqlid and the Religious Institution', *Studia Islamica* 20 (1964), p. 132.

42. Lambton, 'A Reconsideration of the Position of the Marja' al-Taqlid', p. 132. See also Enayat, 'Khomeini', p. 337.

43. Nazih Ayubi, *Political Islam: Religion and Politics in the Arab World* (London and New York: Routledge, 1991), p. 135.

44. Constitution of the Islamic Republic of Iran, Principle 5.

45. See Martin Kramer, 'Redeeming Jerusalem: The Pan-Islamic Premise of Hizballah', in *The Iranian Revolution and the Muslim World*, ed. David Menashri (Boulder, CO: Westview Press, 1990), pp. 122–3; Aziz, 'Popular Sovereignty', p. 280; Lambton, 'A Reconsideration of the Position of the Marja' al-Taqlid', p. 125 et passim.

46. Al-Sayyid Hassan Nasru'llah quoted in *al-'Ahd*, 26 Sha'ban 1407.

47. Muhammad Muhsin, 1 March 1997.

48. Muhammad Ra'id, 9 March 1998.

49. 'Ammar al-Mussawi, 'Interview: Ammar al-Mussawi', interview by Giles Trendle, *Lebanon Report* 5, no. 12 (December 1994), p. 10.

50. Al-Sayyid 'Abbas al-Mussawi, Ba'albakk, *Amiru'l-Zakira*, 10 Muharram 1410, p. 212.

51. Al-Sayyid Hassan Nasru'llah, 'Jerusalem Day' southern suburbs of Beirut, al-Manar TV, 24 January 1998.

52. Al-Sayyid Hassan Nasru'llah, 'Jerusalem Day', southern suburbs of Beirut, al-Manar TV, 15 January 1999.

53. Momen, p. 205.

54. Ibid., p. 206.

55. The Iranian constitution was amended after Khumayni's death to permit jurists such as Khamini'i who were not *maraji' at-taqlid* to assume the *Wilayat*. See Ervand Abrahamian, *Khomeinism: Essays on the Islamic Republic* (London: I.B. Tauris, 1993), p. 34.

56. Nasru'llah, 'Jerusalem Day', 7 February 1997.

57. Ibid., 15 January 1999.

58. Ibid., 7 February 1997.

59. As explained by 'Ali Fayyad, 2 March 1997.

60. Ibid.

61. Husayn al-Mussawi quoted in Simon Shapira, 'The Origins of Hizballah', *Jerusalem Quarterly*, no. 46 (Spring 1998), p. 125.

62. Fayyad, 2 March 1997.

63. See As'ad AbuKhalil, 'The Incoherence of Islamic Fundamentalism: Arab Islamic Thought at the End of the Twentieth Century', *Middle East Journal* 48, no. 4 (Autumn 1994), p. 690, and Lambton, 'A Reconsideration of the Position of the Marja' al-Taqlid', p. 126.

64. See *al-Burnamij al-Intikhabi li-Hizbu'llah*, 1992; 'Ammar al-Mussawi quoted in Trendle, p. 10; Nasru'llah, Orbit TV, May 1997; Nasru'llah, LBC, March 1997.

65. 'Text of Open Letter Addressed by Hizballah to the Downtrodden of Lebanon and the World', in *Amal and the Shi'a: Struggle for the Soul of Lebanon*, Augustus Richard Norton (Austin, TX: University of Texas Presss, 1987), p. 168.

66. Nasru'llah, LBC, March 1997.

67. *Al-'Ahd*, 12 Sha'ban 1407.

68. Nasru'llah, Orbit TV, May 1997.

69. Martin Kramer, 'The Moral Logic of Hizballah', in *Origins of Terrorism, Psychologies, Ideologies, Theologies, States of Mind*, ed. Walter Reich (New York: Cambridge University Press, 1990), p. 155.

70. See Sivan, 'Sunni Radicalism', p. 21, and Magnus Ranstorp, *Hizb'allah in Lebanon: The Politics of the Western Hostage Crisis* (New York: St. Martin's Press, 1997), p. 47.

71. Muhammad Fnaysh, 15 August 1997; Muhsin, 1 March 1997. See also Nasru'llah, Orbit TV, May 1997.

72. Muhsin, 1 March 1997.

73. Shaykh Na'im Qasim, 17 March 1998. See also Nasru'llah, Orbit TV, May 1997 and *al-'Ahd*, 21 November 1997.

74. Al-Sayyid 'Abbas al-Mussawi, southern suburbs of Beirut, *Amiru'l-Zakira*, Dhu al-Hujja 1406, p. 197.

75. Ibrahim al-Amin al-Sayyid quoted in Kramer, 'Redeeming Jerusalem', p. 116.

76. *Al-Maokif*, no. 22, p. 2.

77. Nasru'llah quoted in *ad-Diyar*, 19 December 1993.

78. Fnaysh, 15 August 1997.

79. Muhsin, 1 March 1997.

80. Fnaysh, 15 August 1997.

Chapter 4

1. *Al-'Ahd*, 5 Shawal 1404.

2. Ibid., 10 Safar 1406.

3. Ibid., 12 Sha'ban 1407.

4. Ibid., 10 Safar 1406.

5. Quoted in Martin Kramer, 'The Moral Logic of Hizballah', in *Origins of Terrorism, Psychologies Ideologies, States of Mind*, ed. Walter Reich (New York: Cambridge University Press, 1990), p. 132.

6. *Al-'Ahd*, 5 Shawal 1404.

7. Mussawi quoted in Ghassan 'Azi, *Hizbu'llah: Min al-Hilm ila al-Waqi'yya al-Siyasiyya* (Kuwait: Qurtas Publishing, 1998), p. 65.

8. Ibid.

9. *Al-'Ahd*, n.d.

10. Kramer, 'The Moral Logic of Hizballah', pp. 132–3.

11. 'Text of Open Letter Addressed by Hizballah to the Downtrodden of Lebanon and the World', in *Amal and the Shi'a: Struggle for the Soul of Lebanon*, Augustus Richard Norton (Austin, TX: University of Texas Press, 1987), p. 169.

12. Ibid., p. 168 and p. 169.

13. *Al-'Ahd*, 24 Safar 1408.

14. *As-Safir*, 31 July 1998.

15. *Al-'Ahd*, 2 June 1995.

16. Ibid., 27 January 1995.

17. Martin Kramer, 'Redeeming Jerusalem: The Pan-Islamic Premise of Hizballah', in *The Iranian Revolution and the Muslim World*, ed. David Menashri (Boulder, CO: Westview Press, 1990), p. 110.

18. Nasru'llah, C33 TV, May 1996.

19. Ibid.
20. Shaykh Hassan Trad, quoted in 'Azi, *Hizbu'llah*, p. 66.
21. Ibrahim al-Amin al-Sayyid, quoted in ibid.
22. *Al-'Ahd*, 24 Safar 1408. See also party quote in 'Azi, *Hizbu'llah*, p. 64: 'We are an inextricable part of the Islamic Revolution.'
23. *Al-'Ahd*, 2 June 1995.
24. Farthang Rajaee, 'Iranian Ideology and Worldview: The Cultural Export of Revolution', in *The Iranian Revolution: Its Global Impact*, ed. John L. Esposito (Miami: Florida International University Press; Gainsville, FL: Orders, University Press of Florida, 1990), p. 68.
25. See al-Sayyid 'Abbas al-Mussawi, Shabiyya, *Amiru'l Zakira*, 20 Jamadi ath-Thani 1408, p. 203; *al-'Ahd*, 2 June 1995; Husayn al-Mussawi, 21 August 1997.
26. Hamas Charter, Article 14.
27. *Al-'Ahd*, 21 Dhu al-Hujja 1404.
28. Nasru'llah, 'Jerusalem Day', 15 January 1999.
29. Ibid.
30. Ibid.
31. Nasru'llah, Nabishit, *Amiru'l-Zakira*, 27 March 1992, p. 170.
32. Hala Jaber, *Hezbollah: Born with a Vengenace* (London: Fourth Estate Ltd, 1997), p. 59.
33. Yussef Meri', 10 April 1998.
34. For example, see Nasru'llah, 'Jerusalem Day', 7 February 1997, and *al-Maokif*, no. 7, p. 5.
35. 'Open Letter', p. 179.
36. 'Abbas al-Mussawi, *Amiru'l-Zakira*, 20 Jamadi ath-Thani 1408, p. 203.
37. Al-Sayyid Hassan Nasru'llah, 'Martyrs' Day', southern suburbs of Beirut, al-Manar TV, 28 June 1996.
38. See *al-'Ahd*, 2 June 1995, and al-Sayyid 'Abbas al-Mussawi, Mashghara, *Amiru'l-Zakira* 17 Muharram 1410, p. 209.
39. 'Abbas al-Mussawi, 'Min Jibshit'.
40. 'Open Letter', p. 184.
41. Al-Sayyid 'Abbas al-Mussawi quoted in 'Azi, *Hizbu'llah*, p. 65.
42. Nasru'llah, 'Jerusalem Day', p. 1997.
43. Al-Sayyid Hassan Nasru'llah, southern suburbs of Beirut, al-Manar TV, 8 August 1997.
44. 'Ali Fayyad, 2 March 1997.
45. Al-Sayyid 'Abbas al-Mussawi, Ba'albakk, *Amiru'l-Zakira*, 10 Muharram 1410, p. 212.
46. 'Open Letter', p. 184.
47. Al-Sayyid 'Abbas al-Mussawi, Kafra, *Amiru'l-Zakira*, 10 Dhu al-Qa'da, p. 219.
48. *Al-'Ahd*, 17 Dhu al-Hujja 1406.
49. Al-Sayyid 'Abbas al-Mussawi, Deir Qanun al-Nahr, *Amiru'l-Zakira*, 29 Rabi' al-Awwal 1408, p. 205.
50. Meri', 10 April 1998.
51. *Sam wa 'Assal*, presented by As'ad Majid, al-Manar TV, 7 August 1994.
52. 'Abbas al-Mussawi, Islamabad, *Amiru'l-Zakira*, Ramadan 1410, p. 216.
53. Nasru'llah, LBC, March 1997.

54. *Daily Star*, 23 January 1997.
55. Meri', 10 April 1998.
56. Nasru'llah, LBC, March 1997.
57. Shaykh Na'im Qasim, 17 March 1998.
58. Meri', 10 April 1998.
59. Fayyad, 2 March 1997.
60. Ibid. See also Nasru'llah, LBC, March 1997.
61. *Al-'Ahd*, 10 Safar 1406.
62. See *al-'Ahd*, 26 Sha'ban 1405, and *al-'Ahd*, 12 Muharram 1406.
63. *Al-'Ahd*, 26 Sha'ban 1405.
64. Ibid.
65. Al-Sayyid Hassan Nasru'llah, 'Martyrs' Funeral', southern suburbs of Beirut, al-Manar TV, 5 August 1997.
66. *Al-Maokif*, no. 18, p. 1.
67. *Al-'Ahd*, 6 Rabi' al-Awwal 1407.
68. *Daily Star*, 24 December 1998.
69. 'Abbas al-Mussawi, *Amiru'l-Zakira*, 29 Rabi' al-Awwal 1408, p. 204.
70. Al-Sayyid 'Abbas al-Mussawi, Beirut, *Amiru'l-Zakira*, Rabi' ath-Thani 1405, p. 190.
71. *Al-'Ahd*, 2 June 1995.
72. Nasru'llah, Nabatiyyeh, al-Manar TV, September 1996.
73. *Al-Ahd*, 12 Sha'ban 1407.
74. Marius Deeb, 'Shi'a Movements in Lebanon: Their Formation, Ideology, Social Basis and Links with Iran and Syria', *Third World Quarterly* 10, no. 2 (April 1988), p. 696.
75. Quoted in Kramer, 'Redeeming Jerusalem', p. 118.
76. Khumayni, *Islam and Revolution: Writings and Declarations of Imam Khomeini*, trans. and ed. Hamid Algar (Berkeley, CA: Mizan Press), p. 332.
77. Al-Sayyid 'Abbas al-Mussawi, southern suburbs of Beirut, *Amiru'l-Zakira*, 3 Dhu al-Hujja 1406, p. 196.
78. 'Abbas al-Mussawi, *Amiru'l-Zakira*, 29 Rabi' al-Awwal 1408, p. 205.
79. *Al-'Ahd*, 23 Shawwal 1405.
80. *Al-'Ahd*, 21 Dhu al-Qa'da 1404.
81. See ibid.; *Al-'Ahd*, 23 Shawwal 1405; Husayn al-Mussawi, 21 August 1997.
82. *As-Safir*, 31 July 1998.
83. *Al-Maokif*, no. 32, p. 3.
84. Muhammad Fnaysh, 15 August 1997, and Fayyad, 2 March 1997.
85. In a similar vein, many Muslim thinkers in the 1950s utilised Arab nationalism as a means of confronting neo-colonialism and Zionism, as recalled by James Piscatori, *Islam in a World of Nation States* (Cambridge: Cambridge University Press, 1986), p. 107.
86. Al-Sayyid Hassan Nasru'llah, 'Palestinian National Congress', Damascus, al-Manar TV, 12 December 1998.
87. See Nasru'llah, 'Jerusalem Day', 7 February 1997; Shaykh Na'im Qasim quoted in *al-Maokif*, no. 15, p. 2; *al-Maokif*, no. 12, p. 3.
88. See Nasru'llah, 'Jerusalem Day', 7 February 1997; *al-Maokif*, no. 20, p. 2; *al-Maokif*, no. 12, p. 3.

89. Fnaysh, 15 August 1997.
90. See, for example, Shaykh Subhi al-Tufayli in *al-'Ahd*, 18 Jamad al-Awwal 1410.
91. 'Abbas al-Mussawi, *Amiru'l Zakira*, 20 Jamadi ath-Thani, p. 202.
92. See *Sam wa 'Assal*, 7 August 1994, for Hizbu'llah's admission of Christian role in *Intifada*.
93. *Daily Star*, 22 September 1997.
94. *Al-'Ahd*, 21 November 1997.
95. *Daily Star*, 22 September 1997.
96. *Al-Maokif*, no. 21, p. 3.
97. Fnaysh, 15 August 1997.
98. *Al-Maokif*, no. 21, p. 3.
99. See Nasru'llah, 'Jerusalem Day', 24 January 1998; *Al Burnamij al-Intikhabi li-Hizbu'llah*, 1992; al-Sayyid Hassan Nasru'llah, southern suburbs of Beirut, *Amiru'l-Zakira*, 24 Dhu al-Qa'da 1412, p. 227.
100. Samuel Huntington, *The Clash of Civilizations and the Remaking of World Order* (London: Simon and Schuster Ltd, 1997; London: Touchstone Books, 1998), p. 43.
101. Fayyad, 18 February 2000.
102. Ibid. Huntington *The Clash of Civilizations*, also makes the same observation on p. 45, as does Bassam Tibi in *The Crisis of Modern Islam: A Preindustrial Culture in the Scientific Age*, trans. Judith von Sivers (Salt Lake City: University of Utah Press, 1988), p. 51, where he asserts that 'Islam was assimilated into the cultures of the various peoples who were Islamicised.'
103. These are just some of Huntington's criteria which define civilisation, *The Clash of Civilizations*, p. 42.
104. Fayyad, 18 February 2000. See also al-Sayyid Hassan Nasru'llah, Ghobeiri, *Amiru'l-Zakira*, 23 February 1992, p. 139, and Nasru'llah, Orbit TV, May 1997.
105. Fayyad, 18 February 2000.
106. *Al-'Ahd*, 10 Safar 1406. See also Ibrahim al-Amin al-Sayyid quoted in *al-'Ahd*, 12 Muharram 1406.
107. Nasru'llah, Orbit TV, May 1997.
108. Huntington, *The Clash of Civilizations*, p. 256.
109. Ibid., p. 45.
110. Ibid., p. 42.
111. Fayyad, 18 February 2000.
112. Ibid.
113. Nasru'llah, C33 TV, May 1996. See also *al-Maokif*, no. 2, p. 4.
114. Nasru'llah, C33 TV, May 1996.
115. See Nasru'llah, LBC, March 1997; Nasru'llah, Orbit TV, May 1997; 'Azi, *Hizbu'llah*, p. 63.
116. *Al-Maokif*, no. 2, p. 4.
117. Nasru'llah, LBC, March 1997.
118. Fnaysh, 15 August 1997.
119. Nasru'llah, Orbit TV, May 1997.
120. Magnus Ranstorp, *Hizb'allah in Lebanon: The Politics of the Western Hostage Crisis* (New York: St. Martin's Press, 1997), p. 47.

121. See Nasru'llah, Orbit TV, May 1997, and Nasru'llah, C33 TV, May 1996.
122. Ibid.
123. Nasru'llah, C33 TV, May 1996.
124. See *as-Safir*, 4 December 1998; *Schu'un al-Awsat*, no. 59 (January/ February 1997), p. 64 ; Shaykh Nabil Qauk quoted in Jaber, *Hezbollah*, p. 42.
125. Nasru'llah, al-Manar TV, 5 August 1997.
126. Nasru'llah in *al-'Ahd*, 25 February 1994.
127. Nasru'llah quoted in 'Azi, *Hizbu'llah*, p. 63.
128. Nasru'llah, LBC, March 1997, and *al-Maokif*, no. 34, p. 1.
129. Nasru'llah, al-Manar TV, 8 August 1997.
130. See, for example, Nasru'llah, al-Manar TV, 3 November 1997.
131. *Al-'Ahd*, 10 Safar 1406.
132. Muhammad Ra'id, 9 March 1998.
133. Fnaysh, 15 August 1997.
134. Muhammad Muhsin, 1 March 1997.
135. *Al-'Ahd*, 12 Muharram 1406.
136. Fnaysh, 15 August 1997.
137. Qasim, 17 March 1997, and Muhsin, 1 March 1997.
138. Qasim, 17 March 1997.
139. Muhsin, 1 March 1997.
140. Fayyad, 2 March 1997.
141. See Fred Halliday, 'Review Article: the Politics of Islam – a Second Look', *British Journal of Political Studies*, vol. 25 (July 1995), p. 407; Ervand Abrahamian, *Khomeinism: Essays on the Islamic Republic* (London: I.B. Touris and Co., 1993), p. 15; Piscatori, *Islam in a World of Nation States*, p. 112.
142. Piscatori, *Islam in a World of Nation States*, p. 112.
143. Abrahamian, *Khomeinism*, p. 1.
144. Constitution of the Islamic Republic of Iran, Principle 15.
145. Ibid., Principle 115.
146. Ibid., Principle 145.
147. Rahman quoted in Piscatori, *Islam in a World of Nation States*, pp. 110–11.
148. Ra'id, 9 March 1998.
149. Qasim, 17 March 1998.
150. Ibid. See also 'Open Letter', p. 180, for similar view.
151. Nasru'llah, LBC, March 1997. The terms 'Lebanonism' and 'Islamism' are adapted from Ra'id, 9 March 1998.
152. Qasim, 17 March 1998.
153. Ibid.
154. Ra'id, 9 March 1998.

Chapter 5

1. Anoushiravan Ehteshami and Raymond A. Hinnebusch, *Syria and Iran: Middle East Powers in a Penetrated Regional System* (London and New York: Routledge, 1997), p. 125, p. 126 and p. 129.

2. John P. Entelis, 'Civil Society and the Authoritarian Temptation in Algerian Politics: Islamic Democracy Versus the Centralised State', in *Civil Society in the Middle East*, p. 222.
3. Hala Jaber, *Hezbollah: Born with a Vengeance* (London: Fourth Estate Ltd, 1997), p. 56.
4. *Al-'Ahd*, 10 Safar 1406.
5. Samuel Huntington, *The Clash of Civilizations and the Remaking of World Order* (London: Simon and Schuster Ltd, 1997; London: Touchstone Books, 1998), p. 217.
6. 'Abbas al-Mussawi, *Amiru'l-Zakira*, 29 Rabi' al-Awwal 1408, p. 204.
7. Huntington, *The Clash of Civilizations*, p. 128.
8. *Al-'Ahd*, 23 Shawwal 1405.
9. 'Ali Fayyad, 18 February 2000. See also Ibrahim al-Amin al-Sayyid quoted in *al-'Ahd*, 21 Dhu al-Qa'da 1404. Still, it would be an exaggeration to claim, as Huntington has, that this struggle has assumed the form of a 'clash'. For Fayyad, the distinction between the two terms is critical. The imbalance of power between Islamic civilisation and Western civilisation means that Islam is engaged in a 'struggle' with the West and not a 'clash', which can only occur between two adversaries of equal size.
10. According to one of Huntington's definitions of civilisation, *The Clash of Civilizations*, p. 42.
11. *Al-'Ahd*, 27 Rabi' al-Awwal 1407.
12. Yvonne Yazbeck Haddad, 'Islamist Depictions of Christianity in the Twentieth Century: the Pluralism Debate and the Depiction of the Other', *Islam and Christian-Muslim Relations* 7, no. 1 (1996), p. 78.
13. To the extent that the term has become an adjective for depicting Hizbu'llah's enemies. See, for example, Shaykh Subhi al-Tufayli's reference to the Maronites' 'crusader mentality', in *al-'Ahd*, 10 Safar 1406.
14. Haddad, 'Islamist Depictions of Christianity', p. 78.
15. *Al-'Ahd*, 6 Rabi' al-Awwal 1407.
16. Huntington, *The Clash of Civilizations*, p. 48.
17. Ibid., p. 47.
18. *Al-'Ahd*, 6 Rabi'i al-Awwal 1407.
19. See al-Sayyid Hassan Nasru'llah, *Amiru'l- Zakira*, 27 March 1992, p. 167, and 'Text of Open Letter Addressed by Hizballah to the Downtrodden of Lebanon and the World', in *Amal and the Shi'a: Struggle for the Soul of Lebanon*, Augustus Richard Norton (Austin, TX: University of Texas Press, 1987), p. 167 et passim.
20. For example, see Nasru'llah, *Amiru'l-Zakira*, 27 March 1992, p. 170.
21. *Al-'Ahd*, 17 Dhu-Hujja 1406.
22. Ibid., n.d.
23. Ibid., 24 Safar 1408.
24. Na'im Qasim quoted in Jaber, *Hezbollah*, p. 57.
25. *Al-'Ahd*, 10 Safar 1406.
26. *Al-'Ahd*, 21 Dhu al-Qa'da 1404.
27. 'Open Letter', p. 170.

28. See 'Abbas al-Mussawi, *Amiru'l-Zakira*, 17 Muharram 1410, pp. 209–10 and *al- Maokif*, no. 2, p. 1.

29. Just a few examples of this term are cited in *al-'Ahd*, 10 Safar 1406; Nasru'llah, LBC, March 1997; *Al-'Ahd*, 27 Rabi' al-Awwal 1407; Nasru'llah, 'Jerusalem Day', 24 January 1998; Husayn al-Mussawi, 21 August 1997.

30. The *Daily Star*, 13 May 1998, quotes a banner which reads 'Our enemies forever: America and Israel'.

31. 'Abbas al-Mussawi, Beirut, *Amiru'l-Zakira*, Safar 1405, p. 186.

32. 'Open Letter', p. 178.

33. 'Abbas al-Mussawi, *Amiru'l-Zakira*, Safar 1405, p. 186.

34. According to Huntington, *The Clash of Civilizations*, p. 45, Russia is considered by many scholars to be the centre of an Orthodox civilisation, distinct from the West.

35. Huntington, ibid., p. 217, distinguishes between the 'ideological' conflict between the Soviet Union and the West, and the civilisational conflict between Islam and the West.

36. Ibid., p. 214.

37. *Sam wa 'Assal*, presented by As'ad Majid, al-Manar TV, 12 June 1993.

38. *Al-'Ahd*, 21 February 1999.

39. Ibid., 21 Dhu al-Qa'da 1404.

40. Ibid., n.d.

41. Haddad 'Islamist Depictions of Christianity', observes on p. 88 that this is a common perception held by Islamists.

42. *Al-Maokif*, no. 32, p. 3.

43. *Al-'Ahd*, 21 Dhu al-Qa'da 1404.

44. See, for example, Nasru'llah, 'Jerusalem Day', 24 January 1998; al-Sayyid 'Abbas al-Mussawi, Beirut, *Amiru'l-Zakira*, Rabi' ath-Thani 1405, p. 190; *al-'Ahd*, 21 Dhu al-Qa'da 1404.

45. *Sam wa 'Assal*, 12 June 1993.

46. Jaber, *Hezbollah*, p. 57.

47. *Al-Burnamij al-Intikhabi li Hizbu'llah*, 1992.

48. Ibid. See also 'Open Letter', p. 168 and Nasru'llah, 'Jerusalem Day', 24 January 1998.

49. Muhammad Husayn Fadlu'llah, 'Islamic Unity and Political Change: Interview with Shaykh Muhammad Husayn Fadlallah', by Mahmoud Soueid, *Journal of Palestine Studies* 25, no. 1, p. 71. Al-Sayyid Hassan Nasru'llah also shares this view in 'Commemoration of April Invasion', southern suburbs of Beirut, al-Manar TV, 18 April 1997.

50. *Al-Maokif*, no. 25, p. 1.

51· Meir Litvak also makes this observation about Hamas' portrayal of Israel and the West in 'The Islamisation of the Palestinian-Israeli Conflict: The Case of Hamas', *Middle East Studies* 34, no. 1 (January 1998), p. 150.

52. 'Open Letter', p. 179.

53. *Al-Maokif*, no. 24, p. 4.

54. Muhammad Fnaysh, al-Manar TV, October 1997.

55. *Al-'Ahd*, 27 January 1995. See also Nasru'llah, LBC, March 1997.

56. <www.moqawama.org> (Islamic Resistance Support Association website)
57. 'Abbas al-Mussawi, *Amiru'l-Zakira*, Safar 1405, p. 182.
58. *Al-Maokif*, no. 25, p. 5.
59. *Al-'Ahd*, 18 Jamad al-Awwal 1410.
60. Ibid., 27 January 1995.
61. *Al-Maokif*, no. 24, p. 4.
62. *Al-'Ahd*, 27 January 1995.
63. 'Abbas al-Mussawi, 'Min Jibshit'.
64. Fnaysh, 15 August 1997.
65. *TIME*, 147, no. 20, 13 May 1996.
66. Meri', 10 April 1998.
67. See *al-Maokif*, no. 1, p. 4, and Nasru'llah, *Amiru'l-Zakira*, 23 February 1992, p. 138.
68. *Al-Ahd*, n.d.
69. 'Open Letter', p. 171.
70. See ibid., p. 186, and Augustus Richard Norton, 'Lebanon: The Internal Conflict and the Iranian Connection', in *The Iranian Revolution: Its Global Impact*, ed. John L. Esposito (Miami: Florida International University Press; Gainsville, FL: Orders, University Press of Florida, 1990), p. 130.
71. Nasru'llah, C33 TV, May1996.
72. Ibid. See also 'Open Letter', pp. 181–2.
73. Muhammad Muhsin, 1 March 1997. See also Nasru'llah, *Amiru'l-Zakira*, 23 February 1992, p. 138.
74. Nasru'llah, 8 August 1997.
75. Ibid.
76. Ibid.
77. See Nasru'llah, 'Jerusalem Day', 24 January 1998; Nasru'llah, 18 April 1998; Nasru'llah, 8 August 1997.
78. Nasru'llah, 'Jerusalem Day', 24 January 1998.
79. Muhsin, 1 March 1997.
80. Nasru'llah, 18 April 1998.
81. *Al-'Ahd*, 17 Dhu al-Hujja 1406.
82. Meri', 10 April 1998.
83. The use of this term is not confined to the American State Department or even to the American media. As observed by Chris Mowles, 'The Israeli Occupation of South Lebanon', *Third World Quarterly* 8, p. 1363, no. 4 (October 1986), the BBC used it to describe Resistance operations against Israel.
84. *Al-Maokif*, no. 12, p. 5.
85. Fnaysh, Future TV, 2 July 1997.
86. Fnaysh, 15 August 1997. See also Nasru'llah, C33 TV, May 1996.
87. Nasru'llah, C33 TV, May 1996.
88. Ibid.
89. Fnaysh, 15 August 1997. See also Fnaysh, Future TV, 2 July 1997.
90. *Al-Maokif*, no. 6, p. 4.
91. Nasru'llah, *Amiru'l-Zakira*, 23 February 1992, p. 138.
92. *Al-'Ahd*, 8 Safar 1410.

93. Khumayni, *Islam and Revolution: Writings and Declarations of Imam Khomeini*, trans. and ed. Hamid Algar (Berkeley, CA: Mizan Press, 1981), p. 278.

94. Ibid., p. 238.

95. *Al-'Ahd* 8 Safar 1410.

96. See Martin Kramer, 'The Moral Logic of Hizballah', in *Origins of Terrorism, Psychologies, Ideologies, Theologies, States of Mind*, ed. Walter Reich (New York: Cambridge University Press, 1990), p. 548; Nizar Hamzeh and Hrair Dekmejian, 'The Islamic Spectrum of Lebanese Politics', *Journal of South Asian and Middle Eastern Studies* 16, no. 3 (Spring 1993), p. 40; Giles Trendle, 'Islamic Power', *The Middle East* (November 1994), p. 15; Mary-Jane Deeb, 'Militant Islam and the Politics of Redemption', *AAPSS* (November 1992), p. 63; Nizar Hamzeh, 'Lebanon's Hizballah: From Islamic Revolution to Parliamentary Accommodation', *Third World Quarterly* 14, no. 2 (1993), p. 322; Norton, 'Lebanon: the Internal Conflict', p. 128.

97. Jaber, *Hezbollah*, p. 113.

98. In interviews with the author, both Husayn al-Mussawi, 21 August 1997 and Fayyad, 2 March 1997, disavowed any involvement in Islamic Jihad.

99. Fnaysh, 15 August 1997.

100. Subhi al-Tufayli quoted in Jaber, *Hezbollah*, p. 128. This view was also expressed by Fnaysh, 15 August 1997; Fayyad, 2 March 1997; Husayn al-Mussawi, 21 August 1997; Muhammad Muhsin, 1 March 1997. See also *al-'Ahd*, 8 Safar 1410 and Robin Wright, *Sacred Rage: The Crusade of Modern Islam* (New York: Linden Press/Simon and Schuster, 1995), p. 106, for Hizbu'llah's denials of involvement in the kidnappings.

101. As maintained by Muhsin, 1 March 1997, and Husayn al-Mussawi, 21 August 1997.

102. Husayn al-Mussawi, 21 August 1997. See also Jaber, *Hezbollah*, p. 124.

103. Husayn al-Mussawi, 21 August 1997.

104. Jaber, *Hezbollah*, p. 99.

105. Ibid., pp. 116–17.

106. Ibid., p. 117.

107. Ibid., p. 112.

108. Muhammad Ra'id, 9 March 1998. Muhammad Muhsin also alludes to this debate in *Sam wa 'Assal*, presented by As'ad Majid, al-Manar TV, February 1996.

109. Muhsin in *Sam wa 'Assal*, February 1996. Muhsin also declared this to the author in person on 1 March 1997.

110. Muhsin, 1 March 1997.

111. Qasim, 17 March 1998.

112. Fnaysh, 15 August 1997.

113. Nasru'llah, 8 August 1997.

114. Fnaysh, 15 August 1997.

115. Qasim, 17 March 1998. See also Shaykh Na'im Qasim quoted in Jaber, *Hezbollah*, pp. 142–3.

116. Kramer, 'The Moral Logic of Hizballah', p. 150.

117. *Sam wa 'Assal*, 12 June 1993.

118. These terms are borrowed from Kramer's 'The Moral Logic of Hizballah'.
119. Quoted in Kramer, 'The Moral Logic of Hizballah', p. 151.
120. Ibid.
121. Muhsin, 1 March 1997.
122. Qasim, 17 March 1998.
123. Ibid.
124. Husayn al-Mussawi, 21 August 1997.
125. Meri', 10 April 1998.
126. Ibid.
127. Ibid.
128. *Al-'Ahd*, 8 Safar 1410.
129. Meri', 10 April 1998.
130. Husayn al-Mussawi, 21 August 1997. See also Jaber, *Hezbollah*, p. 80; Nasru'llah, MTV, July 1998; Kramer, 'The Moral Logic of Hizballah', p. 142.
131. Fnaysh, 15 August 1997.
132. Quoted in Wright, p. 78.
133. Jaber, *Hezbollah*, p. 78.
134. Ra'id, 9 March 1998. See also Nasru'llah, MTV, July 1998.
135. Meri', 10 April 1998.
136. Ra'id, 9 March 1998.
137. Husayn al-Mussawi, 21 August 1997.
138. Husayn al-Mussawi quoted in Kramer, 'The Moral Logic of Hizballah', p. 142.
139. 'Open Letter', p. 172.
140. See al-'Ahd, 21 November 1997, and al-Maokif, no. 22, p. 4.
141. *Al-'Ahd*, 21 November 1997.
142. *Al-Maokif*, no. 1, p. 5.
143. Ibid., no. 3, p. 3.
144. Husayn al-Mussawi, 21 August 1997.
145. See Magnus Ranstorp, *Hizb'allah in Lebanon: The Politics of the Western Hostage Crisis* (New York: St. Martin's Press, 1997), p. 119, and Martin Kramer, 'Hizballah: The Calculus of Jihad', *Bulletin: The American Academy of Arts and Sciences* 47, no. 8 (May 1994), p. 39.
146. Al-Maokif, no. 20, p. 1.
147. Ibid., no. 1, p. 5.
148. Ibid., no. 3, p. 5.
149. *Al-'Ahd*, 10 Safar 1406.
150. Ibid., 18 Jamad al-Awwal 1990.
151. 'Abbas al-Mussawi, *Amiru'l-Zakira*, 10 Muharram 1410, p. 211.
152. 'Open Letter', p. 178.
153. See Hizbu'llah's Foreign Relations' Unit, *The Message of Hizballah to the Pope on the Occasion of His Visit to Lebanon*, pp. 1–2, and *al-Maokif*, no. 30, p. 6.
154. *Al-'Ahd*, n.d.
155. 'Abbas al-Mussawi, *Amiru'l-Zakira*, 29 Rabi' al-Awwal 1408, p. 204.
156. Jaber, *Hezbollah*, p. 56.
157. *Al-'Ahd*, 24 Safar 1408.

158. *Sam wa 'Assal*, presented by As'ad Majid, al-Manar TV, 19 August 1993.
159. *Sam wa 'Assal*, February 1996.
160. Valerie Hoffmann, 'Muslim Fundamentalists: Psychosocial Profiles', in *Fundamentalisms Comprehended*, vol. 5, *The Fundamentalist Project*, ed. Martin E. Marty and R. Scott Appleby (Chicago: University of Chicago Press, 1995), p. 202. David George notes (in 'Pax Islamica: An Alternative New World Order?', *Islamic Fundamentalism*, no. 2, Twayne's Themes in Right Wing Politics and Ideology Series, ed. Youssef Choueiri (Boston: Twayne Publishers, 1990), p. 87) that this term has now been replaced by the 'cultural assault'.
161. <www.almanar.com.lb> (al-Manar TV website)
162. Qasim, 17 March 1998.
163. *Al-'Ahd*, 24 Safar 1408.
164. Ibid., 27 Rabi' al-Awwal 1407.
165. *Sam wa 'Assal*, presented by As'ad Majid, al-Manar TV, 7 August 1994.
166. Qasim, 17 March 1998.
167. *Al-'Ahd*, 27 January 1995.
168. Ibid., 27 Rabi' al-Awwal 1407.
169. Muhsin, 1 March 1997.
170. Muhsin in *Sam wa 'Assal*, February 1996.
171. Muhsin, 1 March 1997.
172. Nasru'llah, Beirut, 26 February 1998.
173. Muhsin in *Sam wa 'Assal*, February 1996.
174. *Sam wa 'Assal*, 7 August 1994.
175. Ibid., 12 June 1993.
176. Ibid., 19 August 1993.
177. Ibid.
178. Ibid.
179. Ibid.
180. *Sam wa 'Assal*, 12 June 1993.
181. *Al-'Ahd*, 25 February 1992.
182. 'Open Letter', p. 169.
183. See *Sam wa 'Assal*, 7 August 1994, and 'Open Letter', p. 169.
184. *Sam wa 'Assal*, 19 August 1993.
185. Ibid., 7 August 1994.
186. Ibid., 12 June 1993.
187. Ibid.
188. Ibid., 19 August 1993.
189. Ibid., 12 June 1993.
190. Ibid., 19 August 1993.
191. Ibid., 12 June 1993.
192. *Al-'Ahd*, 21 Dhu al-Qa'da 1404.
193. See *al-Burnamij al-Intikhabi li Hizbu'llah*, 1992, and *al-'Ahd*, 18 Jamad al-Awwal 1410.
194. 'Open Letter', p. 170.
195. Ra'id, 9 March 1998.
196. Fnaysh, 15 August 1997, and Meri', 10 April 1998. See also *al-Maokif*, no. 21, p. 5; *al-'Ahd*, 10 Safar 1406.
197. Nasru'llah, 8 August 1997.

198. Muhsin, 1 March 1997.
199. *Daily Star*, 13 May 1998.
200. Fnaysh, 15 August 1997. See also *Daily Star*, 13 May 1998.
201. Fnaysh, 15 August 1997.
202. *Daily Star*, 22 September 1997.
203. For examples see <www.moqawama.org> and *al-Maokif*, no. 12, p. 5.
204. Huntington, *The Clash of Civilizations*, p. 211 et passim.
205. As distinguished by Fayyad, 18 February 2000.
206. Ibid.
207. Ibid. Meri' also makes this distinction, 10 April 1998.
208. Fayyad, 18 February 2000. See also *al-Maokif*, no. 20, p. 5.
209. Meri', 10 April 1998.
210. Ibid.
211. *Al-'Ahd*, 27 Rabi' al-Awwal 1407.
212. Qasim, 17 March 1998. This view is also shared by Muhsin, 1 March 1997.
213. Qasim, 17 March 1998.
214. Husayn al-Mussawi, 21 August 1997.
215. 'Ammar al-Mussawi, 'Interview: Ammar Mussawi', interview by Giles Trendle, *Lebanon Report* 5, no. 12 (December 1994), p. 10.
216. Rima Fakhri, interview by author, tape recording, southern suburbs of Beirut, 23 December 1997.
217. For example, Hizb'ullah MP Husayn al-Hajj Hassan pursued his PhD in France, Muhammad Muhsin completed his PhD in the UK and 'Ali Fayyad did some graduate work in Italy.
218. Fakhri, 23 December 1997.
219. This can be inferred from al-Sayyid 'Abbas al-Mussawi, Jibshit, *Amiru'l-Zakira*, 12 Jamad al-Awwal, p. 193, which discusses the Western exploitation of knowledge/science.
220. *Al-'Ahd*, 27 Rabi' al-Awwal 1407.
221. As revealed by Qasim, 17 March 1998, and Husayn al-Mussawi, 21 August 1997.
222. Emile Sahliyeh, Religious Fundamentalisms Compared: Palestinian Islamists, Militant Lebanese Shi'ites and Radical Sikhs', in *Fundamentalisms Comprehended*, vol. 5, *The Fundamentalist Project*, eds Martin E. Marty and R. Scott Appleby (Chicago: University of Chicago Press, 1995), p. 141.
223. John P. Entelis, 'Islam, Democracy and the State: the Reemergence of Authoritarian Politics in Algeria', in *Islam and Secularism in North Africa*, ed. J. Ruedy (New York: St. Martin's Press, 1994), p. 221.
224. William E. Shepard, 'Islam and Ideology: Towards a Typology', *International Journal of Middle East Studies* 19 (1987), p. 308.
225. *Al-'Ahd*, 27 Rabi' al-Awwal 1407.
226. *Al-Maokif*, no. 24, p. 5.
227. Muhsin, 1 March 1997.

Chapter 6

1. Husayn al-Mussawi, 21 August 1997.
2. Al-Sayyid Hassan Nasru'llah, Nabatiyyeh, al-Manar TV, 6 September 1996.

3. *Ash-Shira'*, 24 August 1998.
4. *Al-'Ahd*, n.d.
5. Al-Sayyid 'Abbas al-Mussawi quoted in *Middle East International*, 26 July 1991, p. 11.
6. *Al-'Ahd*, 23 Shawwal 1405.
7. Ibid., 26 Sha'ban 1405, and 21 Dhu al-Qa'da 1404.
8. Ibid., 26 Sha'ban 1405.
9. *Al-Burnamij al-Intikhabi li Hizbu'llah*, 1992.
10. Husayn al-Mussawi, 21 August 1997.
11. 'Text of Open Letter Addressed by Hizballah to the Downtrodden of Lebanon and the World', in *Amal and the Shi'a: Struggle for the Soul of Lebanon*, Augustus Richard Norton (Austin, TX: University of Texas Press, 1987), p. 170.
12. Muhammad Fnaysh, 15 August 1997.
13. Emmanuel Sivan, 'Islamic Fundamentalism, Anti-Semitism and Anti-Zionism', in *Anti-Zionism and Anti-Semitism in the Contemporary World*, ed. Robert S. Wistrich (London: Macmillan, 1990), p. 76.
14. Faraj quoted in David C. Rapoport, 'Sacred Terror: A Contemporary Example From Islam', in *Origins of Terrorism, Psychologies, Ideologies, Theologies, States of Mind*, ed. Walter Reich (Cambridge: Cambridge University Press, 1990), p. 111.
15. Ibid.
16. Sivan, 'Islamic Fundamentalism', p. 75.
17. *Al-'Ahd*, 21 Dhu al-Qa'da 1404.
18. Magnus Ranstorp, *Hizb'allah in Lebanon: The Politics of the Western Hostage Crisis* (New York: St: Martin's Press, 1997), p. 57 and Chibli Mallat, *Shi'i Thought from the South of Lebanon*, Papers on Lebanon, vol. 7 (Oxford: Centre for Lebanese Studies, 1988), pp. 35–7.
19. Nasru'llah, Orbit TV, May 1997.
20. Fnaysh, 15 August 1997.
21. Nasru'llah, 'Palestinian National Congress'.
22. Husayn al-Mussawi, 21 August 1997.
23. Nasru'llah, 6 September 1996.
24. Nasru'llah, LBC, March 1997.
25. Nasru'llah, 6 September 1996.
26. *Ash-Shira'*, 24 August 1998.
27. Ibid.
28. Fnaysh, 15 August 1997.
29. 'Ali Fayyad, 2 March 1997. See also 'Open Letter', p. 169: 'Each of us is a combat soldier when the call for *jihad* demands it.'
30. Yussef Meri', 10 April 1998.
31. Muhammad Muhsin, 1 March 1997.
32. Ibid.
33. Robin Wright, *Sacred Rage: The Crusade of Modern Islam* (New York: Linden Press/Simon and Schuster, 1995), p. 69.
34. Nasru'llah, C33 TV, May 1996.
35. *Al-'Ahd*, 8 Safar 1410.
36. Nasru'llah, al-Manar TV, n.p., n.d.
37. Ibid.

38. Nasru'llah, LBC, March 1997, and Nasru'llah, 'Jerusalem Day', 7 February 1997.
39. Nasru'llah, 8 August 1997.
40. Nasru'llah, *Amiru'l-Zakira*, 23 February 1992, p. 137, and 'Abbas al-Mussawi, *Amiru'l-Zakira*, 10 Dhu al-Qa'da 1411, p. 218.
41. Fnaysh, 15 August 1997.
42. Fayyad, 2 March 1997.
43. Nasru'llah, LBC, March 1997.
44. Ibid.
45. *As-Safir*, 31 July 1998.
46. 'Abbas al-Mussawi, *Amiru'l-Zakira*, 10 Dhu al-Qa'da 1411, p. 218.
47. Ibid., pp. 217–18.
48. Nasru'llah, *Amiru'l-Zakira*, 23 February 1992, p. 137.
49. Nasru'llah, C33 TV, May 1996.
50. See, for example, *al-Maokif*, no. 20, p. 4; *Daily Star*, 14 March 1997; *ash-Shira'*, 28 December 1998; *al-Hawadith*, 19 March 1999.
51. As defined by Abdul Razaq O.Kilani, 'Jihad: A Misunderstood Aspect of Islam', *Islamic Culture* 70, no. 3 (1996), p. 35.
52. *Al-'Ahd*, n.d.
53. Nasru'llah, '"Ashura Speech', 12 May 1997.
54. Ibid.
55. Quoted in Hala Jaber, *Hezbollah: Born with a Vengeance* (London: Fourth Estate Ltd, 1997), p. 87.
56. Nasru'llah, '"Ashura Speech', 12 May 1997.
57. Kilani, 'Jihad', p. 35.
58. *Al-'Ahd*, n.d. As'ad AbuKhalil, 'Ideology and Practice of Hizballah in Lebanon: Islamization of Leninist Organizational Principles', *Middle Eastern Studies* 27, no. 3 (July 1991), p. 398, also makes the same distinction.
59. *Al-'Ahd*, n.d.
60. Ibid.
61. Ibid.
62. Ibid.
63. In *Al-'Ahd*, n.d., al-Sayyid Hassan Nasru'llah states that *jihad* is as fundamental a requirement of the Islamic faith, as are fasting, praying, alms-giving and pilgrimage.
64. Moojan Momen, *An Introduction to Shi'ite Islam: The History and Doctrines of Twelver Shi'ism* (New Haven and London: Yale University Press, 1985), p. 180.
65. Al-Sayyid Hassan Nasru'llah, al-Manar TV, n.p., n.d.
66. *Al-'Ahd*, 17 Dhu al-Hujja 1406 and al-Sayyid Hassan Nasru'llah, 'Martyrs' Day', southern suburbs of Beirut, al-Manar TV, 28 June 1996.
67. Nasru'llah, '"Ashura Speech', 9 May 1997.
68. Al-Sayyid Hassan Nasru'llah quoted in *al-Maokif*, no. 2, p. 1. Husayn al-Mussawi, 21 August 1997, interprets the Karbala drama in a similar way when he asserts that Imam Husayn's teaching was that 'subjugation is death in your life'. See also *al-Maokif*, no. 5, p. 8, for Shaykh Na'im Qasim's view.
69. *Al-'Ahd*, n.d.

70. Nasru'llah, "*Ashura* Speech', 9 May 1997.
71. *Al-Maokif*, no. 2, p. 1.
72. Nasru'llah, LBC, March 1997. See also *Al-'Ahd*, 24 Safar 1408; *as-Safir*, 24 August 1998; 'Abbas al-Mussawi, 20 Jamadi ath-Thani 1408, *Amiru'l-Zakira*, p. 202, for references to 'religious legal obligation'.
73. Nasru'llah, LBC, March 1997; Nasru'llah, 'Martyrs' Day'; Nasru'llah, 26 February 1998.
74. *Al-'Ahd*, n.d.
75. Meir Litvak, 'The Islamisation of the Palestinian-Israeli Conflict: The Case of Hamas', *Middle East Studies* 34, no. 1 (January 1998), p. 156.
76. *Al-'Ahd*, n.d.
77. Nasru'llah, LBC, March 1997.
78. Nasru'llah, n.p., n.d.
79. Muhsin, 1 March 1997.
80. *Al-Maokif*, no. 2, p. 2, and Nasru'llah, C33 TV, May 1996.
81. Meri', 10 April 1998.
82. Ibid.
83. *Al-'Ahd*, 24 Safar 1408, and 'Abbas al-Mussawi, *Amiru'l-Zakira*, 20 Jamadi ath-Thani 1408, p. 203.
84. Qasim, 17 March 1998.
85. Muhsin, 1 March 1997.
86. Nasru'llah, 'Martyrs' Day'.
87. *Al-'Ahd*, 24 Safar 1408.
88. Nasru'llah, 'Jerusalem Day', 7 February 1997.
89. *Ash-Shira'*, 24 August 1998.
90. Nasru'llah, "*Ashura* Speech', 9 May 1997.
91. See *Daily Star*, 11 July 1997, and 16 January 1998.
92. *Ash-Shira'*, 24 August 1998.
93. Nasru'llah, C33 TV, May 1996.
94. Nasru'llah, "*Ashura* Speech', 12 May 1997.
95. 'Abbas al-Mussawi, 'Min Jibshit'.
96. *Al-'Ahd*, 24 Safar 1408.
97. *Al-Hawadith*, 19 March 1999.
98. Shaykh Na'im Qasim quoted in Matts Warn, 'A Voice of Resistance: The Point of View of Hizballah', Advanced Course in Political Science, Stockholm University (May 1997), p. 35.
99. *Al-'Ahd*, 12 Sha'ban 1407.
100. Nasru'llah, "*Ashura* Speech', 12 May 1997.
101. Ibid.
102. Ibid., and Nasru'llah, 3 November 1997.
103. Ibid.
104. Nasru'llah, 5 August 1997.
105. Ibid.
106. Nasru'llah, LBC, March 1997.
107. Nasru'llah, 'Commemoration of April Invasion'.
108. *Al-Hawadith*, 19 March 1999.
109. 'Speaking Out for Terror', *World Press Review* (January 1998), p. 47.
110. Ibid.
111. Nasru'llah, "*Ashura* Speech', 9 May 1997.

112. 'Speaking out for Terror', p. 47.
113. Nasru'llah, 5 August 1997.
114. Nasru'llah, "*Ashura* Speech', 12 May 1997.
115. Nasru'llah, 5 August 1997.
116. Ibid.
117. 'Ali Fayyad, 2 March 1997.
118. Nasru'llah, "*Ashura* Speech', 12 May 1997, and Nasru'llah, C33 TV, May 1996.
119. Fayyad, 18 February 2000, concurs with this inference.
120. Nasru'llah, "*Ashura* Speech', 12 May 1997.
121. *Al-'Ahd*, 10 Safar 1406.
122. Quoted in Martin Kramer, 'The Moral Logic of Hizballah', in *Origins of Terrorism, Psychologies, Ideologies, Theologies, States of Mind*, ed. Walter Reich (New York: Cambridge University Press, 1990), p. 20.
123. Nasru'llah, C33 TV, May 1996.
124. See Kramer, 'The Moral Logic', p. 145: 'Such an undertaking differs little from that of a soldier who fights and knows that in the end he will be killed. The two situations lead to death; except that one fits in with conventional procedures of war, and the other does not.'
125. See Nasru'llah, on C33 TV, May 1996, for Hizbu'llah's view and Martin Kramer, 'Hizballah: the Calculus of Jihad', *Bulletin: The American Academy of Arts and Sciences* 47, no. 8 (May 1994), p. 32, for Fadlu'llah's invocation of this argument.
126. Nasru'llah, C33 TV, May 1996.
127. *Al-'Ahd*, 10 Safar 1406.
128. Nasru'llah, C33 TV, May 1996.
129. Nasru'llah, LBC, March 1997.

Chapter 7

1. Anoushiravan Ehteshami and Raymond A. Hinnebusch, *Syria and Iran: Middle East Powers in a Penetrated Regional System* (London and New York: Routledge, 1997), p. 154.
2. *Al-'Ahd*, 26 Sha'ban 1405.
3. Na'im Qasim, 17 March 1998.
4. Muhammad Ra'id, 9 March 1998.
5. *Sam wa 'Assal*, 7 August 1994.
6. *Al-Burnamij al-Intikhabi li Hizbu'llah*, 1992.
7. *Al-'Ahd*, 25 February 1994.
8. Al-Sayyid Hassan Nasru'llah, MTV, July 1998.
9. Yehoshafat Harkabi, 'On Arab Anti-Semitism Once More', in *Anti-Semitism Through the Ages*, ed. Shmuel Almog, trans. Nathan H. Reisner (Oxford: Pergamon Press, 1988), p. 230.
10. *As-Safir*, 24 August 1998.
11. Muhammad Fnaysh, 15 August 1997. See also Nasru'llah, LBC, March 1997.
12. *Al-'Ahd*, 18 Jamad al-Awwal 1410 and Fayyad, 18 February 2000. See also Meir Litvak, 'The Islamisation of the Palestinian-Israeli Conflict: The Case of Hamas', *Middle East Studies* 34, no. 1 (January 1998), p. 150,

for Hamas' depiction of the struggle as 'an existential battle and not just a question of borders'.

13. 'Abbas al-Mussawi, *Amiru'l-Zakira*, 15 Muharram 1407, p. 202.
14. Ibid., 17 Muharram 1410, pp. 209–10.
15. *Al-'Ahd*, 18 Jamad al-Awwal 1410, and Nasru'llah, 5 August 1997.
16. *Al-'Ahd*, 18 Jamad al-Awwal 1410.
17. Nasru'llah, 'Commemoration of April Invasion'.
18. Nasru'llah, n.p., al-Manar TV, n.d.
19. Muhammad Muhsin, 1 March 1997.
20. *Al-'Ahd*, 27 January 1995.
21. Fnaysh, 15 August 1997, and *al-Maokif*, no. 8, p. 6.
22. *Al-'Ahd*, 27 January 1995; Nasru'llah, *Amiru'l-Zakira*, 23 February 1992, p. 137; *al-Maokif*, no. 20, p. 2.
23. Robert Fisk, *Pity the Nation: Lebanon at War* (London: Andre Deutsch Ltd, 1990), p. 366.
24. Anonymous party source, interview by author, tape recording, Beirut, 13 February 2000.
25. Ibid.
26. 'Abbas al-Mussawi, *Amiru'l-Zakira*, 10 Dhu al-Hujja 1406, p. 200.
27. Ibid.
28. Nasru'llah, C33 TV, May 1996.
29. 'Abbas al-Mussawi, Beirut, *Amiu'l-Zakira*, 21 Muharram 1409, p. 207.
30. *Al-Hawadith*, 19 March 1999, p. 19.
31. Nasru'llah, C33 TV, May 1996.
32. Nasru'llah, 5 August 1997, and Nasru'llah, Biqa', al-Manar TV, 13 May 1998.
33. Nasru'llah, 5 August 1997.
34. Nasru'llah, 13 May 1998.
35. Anonymous party source, 13 February 2000.
36. Ibid.
37. Ibid.
38. 'Text of Open Letter Addressed by Hizballah to the Downtrodden of Lebanon and the World', in *Amal and the Shi'a: Struggle for the Soul of Lebanon*, Augustus Richard Norton (Austin, TX: University of Texas Press, 1987), p. 179.
39. *Al-Hawadith*, 19 March 1999, and *al-Watan al-'Arabi*, 5 December 1999.
40. *Daily Star*, 16 January 1999, and *al-Maokif*, no. 32, p. 1.
41. *Al-Maokif*, no. 32, p. 1.
42. *TIME*, 147, no. 20, 13 May 1996.
43. Fnaysh, 15 August 1997.
44. Fnaysh, al-Manar TV, October 1997.
45. Ibid.
46. *TIME*, 13 May 1996.
47. *Al-Maokif*, no. 4, p. 4.
48. *Al-Watan al-'Arabi*, 5 December 1999.
49. Fnaysh, 15 August 1997.
50. *Al-Watan al-'Arabi*, 5. December 1999.
51. Nasru'llah admits as much in *al-Watan al-'Arabi*, 5 December 1999, when he states that these *'thawabit'* are adhered to by 'everyone'.

52. Fnaysh, al-Manar TV, October 1997.
53. Fnaysh, 15 August 1997.
54. Nasru'llah, *Amiru'l-Zakira*, 24 Dhu al-Qa'da 1412, pp. 222–3.
55. Nasru'llah, 8 August 1997, and *al-Maokif*, no. 18, p. 1.
56. *Al-Maokif*, no. 15, p. 4, and 'Abbas al-Mussawi, *Amiru'l-Zakira*, 10 Dhu al-Qa'da 1411, p. 217.
57. Al-Mussawi, *Amiru'l-zakira*, 10 Dhu al-Qa'da 1411, p. 218, and Fnaysh, 15 August 1997.
58. <www.moqawama.org> (Islamic Resistance Support Association website)
59. Ibid.
60. *Sam wa 'Assal*, 19 August 1993.
61. Nasru'llah, 'Jerusalem Day', 24 January 1998. In this speech, Nasru'llah even blames the internecine conflict in Algeria on the Zionists.
62. *Al-Maokif*, no. 32, p. 2.
63. Nasru'llah, LBC, March 1997.
64. *Sam wa 'Assal*, 19 August 1993.
65. As declared by Fnaysh, 15 August 1997; Qasim, 17 March 1998; Yussef Meri', 10 April 1998; Nasru'llah, quoted in *TIME*, 13 May 1996.
66. Muhsin, 1 March 1997, and Qasim, 17 March 1998.
67. Qasim, 17 March 1998. Muhsin, 1 March 1997, also echoes this view.
68. Murtada quoted in Matts Warn, 'A Voice of Resistance: The Point of View of Hizballah', Advanced Course in Political Science, Stockholm University, May 1997, p. 56.
69. Nasru'llah, C33 TV, May 1996.
70. Muhsin, 1 March 1997.
71. Qasim, 17 March 1998.
72. Nasru'llah, 'Jerusalem Day', 7 February 1997.
73. Muhsin, 1 March 1997.
74. Qasim, 17 March 1998.
75. Meri', 10 April 1998.
76. Husayn al-Mussawi, 21 August 1997.
77. Qasim, 17 March 1998.
78. 'Ali Fayyad, 2 March 1997.
79. Fnaysh, 15 August 1997.
80. Ibid.
81. With the exceptions of the US State Department, which annually brands Hizbu'llah a terrorist group, and French Premier Lionel Jospin who, on 24 February 2000, described Hizbu'llah's Resistance activities as 'terrorist' acts.
82. Meri', 10 April 1998.
83. Fayyad, 2 March 1997.
84. *Al-'Ahd*, 25 February 1994.
85. See Nasru'llah, 'Jerusalem Day', 7 February 1997; *al-Maokif*, no. 12, p. 3; *al-Maokif*, no. 15, p. 3; Nasru'llah, 5 August 1997.
86. Fnaysh, 15 August 1997.
87. *Al-Maokif*, no. 15, p. 3; Nasru'llah, 'Jerusalem Day', 7 February 1997; Fnaysh, 15 August 1997.
88. Nasru'llah, 5 August 1997.

89. Nasru'llah, 'Jerusalem Day', 7 February 1997; Nasru'llah, 8 August 1997; Nasru'llah, 5 August 1997.
90. Nasru'llah, 8 August 1997.
91. Nasru'llah, 'Rally Denouncing the Wye Plantation Accord', southern suburbs of Beirut, al-Manar TV, 1 November 1998.
92. Ibid.
93. Nasru'llah, 8 August 1997.
94. Ibid.
95. See *al-Maokif*, no. 15, p. 3; Nasru'llah, 'Wye Plantation'; Nasru'llah, 'Palestinian National Congress'.
96. *Al-Maokif*, no. 25, p. 1.
97. *Al-Maokif*, no. 30, p. 1.
98. Nasru'llah, 'Wye Plantation', 1 November 1998.
99. Muhammad Ra'id, 9 March 1998.
100. Qasim, 17 March 1998. Also stated by Ra'id, 10 April 1998; Fnaysh, 15 August 1997; Muhsin, 1 March 1997.
101. Murtada quoted in Warn, p. 56.
102. Husayn al-Mussawi, 21 August 1997.
103. Ra'id, 9 March 1998.
104. *Al-Maokif*, no. 15, p. 4.
105. Ibid.
106. Ibid.
107. Ra'id, 9 March 1998.
108. Ibid.
109. The exact words he used were, 'When Kiryat Shmona will burn, Lebanon's land will burn! One is linked with the other. Blood for blood, life for life, child for child.'
110. None were cited in any of the Hizbu'llah web site news archives, and none were reported by Hizbu'llah's Central Press Office.
111. Hizbu'llah's radio station, an-Nur, quoted in *Jerusalem Post*, 25 February 2000
112. Husayn al-Mussawi, 21 August 1997.
113. 'Abbas al-Mussawi, *Amiru'l-Zakira*, 10 Dhu al-Hujja 1406, p. 199.
114. 'Open Letter', p. 179.
115. Ibid., p. 179 and Nasru'llah, MTV, July 1998.
116. *Al-'Ahd*, 9 September 1994.
117. Nasru'llah, 'Palestinian National Congress'.
118. Qasim quoted in *Monday Morning*, 17 October 1994.
119. See Nasru'llah, 'Wye Plantation'; *al-'Ahd*, 19 September 1997; Nasru'llah, 'Jerusalem Day', 15 January 1999.
120. Nasru'llah, 'Jerusalem Day', 15 January 1999.
121. *Al-Iman*, 21 August 1998.
122. Ibid.
123. Husayn al-Mussawi, 21 August 1997.
124. Nasru'llah, ''Ashura Speech', 9 May 1997.
125. Nasru'llah, 'Jerusalem Day', 24 January 1998.
126. Ibid.
127. Nasru'llah, 'Jerusalem Day', 7 February 1997.

128. Ibid. and 'Ammar al-Mussawi, 'Interview: Ammar Mussawi', Interview by Giles Trendle, *The Lebanon Report* 5, no. 12 (December 1994), p. 10.

129. *Al-Maokif*, no. 1, p. 7.

130. Ibid., no. 1, p. 7.

131. 'Abbas al-Mussawi, 'Min Jibshit', and Husayn al-Mussawi, 21 August 1997.

132. Fnaysh, 15 August 1997.

133. Ibid.

134. Muhammad Husayn Fadlu'llah, 'Islamic Unity and Political Change: Interview with Shaykh Muhammad Hussayn Fadlallah', interview by Mahmoud Soueid, *Journal of Palestine Studies* 25, no. 1 (Autumn 1995), p. 75.

135. *Al-'Ahd*, n.d. 'Abbas al-Mussawi also expresses his rejection of Resolution 425 in *Amiru'l-Zakira*, Dhu-Hujja 1406, p. 197.

136. 'Abbas al-Mussawi, *Amiru'l-Zakira*, 10 Dhu al-Hujja 1406, p. 199.

137. Ibid.

138. Nasru'llah, LBC, March 1997.

139. *Al-Ahd*, n.d.

140. According to Eyal Zisser ('Hizballah in Lebanon – at the Crossroads', in *Religious Radicalism in the Greater Middle East*, eds Bruce Maddy Weitzman and Efraim Inbar (London: Frank Cass, 1996), p. 104), this is proof of Hizbu'llah's 'Lebanonisation'.

141. *Al-Maokif*, no. 2, p. 1, and Nasru'llah, MTV, July 1998.

142. 'Open Letter', p. 179.

143. <www.mideastinsight.org>, *Middle East Insight* website Nasru'llah, 'Peace Requires Departure of Palestinians: Interview with Sheikh Hassan Nasru'llah', interview by Antoine K. K. Kehdy, *Middle East Insight* 15, no. 2 (March/April 2000).

144. Nasru'llah, C33 TV, May 1996, and Nasru'llah, LBC, March 1997.

145. Nasru'llah, C33 TV, May 1996.

146. Nasru'llah, 'Peace Requires Departure of Palestinians'.

147. Ibid.

148. Ibid. See also Ehteshami's and Hinnebusch's assessment, *Syria and Iran*, p. 142.

149. See, for example, Nasru'llah, C33 TV, May 1996; Nasru'llah, 26 February 1998; *al-Maokif*, no. 6, p. 5.

150. Nasru'llah, 26 February 1998.

151. Nasru'llah, C33 TV, May 1996.

152. Nasru'llah, 26 February 1998.

153. Husayn al-Mussawi, 21 August 1997.

154. Fayyad, 2 March 1997. See also *al-Maokif*, no. 6, p. 5, which also cites Lebanon's weakness as a justification for the party's calls for a single track in the negotiations.

155. For the time being, Hizbu'llah's resistance against Israel coincides with Syrian interests, insofar as it provides Syria with a valuable tool in the peace negotiations. Should Syria make peace with Israel, however, the nature of Syria's relations with Hizbu'llah will almost certainly be affected, very possibly for the worse.

156. *Al-Maokif*, no. 6, p. 5.

157. Qasim, 17 March 1998; Ra'id, 9 March 1998; Meri', 10 April 1998; Fayyad, 2 March 1997.
158. Nasru'llah, LBC, March 1997, and *al-'Ahd*, 27 January 1995.
159. Nasru'llah, C33 TV, May 1996.
160. Ibrahim al-Amin al-Sayyid, February 1997.
161. Nasru'llah, LBC, March 1997.
162. Meri' quoted in Warn, 'A Voice of Resistance', p. 51.
163. Nasru'llah, 'Peace Requires Departure of Palestinians'.
164. Qasim, 17 March 1998. Fnaysh, 15 August 1997, echoes this reasoning.
165. *Al-Maokif*, no. 15, p. 3.
166. Husayn Khalil quoted in *al-'Ahd*, n.d.
167. *Al-Maokif*, no. 11, p. 3.
168. Fayyad, 2 March 1997.
169. Ibid., and Qasim, 17 March 1998.
170. Fnaysh, 15 August 1997.
171. Nasru'llah, 'Jerusalem Day', 24 January 1998.
172. Fnaysh, 15 August 1997.
173. Ibid., and Fayyad, 2 March 1997. While no mention is made of the possibility of resorting to security means to penalise those who normalise economic or social relations with the Israelis and to deter others from following suit – as Ehteshami and Hinnebusch, *Syria and Iran*, p. 147, believe will be the case – it cannot be ruled out.
174. Fnaysh, 15 August 1997.
175. Nasru'llah, 'Palestinian National Congress'.
176. *Al-'Ahd*, 18 Jamad al-Awwal 1410, and 'Open Letter', p. 179.
177. Nasru'llah, 'Jerusalem Day', 15 January 1999.
178. Husayn al-Mussawi, 21 August 1997, and Qasim, 17 March 1998. The same view is held by Hamas, Augustus Richard Norton, 'Lebanon: The Internal Conflict and the Iranian Connection', in *The Iranian Revolution: Its Global Impact*, ed. John L. Esposito (Miami: Florida International University Press; Gainsville, FL: Orders, University Press of Florida, 1990), p. 155.
179. Nasru'llah, *Amiru'l-Zakira*, 23 February 1992, p. 139, and Nasru'llah, 8 August 1997.
180. Qasim, 17 March 1998. Ra'id, 9 March 1998, echoes this view.
181. 'Open Letter', p. 173.
182. *Al-'Ahd*, 26 Sha'ban 1405.
183. *Al-'Ahd*, 17 Dhu al-Hujja 1406. See also *al-'Ahd*, 12 Muharram 1406.
184. Fnaysh, Future TV, 2 July 1997, and 'Open Letter', p. 179.
185. *Al-'Ahd*, 12 Muharram 1406, and Fnaysh, Future TV, 2 July 1997.
186. *Al-'Ahd*, n.d. See also *al-'Ahd*, 24 Safar 1408.
187. Nasru'llah, *Amiru'l-Zakira*, 23 February 1992, p. 168.
188. Nasru'llah, 'Jerusalem Day', 15 January 1999, and Meri', 10 April 1998.
189. *Al-'Ahd*, 12 Sha'ban 1407, and *al-'Ahd*, 10 Safar 1406.
190. Husayn al-Mussawi, 21 August 1997.
191. Fnaysh, 15 August 1997.
192. Qasim, 17 March 1998.
193. Nasru'llah, LBC, March 1997.
194. Ra'id, 9 March 1998; Meri' 10 April 1998; Fayyad, 2 March 1997; Muhsin, 1 March 1997; Qasim, quoted in Ehteshami and Hinnebusch,

Syria and Iran, p. 141; Shaykh Nabil Qauk quoted in the *Daily Star*, 26 May 1998.

195. Ra'id, 9 March 1998.
196. Meri', 10 April 1998.
197. Ibid. See also May Chartouni-Dubarry, 'Hizballah: From Militia to Political Party', in *Lebanon on Hold: Implications for Middle East Peace*, eds Nadim Shehadi and Rosemary Hollis (London: Royal Institute of International Affairs; Oxford: Centre for Lebanese Studies, 1996), p. 120, for similar assessment.
198. Examples of this term can be found in *Daily Star*, 21 October 1997; *al-Maokif*, no. 20, p. 4; Ra'id, 9 March 1998; Qasim, 17 March 1998; *al-'Ahd*, 25 February 1994; Nasru'llah, LBC, March 1997; *al-Hawadith*, 19 March 1999; *al-Maokif*, no. 12, p. 1; Nasru'llah, 'Peace Requires Departure of Palestinians'.
199. Nasru'llah, LBC, March 1997; *al-Hawadith*,19 March 1999; *Daily Star*, 21 October 1997.
200. See Fnaysh, Future TV, 2 July 1997, and Fnaysh quoted in *al-Maokif*, no. 21, p. 6.
201. Fnaysh, al-Manar TV, October 1997.
202. Ibid.
203. Muhsin, 1 March 1997, and Ra'id, 9 March 1998.
204. Muhsin, 1 March 1997.
205. Fnaysh, al-Manar TV, October 1997. Muhsin, 1 March 1997, also expresses this belief.
206. *Al-'Ahd*, 24 Safar 1408. See also Martin Kramer, 'The Oracle of Hizballah: Seyyid Muhammad Husayn Fadallah', *Spokesmen for the Despised Fundamentalist Leaders in the Middle East*, ed. R. Scott Appleby (Chicago: University of Chicago Press, 1997), p. 121, for Fadlu'llah's view: 'the liberation of Jerusalem would be done "only in future generations" '.
207. Nasru'llah, *Amiru'l-Zakira*, 23 February 1992, p. 170.
208. Ra'id, 9 March 1998.
209. See *al-Maokif*, no. 32, p. 1, and *al-'Ahd*, 22 January 1999.

Chapter 8

1. Muhammad Fnaysh, 15 August 1997.
2. Ibid., and Muhammad Muhsin, 1 March 1997.
3. Fnaysh, 15 August 1997, and Ibrahim al-Amin al-Sayyid, *Mukhtasar Mufid*, NBN, 20 September 1999.
4. Na'im Qasim, 17 March 1998.
5. 'Ammar al-Mussawi, 'Interview: Ammar Mussawi', interview by Giles Trendle, *Lebanon Report* 5, no. 12 (December 1994), p. 10, and Muhammad Ra'id, 9 March 1998.
6. Both Qasim, 17 March 1998, and Husayn al-Mussawi, 21 August 1997, use this term.
7. Fnaysh, 15 August 1997.
8. Ibid.
9. Qasim, 17 March 1998.
10. Ibid.

11. For reference to 'Jewish Zionists' see, al-Sayyid Hassan Nasru'llah, 'Wye Plantation'; Nasru'llah, 'Jerusalem Day', 24 January 1998; Nasru'llah, 8 August 1997.
12. See, for example, Fnaysh, al-Manar TV, October 1997, and Nasru'llah, 'Jerusalem Day', 24 January 1998, for usage of both terms in the same text.
13. Fnaysh, al-Manar TV, October 1997. See also Nasru'llah, 'Commemoration of April Invasion', and Nasru'llah, *Amiru'l-Zakira*, 23 February 1992, p. 138.
14. Fnaysh, al-Manar TV, October 1997.
15. Ra'id, 9 March 1998. See also Meir Litvak, 'The Islamisation of the Palestinian-Israeli Conflict: The Case of Hamas', *Middle East Studies* 34, no. 1 (January 1998), p.152, for comparison with Hamas which echoes this view: 'Zionism is simply a racist entity responsible for translating the aggressive Jewish idea into a belligerent reality.'
16. Fnaysh, 15 August 1997.
17. *Al-Maokif*, no. 25, p. 1.
18. See for example, 'Speaking Out for Terror', *World Press Review* (January 1998), p. 47.
19. *Al-Maokif*, no. 25, p. 1.
20. Fnaysh, 15 August 1997.
21. Ra'id, 9 March 1998.
22. Muhsin, 1 March 1997.
23. *Al-'Ahd*, 7 February 1997.
24. See Nasru'llah, 8 August 1997, and Nasru'llah, "*Ashura* Speech', 9 May 1997.
25. Nasru'llah, 8 August 1997.
26. Nasru'llah, *Amiru'l-Zakira*, 23 February 1992, p. 139.
27. *Al-Maokif*, no. 32, p. 2.
28. Nasru'llah, *Amiru'l-Zakira*, 23 February 1992, p. 139.
29. Ibid., and Nasru'llah, 'Jerusalem Day', 15 January 1999.
30. See, for example, Bernard Lewis, 'The Arab World Discovers Anti-Semitism', in *Anti-Semitism in Times of Crisis*, eds Sander L. Gilman and Steven Katz (New York: New York University Press, 1991), pp. 343–52, and Emmanuel Sivan, 'Islamic Fundamentalism Anti-Semitism and Anti-Zionism', in *Anti-Zionism and Anti-Semitism in the Contemporary World*, ed. Robert S. Wistrich (London: Macmillan, 1990), pp. 74–84.
31. Martin Luther quoted in <www.digital.net/~billw/ANTI/anti-semitism>
32. Charles Y. Glock and Rodney Stark , *Christian Beliefs and Anti-Semitism*, quoted in <www.us-israel.org/jsource/> (Jewish Virtual Library website)
33. Ra'id, 9 March 1998.
34. As defined by Lewis, 'The Arab World Discovers Anti-Semitism', p. 230 and Yehoshafat Harkabi, 'On Arab Anti-Semitism Once More', in *Anti-Semitism Through the Ages*, ed. Shmuel Almog, trans. Nathan H. Reisher (Oxford: Pergamon Press, 1988), p. 346.
35. Lewis, 'The Arab World Discovers Anti-Semitism', p. 347.
36. See, for example, Harkabi, 'On Arab Anti-Semitism', p. 227.
37. Lewis, 'The Arab World Discovers Anti-Semitism', p. 346.
38. 'Abbas al-Mussawi, *Amiru'l-Zakira*, Dhu al-Hujja 1406, p. 197.
39. Ibid.

40. Although there are many Hizbu'llah statements which correspond to these Qur'anic verses, or which resonate their demonic themes, as an extra precaution, I have had these verses reviewed by a Hizbu'llah official who agreed that they accurately reflect Hizballah's view of the Jews.

41. An exegesis of the *hadith* concerning Jews, will not be employed here for the simple reason that Hizbu'llah does not cite any *hadith* in its demonisation of the Jews, but relies exclusively on Qur'anic verses.

42. See, for example, 'Text of Open Letter Addressed by Hizballah to the Downtrodden of Lebanon and the World', in *Amal and the Shi'a: Struggle for the Loul of Lebanon*, Augustus Richard Norton (Austin, TX: University of Texas Press, 1987), p. 171, and Nasru'llah, 'Jerusalem Day', 24 January 1998.

43. Husayn al-Mussawi, 21 August 1997.

44. Nasru'llah, 8 August 1997.

45. Ibid.

46. Ibid.

47. Husayn al-Mussawi, 21 August 1997; Nasru'llah, 'Jerusalem Day', 24 January 1998; *Sam wa 'Assal*, February 1996; Ra'id, 9 March 1998.

48. As in Nasru'llah, 'Jerusalem Day', 15 January 1999, and Nasru'llah, *Amiru'l-Zakira*, 23 February 1992, p. 139.

49. Nasru'llah, 8 August 1997.

50. See, for example, Nasru'llah, 8 August 1997; Nasru'llah, "*Ashura* Speech', 9 May 1997; *Sam wa 'Assal*, 7 August 1994; Nasru'llah, 16 February 1999, for such portrayals.

51. Ra'id, 9 March 1998.

52. Qasim, 17 March 1998.

53. Nasru'llah, 8 August 1997.

54. 'Abbas al-Mussawi, *Amiru'l-Zakira*, Dhu al-Hujja 1406, p. 197.

55. Nasru'llah, 'Jerusalem Day', 24 January 1998.

56. Fnaysh, 15 August 1997; *Sam wa 'Assal*, February 1996; Nasru'llah, 'Jerusalem Day', 24 January 1998.

57. Nasru'llah, 'Jerusalem Day', 24 January 1998.

58. See <www.us-israel.org/jsource/>

59. Nasru'llah, 'Jerusalem Day', February 1998 and *Sam wa 'Assal*, February 1996.

60. *Sam wa 'Assal*, February 1996.

61. Ra'id, 9 March 1998, and Fnaysh, 15 August 1997.

62. Ra'id, 9 March 1998.

63. Ibid.

64. Ra'id , 9 March 1998; Fayyad, 18 February 2000; Husayn al- Mussawi, 21 August 1997.

65. Fayyad, 18 February 2000.

66. Ra'id, 9 March 1998.

67. As believed by Fayyad, 18 February 2000.

68. Ibid.

69. Fnaysh, 15 August 1997.

70. Fayyad, 18 February 2000.

71. Qasim, 17 March 1998.

72. Fnaysh, 15 August 1997.

73. Fayyad, 18 February 2000.

Select Bibliography

Many of the detailed references which this text has used can be found in my PhD dissertation, 'The Intellectual Structure of Hizbu'llah: Preservation and Adaptation', which was completed in September 2000 and is now located at the University of Birmingham, UK. Here I will include those references which would be especially useful to those interested in reading further about Hizbu'llah and to students of Islam and the Middle East in general.

Articles and Books

Abrahamian, Ervand, 'Khomeini: A Fundamentalist?' in *Fundamentalism in Comparative Perspective*, ed. Lawrence Kaplan (Amherst: University of Massachusetts Press, 1992), pp. 109–25.
——, *Khomeinism: Essays on the Islamic Republic*. London: I.B. Tauris and Co., 1993.
AbuKhalil, As'ad, 'Ideology and Practice of Hizballah in Lebanon: Islamization of Leninist Organizational Principles', *Middle Eastern Studies* 27, no. 3 (July 1991), pp. 390–403.
——, The Incoherence of Islamic Fundamentalism: Arab Islamic Thought at the End of the Twentieth Century', *Middle East Journal* 48, no. 4 (Autumn 1994), pp. 677–94.
Ajami, Fuad, *The Vanished Imam: Musa al-Sadr and the Shi'a of Lebanon*. London: I.B. Tauris and Co., 1986.
Almond, Gabriel, Emmanuel Sivan and R. Scott Appleby, 'Fundamentalism: Genus and Species', in *Fundamentalisms Comprehended*, vol. 5, *The Fundamentalist Project*, eds Martin E. Marty and R. Scott Appleby (Chicago: University of Chicago Press, 1995), pp. 399–425.
Anderson, Lisa, 'Fulfilling Prophesies: State Policy and Islamic Radicalism', in *Political Islam: Revolution, Radicalism or Reform?* ed. John L. Esposito (Boulder, Co.: Lynne Reiner Publishers, 1997), pp. 17–31.
Ayubi, Nazih, *Political Islam: Religion and Politics in the Arab World*. London and NY: Routledge, 1991.
——, 'State Islam and Communal Plurality', *Annals of the American Academy of Political and Social Sciences* 524 (November 1992), pp. 79–91.
'Azi, Ghassan, *Hizbu'llah: Min al-Hilm ila al-Waqi'yya al-Siyasiyya*. Kuwait: Qurtas Publishing, 1998.
Aziz, T.M., 'Popular Sovereignty in Contemporary Shi'i Political Thought', *The Muslim World* 36, nos. 3–4 (July-October 1996), pp. 273–93.
Bayat, Mangol, 'The Iranian Revolution of 1978–79: Fundamentalist or Modern?' *Middle East Journal*, no.1 (Winter 1983), pp. 30–42.
——, 'Khomeini', in *Expectation of the Millennium: Shi'ism in History*, eds. Seyyed Hossein Nasr, Hamid Dabashi and Seyyed Vali Reza Nasr (Albany: State University of New York Press, 1989), pp. 343–55.

Ben-Shammai, Haggai, 'Jew Hatred in the Islamic Tradition and the Koranic Exegesis', in *Anti-Semitism Through the Ages*, ed. Shmuel Almog, trans. Nathan H. Reisner (Oxford: Pergamon Press, 1988), pp. 161–9.

Budeiri, K. Musa, 'The Nationalist Dimension of Islamic Movements in Palestinian Politics', *Journal of Palestine Studies* 24, no. 3 (Spring 1995), pp. 89–95.

al-Burnamij al-Intikhabi li Hizbu'llah, 1992.

Calder, Norman, 'Accommodation and Revolution in Imami Shi'i Jurisprudence: Khumayni and the Classical Tradition', *Middle Eastern Studies* 18, no. 1 (1982), pp. 3–20.

Chartouni-Dubarry, May, 'Hizballah: From Militia to Political Party', in *Lebanon on Hold: Implications for Middle East Peace*, eds Nadim Shehadi and Rosemary Hollis (London: Royal Institute of International Affairs; Oxford: Centre for Lebanese Studies, 1996), pp. 59–62.

Choueiri, Youssef, 'The Political Discourse of Contemporary Islamist Movements', in *Islamic Fundamentalism*, no. 2, Twayne's Themes in Right Wing Politics and Ideology Series, ed. Youssef Choueiri (Boston: Twayne Publishers, 1990), pp. 19–33.

Cobban, Helena, 'The Growth of Shi'i Power in Lebanon and its Implications for the Future', in *Shi'ism and Social Protest*, eds Juan R.I. Cole and Nikki R. Keddie (London: Yale University Press, 1986), pp. 137–55.

Cole, Juan R.I. and Nikki R. Keddie, Introduction to *Shi'ism and Social Protest*, eds Juan R.I. Cole and Nikki R. Keddie (London: Yale University Press, 1986), pp. 1–29.

'Constitution of the Islamic Republic of Iran', *Middle East Journal* 34 (1980), pp. 184–204.

Crighton, Elizabeth and Martha Abele MacIver, 'The Evolution of Protracted Ethnic Conflict: Group Dominance and Political Underdevelopment in Northern Ireland and Lebanon', *Comparative Politics* 23, no. 2 (January 1991), pp. 121–42.

Deeb, Marius, 'Shi'a Movements in Lebanon: Their Formation, Ideology, Social Basis and Links with Iran and Syria', *Third World Quarterly* 10, no. 2 (1988), pp. 683–98.

Ehteshami, Anoushiravan and Raymond A. Hinnebusch, *Syria and Iran: Middle East Powers in a Penetrated Regional System*. London and New York: Routledge, 1997.

Enayat, Hamid, 'Khomeini', in *Expectation of the Millennium: Shi'ism in History*, eds Seyyed Hossein Nasr, Hamid Dabashi and Seyyed Vali Reza Nasr (Albany: State University of New York Press, 1989), pp. 334–43.

——, 'Martyrdom', in *Expectation of the Millennium: Shi'ism in History*, eds Seyyed Hossein Nasr, Hamid Dabashi and Seyyed Vali Reza Nasr (Albany: State University of New York Press, 1989), pp. 52–7.

Esposito, John L, *The Islamic Threat: Myth or Reality?* New York: Oxford University Press, 1992.

——, Introduction to *Political Islam: Revolution, Radicalism or Reform?* ed. John L. Esposito (Boulder, Co.: Lynne Reiner Publishers, 1997), pp. 1–14.

Esposito, John L. and John O. Voll, *Islam and Democracy*. Oxford: Oxford University Press, 1996.

Fadlu'llah, Muhammad Husayn, 'Islamic Unity and Political Change: Interview with Shaykh Muhammad Hussayn Fadlallah', Interview by Mahmoud Soueid, *Journal of Palestine Studies* 25, no. 1 (Autumn 1995), pp. 61–75.

Faksh, Mahmud A., 'The Shi'a Community of Lebanon: A New Assertive Political Force', *Journal of South Asian and Middle East Studies* 14, no. 3 (Spring 1991), pp. 33–56.

George, David, 'Pax Islamica: An Alternative New World Order?' in *Islamic Fundamentalism*, no. 2, Twayne's Themes in Right Wing Politics and Ideology Series, ed. Youssef Choueiri (Boston: Twayne Publishers, 1990), pp. 71–90.

Haddad, Yvonne Yazbeck, 'Islamist Depictions of Christianity in the Twentieth Century: the Pluralism Debate and the Depiction of the Other', *Islam and Christian-Muslim Relations* 7, no. 1 (1996), pp. 75–93.

Halawi, Majed, *A Lebanon Defied: Musa al-Sadr and the Shi'a Community*. Boulder, Co.: Westview Press, 1992.

Halliday, Fred, 'Review Article: the Politics of Islam – a Second Look', *British Journal of Political Studies* vol. 25 (July 1995), pp. 399–417.

Hamzeh, Nizar, 'Lebanon's Hizballah: From Islamic Revolution to Parliamentary Accommodation', *Third World Quarterly* 14, no. 2 (1993), pp. 321–37.

——, 'Clan Conflicts, Hezbollah and the Lebanese State', *Journal of Social, Political and Economic Studies* 19, no. 4 (Winter 1994), pp. 433–46.

Harik, Judith, 'Between Islam and the System: Sources and Implications of Popular Support for Lebanon's Hizballah', *Journal of Conflict Resolution* 40, no. 1 (March 1996), pp. 41–67.

Harkabi, Yehoshafat, 'On Arab Anti-Semitism Once More', in *Anti-Semitism Through the Ages*, ed. Shmuel Almog, trans. Nathan H. Reisner (Oxford: Pergamon Press, 1988), pp. 227–39.

Hitti, Nassif, 'Lebanon in Iran's Foreign Policy: Opportunities and Constraints', In *Iran and the Arab World*, eds Hooshang Amirahmadi and Nader Entessar (New York: St. Martin's Press, 1993), pp. 180–97.

Hizbu'llah, al-Wahda al-'Ilamiyya al-Markaziyya, *Amiru'l-Zakira*. N.p., Manshurat al-Wala', 1993.

Hoffman, Valerie, 'Muslim Fundamentalists: Psychosocial Profiles', in *Fundamentalisms Comprehended*, vol. 5, *The Fundamentalist Project*, eds Martin E. Marty and R. Scott Appleby (Chicago: University of Chicago Press, 1995), pp. 199–230.

Hudson, Michael, *The Precarious Republic: Political Modernization in Lebanon*. New York: Random House, 1968.

Huntington, Samuel, *The Clash of Civilizations and the Remaking of World Order*. London: Simon and Schuster Ltd, 1997; London, Touchstone Books, 1998.

Hussein, Jassim, 'Messianism and the Mahdi', in *Expectation of the Millennium: Shi'ism in History*, eds Seyyed Hossein Nasr, Hamid Dabashi and Seyyed Vali Reza Nasr (Albany: State University of New York press, 1989), pp. 11–24.

Jaber, Hala, *Hezbollah: Born with a Vengeance*. London: Fourth Estate Ltd, 1997.

Kelidar, Abbas, 'The Shi'i Imami Community and the Politics of the Arab East', *Middle East Studies* 19, no. 1 (1983), pp. 3–15.

Khashan, Hilal, *Inside the Lebanese Confessional Mind*. Lanham, Md: University Press of America, 1992.

Khumayni, Ayatu'llah Seyyid Ruhu'llah Mussawi, *Islam and Revolution: Writings and Declarations of Imam Khomeini*, trans. and ed. Hamid Algar. Berkeley, CA: Mizan Press, 1981.

——, 'Khomeini', in *Expectation of the Millennium: Shi'ism in History*, eds Seyyed Hossein Nasr, Hamid Dabashi and Seyyed Vali Reza Nasr (Albany: State University of New York Press, 1989), pp. 356–67.

Kilani, Abdul Razaq O., 'Jihad: A Misunderstood Aspect of Islam', *Islamic Culture* 70, no. 3 (1996), pp. 35–46.

Kramer, Martin, 'The Moral Logic of Hizballah', in *Origins of Terrorism, Psychologies, Ideologies, Theologies, States of Mind*, ed. Walter Reich (New York: Cambridge University Press, 1990), pp. 131–51.

——, 'Redeeming Jerusalem: The Pan-Islamic Premise of Hizballah', in *The Iranian Revolution and the Muslim World*, ed. David Menashri (Boulder, CO: Westview Press, 1990), pp. 105–30.

——, 'Islam Vs. Democracy', *Commentary* 95 (January 1993), pp. 35–42.

——, 'Hizballah: The Calculus of Jihad', *Bulletin: The American Academy of Arts and Sciences* 47, no. 8 (May 1994), pp. 20–43.

——, 'The Oracle of Hizballah: Seyyid Muhammad Husayn Fadlallah', in *Spokesmen for the Despised: Fundamentalist Leaders in the Middle East*, ed. R. Scott Appleby (Chicago: University of Chicago Press, 1997), pp. 83–181.

Lambton, Anne, 'A Reconsideration of the Position of the Marja' al-Taqlid and the Religious Institution', *Studia Islamica* 20 (1964), pp. 115–35.

Lewis, Bernard, 'The Arab World Discovers Anti-Semitism', in *Anti-Semitism in Times of Crisis*, eds Sander L. Gilman and Steven Katz (New York: New York University Press, 1991), pp. 343–52.

Litvak, Meir, 'The Islamisation of the Palestinian-Israeli Conflict: The Case of Hamas', *Middle East Studies* 34, no. 1 (January 1998), pp. 148–63.

al-Maktab al-Siyasi, Lijnat al-Tahlil wal Dirasat. *Wathiqat al-Ta'if: Dirasa fi al-Madmun*. Beirut, 1989.

Mallat, Chibli, *Shi'i Thought from the South of Lebanon*. Papers on Lebanon, vol. 7. Oxford: Centre for Lebanese Studies, 1988.

Marty, Martin E., 'Fundamentals of Fundamentalism', in *Fundamentalisms in Comparative Perspective*, ed. Lawrence Kaplan (Amherst: University of Massachusetts Press, 1992), pp. 15–23.

Momen, Moojan, *An Introduction to Shi'ite Islam: The History and Doctrines of Twelver Shi'ism*. New Haven and London: Yale University Press, 1985.

Mowles, Chris, 'The Israeli Occupation of South Lebanon', *Third World Quarterly* 8, no. 4 (October1986), pp. 1351–66.

al-Mussawi, 'Ammar, 'Interview: Ammar Mussawi', interview by Giles Trendle, *Lebanon Report* 5, no. 12 (December 1994), p. 10.

Nasr, Nahfat and Monte Palmer, 'Alienation and Political Participation in Lebanon', *International Journal of Middle East Studies* 8 (1977), pp. 493–516.

Nasr, Seyyed Hossein, 'Jihad', in *Expectation of the Millennium: Shi'ism in History*, eds Seyyed Hossein Nasr, Hamid Dabashi and Seyyed Vali Reza Nasr (Albany: State University of New York Press, 1989), pp. 58–60.

Norton, Augustus Richard, 'Shi'ism and Social Protest', in *Shi'ism and Social Protest*, eds. Juan R.I. Cole and Nikki R. Keddie (London: Yale University Press, 1986), pp. 156–78.

——, *Amal and the Shi'a: Struggle for the Soul of Lebanon*. Austin, TX: University of Texas Press, 1987.

——, 'The Origins and Resurgence of Amal', in *Shi'ism, Resistance and Revolution*, ed. Martin Kramer (Boulder, CO: Westview Press, 1987), pp. 203–18.

——, 'Lebanon: The Internal Conflict and the Iranian Connection', in *The Iranian Revolution: Its Global Impact*, ed. John L. Esposito (Miami: Florida International University Press; Gainsville, FL: Orders, University Press of Florida, 1990), pp. 116–37.

——, 'Hizballah: From Radicalism to Pragmatism?' *Middle East Policy* 5, no. 4 (January 1998), pp. 147–58.

Picard, Elizabeth, 'Political Identities and Communal Identities: Shifting Mobilization Among the Lebanese Shi'a Through Ten Years of War, 1975–1985', in *Ethnicity, Politics and Development*, eds. Dennis L. Thompson and Dov. Ronen (Boulder, CO: Lynne Rienner Publishers, 1986), pp. 159–73.

Piscatori, James, *Islam in a World of Nation States*. Cambridge: Cambridge University Press, 1986.

Rajaee, Farhang, 'Iranian Ideology and Worldview: The Cultural Export of Revolution', in *The Iranian Revolution: Its Global Impact*, ed. John L.Esposito (Miami: Florida International University Press; Gainsville, FL: Orders, University Press of Florida, 1990), pp. 63–80.

Ranstorp, Magnus, *Hizb'allah in Lebanon: The Politics of the Western Hostage Crisis*. With a foreword by Terry Waite. New York: St. Martin's Press, 1997.

Rapoport, David C., 'Messianic Sanctions for Terror', *Comparative Politics* 20 (January 1988), pp. 195–213.

——, 'Sacred Terror: A Contemporary Example from Islam', in *Origins of Terrorism, Psychologies, Ideologies, Theologies, Sates of Mind*, ed. Walter Reich (New York: Cambridge University Press, 1990), pp. 103–30.

Rose, Gregory, 'Velayet-e-Faqih and the Recovery of Islamic Identity in the Thought of Ayatollah Khomeini', in *Religion and Politics in Iran*, ed. Nikki R. Keddie (New Haven and London: Yale University Press, 1983), pp. 166–88.

Sachedina, Abdulaziz A., 'Martyrdom', in *Expectation of the Millennium: Shi'ism in History*, eds Seyyed Hossein Nasr, Hamid Dabashi and Seyyed Vali Reza Nasr (Albany: State University of New York Press, 1989), 45–52.

——, 'Activist Shi'ism in Iraq, Iran and Lebanon', in *Fundamentalisms Observed*, vol. 1, *The Fundamentalist Project*, eds Martin E. Marty and R. Scott Appleby (Chicago and London: University of Chicago Press, 1991), pp. 403–56.

Sahliyeh, Emile, 'Religious Fundamentalisms Compared: Palestinian Islamists, Militant Lebanese Shi'ites and Radical Sikhs', in *Fundamentalisms Comprehended*, vol. 5, *The Fundamentalist Project*, eds Martin E. Marty and R. Scott Appleby (Chicago: University of Chicago Press, 1995), pp. 135–52.

Shapira, Shimon, 'The Origins of Hizballah', *The Jerusalem Quarterly*, no. 46 (Spring 1988), pp. 115–30.

Shepard, William E., 'Islam and Ideology: Towards a Typology', *International Journal of Middle East Studies* 19 (1987), 307–36.

Sidahmed, Abdel Salam and Anoushiravan Ehteshami, Introduction to *Islamic Fundamentalism*, no. 2, Twayne's Themes in Right Wing Politics and Ideology Series, ed. Youssef Choueiri (Boston: Twayne Publications, 1990), pp. 1–15.

Sivan, Emmanuel, 'Sunni Radicalism in the Middle East and the Iranian Revolution.' *International Journal of Middle East Studies* 21 (1989), pp. 1–30.

——, 'Islamic Fundamentalism, Anti-Semitism and Anti-Zionism', in *Anti-Zionism and Anti-Semitism in the Contemporary World*, ed. Robert S. Wistrich (London: Macmillan 1990), pp. 74–84.

——, 'Eavesdropping on Radical Islam', *Middle East Quarterly* 2, no. 1 (March 1995), pp. 13–24.

Tibi, Bassam, *The Crisis of Modern Islam: A Preindustrial Culture in the Scientific Age*. Translated by Judith von Sivers. Salt Lake City: University of Utah Press, 1988.

Trendle, Giles, 'Hizbollah Serves its Purpose', *The Middle East* (February 1992), p. 3.

——, 'The Grass Roots of Success', *The Middle East* (February 1993), pp. 12–13.

——, 'Islamic Power', *The Middle East* (November 1994), pp. 15–16.

——, 'Hizballah: Pragmatism and Popular Standing', in *Lebanon on Hold: Implications for Middle East Peace*, eds. Nadim Shehadi and Rosemary Hollis (London: The Royal Institute of International Affairs; Oxford: Centre for Lebanese Studies, 1996), pp. 63–67.

Usher, Graham, 'Hizballah, Syria and the Lebanese Elections', *Journal of Palestine Studies* 26, no. 2 (Winter 1997), pp. 56–67.

Vaziri, Haleh, 'Iran's Involvement in Lebanon: Polarization and Radicalization of Militant Islamic Movements', *Journal of South Asian and Middle Eastern Studies* 16, no. 2 (Winter 1992), pp. 1–16.

Venter, Al, 'The Hizbollah Equation', *The Middle East* (June 1996), pp. 8–9.

Voll, John O. and John L.Esposito, 'Islam's Democratic Essence', *Middle East Quarterly* (September 1994), pp. 3–11.

Warn, Matts, 'A Voice of Resistance: The Point of View of Hizballah', Advanced Course in Political Science, Stockholm University, May 1997.

Wege, Carl Anthony, 'Hezbollah Organization', *Studies in Conflict and Terrorism* 17, no. 2 (April–June 1994), pp. 151–64.

Wright, Robin, *Sacred Rage: The Crusade of Modern Islam*. New York: Linden Press/Simon and Schuster, 1995.

<www.digital.net/~billw/ANTI/anti-semitism>

<www.mideastinsight.org.> Nasru'llah, al-Sayyid Hassan, 'Peace Requires Departure of Palestinians: Interview with Sheikh Hassan Nasrallah', Interview by Antoine K. Kehdy (2 February 2000), *Middle East Insight* 15, no. 2 (March-April 2000).

<www.moqawama.org>

<www.us-israel.org/jsource/>

Zaher, Mahmud, 'Hamas: Waiting for Secular Nationalism to Self-Destruct: An Interview with Mahmud Zaher', interview by Hussein Hijazi, *Journal of Palestine Studies* 24, no. 3 (Spring 1995), pp. 81–8.

Zartman, I. William, 'Democracy and Islam: the Cultural Dialectic', *AAAPSS* 524 (November 1992), pp. 181–91.

Zisser, Eyal, 'Hizballah in Lebanon – at the Crossroads', in *Religious Radicalism in the Greater Middle East*, eds Bruce Maddy Weitzman and Efraim Inbar (London: Frank Cass, 1996), pp. 90–110.

Zubaida, Sami, *Islam: The People and the State*. London and New York: I.B. Tauris and Co. Ltd, 1993.

Daily and Weekly Newspapers

Ad-Diyar
Al-'Ahd
Al-Iman
Al-Fasila
Al-Hawadith
Al-Maokif
Al-Massira
Al-Watan al-'Arabi wal Duwali
As-Safir
Ash-Shira'
Harmoun
Monday Morning
Nida' al-Watan
The Daily Star

Interviews by Author

al-Mussawi, al-Sayyid Husayn. Interview by author, 21 August 1997, southern suburbs of Beirut. Tape recording.

Fakhri, Rima. Interview by author, 23 December 1997, southern suburbs of Beirut. Tape recording.

Fayyad, 'Ali. Interview by author, 2 March 1997 and 18 February 2000, Beirut. Tape recording.

Fnaysh, Muhammad. Interview by author, 15 August 1997, Beirut. Tape recording.

Meri', Yussef. Interview by author, 10 April 1998, Beirut. Tape recording.

Muhsin, Muhammad. Interview by author, 1 March 1997, Beirut. Tape recording.

Qasim, Shaykh Na'im. Interview by author, 17 March 1998, southern suburbs of Beirut. Tape recording.

Ra'id, Muhammad. Interview by author, 9 March 1998, Beirut. Tape recording.

Televised Interviews

Fadlu'llah, al-Sayyid Muhammad Husayn. *Kalam al-Nas*, Lebanese Broadcasting.
Corporation (LBC). July 1997.

Fnaysh, Muhammad. *Wujhat Nazar*, Future Television (FTV). 2 July 1997.
——, *Wajhan ila Wajh*, al-Manar Television. October 1997.
Nasru'llah, al-Sayyid Hassan. *Kalam al-Nas*, C33 TV. May 1996.
——, *Kalam al-Nas*, LBC. March 1997.
——, *'Ala al-Hawa*, Orbit Television. May 1997.
——, *Al-Haki Baynatna*, Murr Television (MTV). July 1998.
al-Sayyid, al-Sayyid Ibrahim al-Amin. *Mukhtasar Mufid*, National Broadcasting Network (NBN). 20 September 1999.

Televised Speeches

al-Mussawi, al-Sayyid 'Abbas. 'Min Jibshit ila al-Nabishit,' Biqa'. Al-Manar TV, 16 February 1992.
Nasru'llah, al-Sayyid Hassan. 'Martyrs' Day', southern suburbs of Beirut. Al-Manar TV, 28 June 1996.
——, Nabatiyyeh. Al-Manar TV, 6 September 1996.
——, 'Jerusalem Day', southern suburbs of Beirut. Al-Manar TV, 7 February 1997.
——, 'Commemoration of April Invasion', southern suburbs of Beirut. Al-Manar TV, 18 April 1997.
——, "*Ashura* Speech', southern suburbs of Beirut. Al-Manar TV, 9 May 1997.
——, "*Ashura* Speech', southern suburbs of Beirut. Al-Manar TV 12 May 1997.
——, Southern suburbs of Beirut. Al-Manar TV, 5 August 1997.
——, Southern suburbs of Beirut. Al-Manar TV, 8 August 1997.
——, Southern suburbs of Beirut. Al-Manar TV, 3 November 1997.
——, 'Jerusalem Day', southern suburbs of Beirut. Al-Manar TV, 24 January 1998.
——, Beirut. Al-Manar TV, 26 February 1998.
——, Biqa'. Al-Manar TV, 13 May 1998.
——, 'Rally denouncing Wye Plantation Accord', southern suburbs of Beirut. Al-Manar TV, 1 November 1998.
——, 'Palestinian National Congress', Damascus. Al-Manar TV, 12 December 1998.
——, 'Jerusalem Day', southern suburbs of Beirut. Al-Manar TV, 15 January 1999.
al-Sayyid, al-Sayyid Ibrahim al-Amin. Parliamentary address, Beirut. Al-Manar TV, February 1997.

Television Programmes

Sam wa 'Assal. Presented by As'ad Majid. Al-Manar TV, 12 June 1993.
——, Presented by As'ad Majid. Al-Manar TV, 19 August 1993.
——, Presented by As'ad Majid. Al-Manar TV, 7 August 1994.
——, Presented by As'ad Majid. Special commentary by Muhammad Muhsin. Al-Manar TV, February 1996.

Index

Compiled by Auriol Griffith-Jones

U.W.E.L. LEARNING RESOURCES